Secular Socialists

The CCF/NDP in Ontario, A Biography

Secular Socialists is a comprehensive history of the NDP in Ontario – and its predecessor, the CCF – from its beginnings in the early 1930s to the contemporary period. It is also a provocative analysis of the survival of the CCF/NDP in the ideologically hostile environment of Ontario. Morley considers the party structure, the ideological forces that have shaped the party platform, the relationship between the caucus and the party executive and membership, the membership and ordinary conventions, and such factional disputes as the expulsion of Communists and the Waffle affair.

Morley draws an analogy between the "party individual" and the "human individual." His description of party development has a biographical character and allows an analysis of the complex relationships that exist between the party and the environment in which it grows. That environment, generally the political culture of Ontario, more specifically labelled the union class culture of Ontario, shapes the party's organizational, ideological, and political choices.

The author also critically examines several prevailing theories about CCF/NDP development, including the view that over the years the party has consistently drifted towards the right – a view that is specifically contradicted here.

J.T. Morley is a member of the Department of Political Science at the University of Victoria.

J.T. MORLEY

Secular Socialists
The CCF/NDP in Ontario,
A Biography

McGill-Queen's University Press
Kingston and Montreal

© McGill-Queen's University Press 1984
ISBN 0-7735-0389-7 (cloth)
ISBN 0-7735-0390-0 (paper)

Legal deposit third quarter 1984
Bibliothèque nationale du Québec

Printed in Canada

This book has been published with the help of a grant from the Social
Science Federation of Canada, using funds provided by the Social Sciences
and Humanities Research Council of Canada. Publication has also been
assisted by the Canada Council under its block grant program.

Canadian Cataloguing in Publication Data
Morley, John Terence, 1943–
Secular socialists : the CCF/NDP in Ontario

Includes bibliographical references and index.
ISBN 0-7735-0389-7 (bound). – ISBN 0-7735-0390-0 (pbk.)

1. New Democratic Party of Ontario – History.
2. Co-operative Commonwealth Federation.   Ontario
Section – History.   3. Ontario – Politics and government –
1923–1961.*   4. Ontario – Politics and government –
1961–   *   I. Title.

JL279.A54M67 1984   324.2713'07   c84-098403-0

Cover Stephen Lewis and Donald C. MacDonald campaigning in Scarborough
West in 1963. Photo by *The Globe and Mail*, Toronto.

For Jane Brewin Morley
to her family and to ours
this book is dedicated

Contents

Tables

Foreword

Compared with other provinces and regions in Canada, Ontario has failed to attract both popular and scholarly analysis. Professor Peter Oliver, of York University, has observed that as far as written history is concerned Ontario is "a have-not province ... in a scholarly sense an underdeveloped region." So much so that in 1970–1 Premier John Robarts established an independent board of trustees which launched the Ontario Historical Studies Series. Works have been commissioned to fill the scholarly vacuum, and slowly a fuller record of Ontario history and politics is becoming available.

Supplementing this organized effort at a renaissance in Ontario studies has been a trickle of individual efforts. Outstanding among these have been H.V. Nelles's *The Politics of Development* (1974), a definitive work on the development of mining, forestry, and hydro, and Albert Tucker's *Steam into Wilderness*, a colourful history of the Ontario Northland Railway; and more popular volumes such as Jonathan Manthorpe's *The Power and the Tories* (1974). Terry Morley's study of the CCF/NDP is a welcome addition to these individual efforts, particularly since there are no plans within the Ontario Historical Studies Series for a focus on Ontario political parties as such.

Secular Socialists is a valuable piece of historical research and analysis. It is developed in the context of an interesting thesis: that in their evolution political parties are like human beings. Thus, the study is subtitled a biography. Morley contends that "the development of any institution from sectarianism to secularism is typical and normal and parallels the development of the human personality from childhood (where one is, in a certain sense, incarcerated or confined) to adulthood (where one is potentially free)." "It is my hypothesis," Morley states, "that political parties survive by integrating, though imperfectly, with the external world and that this integration can be described as a process of secularization." Further, "in this study, the CCF/NDP 'personality' has a character (consistency, order, form, structure) which can be described and analysed, and which patterns the internal crises of the party and constrains the effect of external stimuli from the political milieu of Ontario."

This hypothesis forms a cohesive framework within which Morley considers the chronological development of the party from its inception in 1932, through the euphoria of election victories and the vicissitudes of election defeats, through the evolution into the New Democratic Party, to the quest for power in the years 1964–71. He then dwells in more analytical detail on various aspects of the party – its structure, its ideas, its internal democracy, its discipline, the role of its leaders, and its relationship with the caucus. As an overview, he notes the maturing of the party as evidenced by its capacity to adapt to change. And he concludes that "the party's personality is stable, but not rigid; it is always coherent and recognizable but it responds to external circumstances." These analyses are not only considered in relation to Morley's basic hypothesis but also subjected to a critical assessment in light of classic theories of party organization and operation set out by scholars such as Robert Michels.

Morley's work has the benefit of detailed personal knowledge gained while working at all levels of the CCF/NDP, including two years as executive assistant to the leader in the NDP caucus at Queen's Park. With that wealth of personal experience, he completed his doctoral studies at Queen's University where first-hand knowledge was integrated with an assessment of the CCF/NDP development in the broader context of Ontario political history and the fragmentary studies which had already been done. Finally, Morley moved to the yeasty atmosphere of British Columbia politics where, on the history staff of the University of Victoria, he prepared this work for publication with the perspective of both time and distance. The result is a volume which provides insights into the character, and details in the development, of the Ontario CCF/NDP which will be of interest to students now and an invaluable source material for future scholars.

I cannot conclude without expressing the hope that other historians and political scientists will rescue Ontario political parties from the general neglect of the past. Studies of the CCF/NDP have been piecemeal: Gerry Caplan's *The Dilemma of Canadian Socialism* looks at the CCF from its inception to the end of the Second World War. Morley's book covers these early years and carries the examination forward to 1972; a study of the party during the last decade remains to be done. And there have been no studies of the Progressive Conservative or Liberal parties in Ontario.

Donald C. MacDonald
Atkinson College
York University
December 1983

Preface

The New Democratic Party has attracted more than its share of academic and literary attention. The party, in its present life and in its pre-1961 guise as the Co-operative Commonwealth Federation, has always fascinated scholars and writers: often in an inverse proportion to the fascination seemingly felt by a somewhat suspicious Canadian electorate. The major and best-known works such as Walter Young's *Anatomy of a Party* and Gad Horowitz's *Canadian Labour in Politics* have generally focused on the national party organization and on its fortunes in the federal political arena. Yet from the beginning provincial parties have had significant autonomy and have been responsible for most of the organizational effort. This sense of autonomy and independence has increased with the passing years. Most important, the party has fared rather better among provincial electorates, forming governments in Saskatchewan, Manitoba, and British Columbia and enjoying the status of the official opposition for one period in Nova Scotia and for three in Ontario.

Certainly there have been a good many books and articles primarily focused on the ccf/ndp in a provincial setting, notably Martin Lipset's *Agrarian Socialism*, a widely acclaimed study of the ccf in Saskatchewan. Nothing comparable has been published about the Ontario party, although Gerry Caplan's *The Dilemma of Canadian Socialism* admirably sets down and explains the story of the Ontario ccf before 1946 and Leo Zakuta's *A Protest Movement Becalmed: A Study of Change in the CCF* provides some useful insights into party life in the 1950s.

This present volume is essentially a political history of the Ontario party from its inception in 1932 to 1972. Throughout the book I make use of an analogy between the individual political party (the Ontario CCF/NDP) and the individual human personality. Essentially I argue that this party, this individual, survives and grows to maturity by developing an integrated "persona" capable of adjusting to its changing environment without losing its specific identity and becoming an unrecognizable entity. A similar generalization about the individual human personality underpins much of the writing by social psychologists and conforms to commonsensical notions about the growth and development of humans.

I do not want to make too much of this analogy. It does not yield a new theory of parties which makes all previous literature obsolete. I do not, however, want to make too little of it. The idea of an institutional personality provides an organizing principle for a study of this kind and makes comprehensible the jumble of facts about party organization, party program, electoral failure and success, and internal struggle and external pressures. The Ontario CCF/NDP is a collectivity which interacts – "lives" would be a better word – with other collectivities. In detailing changes in the personnel, program, and structure of an organization, it is necessary to have some vision of the organization as something other than a random collection of people and events. The analogy with the human personality serves this purpose, and, I believe, provides an understanding of Ontario politics not available elsewhere.

The reader should note that this study has an arbitrary beginning and end: 1932 to 1972. There is, of course, some mention of events that occur before 1932 and more mention of those after 1972, particularly in the Afterword. At the same time this focus on a forty-year span necessarily limits the evidence and, hence, the conclusions.

In the long process of bringing this project to the point of publication I have incurred many debts. For his encouragement and friendship I would like to thank Professor Edwin R. Black of Queen's University. He and others, particularly Donald Blake, Paul Fox, George Perlin, and George Rawlyk, provided much helpful advice which, when I followed it, greatly improved the manuscript. I am grateful to Ed Black and George Rawlyk for urging me to send the manuscript to McGill-Queen's University Press.

I have also been fortunate in the interest shown by those connected with McGill-Queen's. Kerry McSweeney gently kept after me to complete revisions. Donald Akenson quickly set the wheels of the publishing process in motion after receiving an inevitably late revised version. Audrey Hlady, as editor, took in a somewhat disorganized manuscript copy, thoroughly reformed it, and has undoubtedly saved me much embarrassment. The manuscript has been typed and retyped by Barbara Johnson, Frances Bird, Evelyn Rawcliffe, and Jill Randall.

In some sense I owe my greatest debts to all those who have valiantly struggled over the years to build the Ontario CCF/NDP. I have been a party activist myself and know the sacrifices that a commitment to such a cause can require. I hope the book, in part, will be seen as a celebration of their effort. Some individuals active in the party have been particularly helpful. All those who submitted to lengthy interviews were most generous with their time and with their knowledge and insight. They are listed in the Appendix. I am also grateful to Morden Lazarus, who has been very kind in writing to encourage me and to make useful suggestions. Desmond Morton provided helpful comments in the early stages of revision as did two anonymous reviewers for McGill-Queen's and the Social Science Federation of Canada.

The whole project would have been much more difficult, if not impossible, had Queen's University not acquired the Ontario CCF/NDP papers. I am grateful to George Rawlyk for pushing forward this acquisition; to Ian Wilson, then the university archivist, for his many kindnesses; to the university itself; and to my then colleagues on the Ontario NDP provincial executive who agreed that Queen's was the best depository. They agreed in large measure because a well-known Queen's alumnus, Donald C. MacDonald, had already decided to donate his papers to his alma mater. If there is any central figure in the historical drama of the Ontario party, it is Donald MacDonald. Almost single-handedly he kept the party alive in the darkest days and since then has served it without fear or favour and with no thought for his own desires. This book could not have been written without him and I am particularly pleased that he graciously consented to write the Foreword.

Finally I want to mention Walter Young. His book *Anatomy of a Party: The National CCF, 1932–1961* has provided an inspiration and a standard for all who venture to write about political parties in Canada, particularly about the CCF/NDP. I have not reached his standard but I will always be grateful for his inspiration given as a colleague and as a friend. His death in 1984, at age fifty, has left a void in the community of scholars, and in the wider community, that cannot be filled.

All these people, and many more, have given this book life. Despite their generous assistance there are still flaws and undoubtedly some errors. These, of course, are of my own making. For all that, the book has been an important and exciting part of my life, though there have been times I am sure when my wife, Jane, and my three sons, Gareth, James, and Simon, would have benefited from a little less scholarly excitement and a little more attention from a distracted husband and father.

PART ONE

A Perspective

1

An Analogy: The Party Personality

Political parties fascinate their students. The great figures of history provoke a similar scholarly interest and, as historians delight in biography, so political scientists enjoy the morphology and dissection of party life. In particular the growth of parties, their survival, and, occasionally, their decline and destruction are processes which continue to attract considerable attention. The problem of explaining these processes of party life and death is obviously difficult, yet interesting and important; it provides the focus for what follows.

The Co-operative Commonwealth Federation (CCF) first ran candidates in an Ontario general election in 1934. One CCF member was elected to the 90-seat Legislative Assembly. Not until 1943 did the CCF have better success when it elected thirty-four members and became the official opposition in a minority assembly. The party continued to play an important role in Ontario politics until the election of 1951 when it was reduced to 2 seats. It slowly rebuilt its legislative strength through the 1950s and early 1960s, and in 1967 the party, in its metamorphosis as the New Democratic Party (NDP), gained 20 of the 108 seats in the assembly. In the four elections from 1971 to 1981 the NDP consistently returned a significant number of members to the assembly, forming the official opposition after the 1975 election.

The party's rise and fall and resurrection calls out for explanation, and the variety offered is fascinating. Desmond Morton, a historian at the University of Toronto, argues that the 1967 recovery was in large measure a consequence of the party's new-found organizational strength and capacity.[1] Others, notably Fred Englemann and Stanley Knowles, focus on party ideology and program as a determining factor of electoral success or failure.[2] Gad Horowitz in his book

Canadian Labour in Politics suggests that the health of the party's continuing relationship with the trade union movement has been a factor in the growth and decline of the CCF/NDP.[3] John Wilson contends that party growth is dependent on demographic trends and that the NDP has made electoral gains in those areas of Ontario that are newly industrialized and therefore contain new industrial workers who increasingly come to see themselves as working class.[4]

Undoubtedly variants of these hypotheses and indeed other attempts at explanation could be made. But though all the preceding explanations are stimulating, they remain unsatisfying. Since they all share a determinist form in which an independent variable explains or causes the circumstances of the dependent variable, they willy-nilly rely upon axioms which are, in some sense, plucked from the void. They ignore the interaction between the institution and its environment and are incomplete.

In place of these conflicting determinist explanations for party growth and survival, an analogy between the "individual" political party and the individual human personality suggests that party growth and survival are akin to the human organism's growth and survival. Both result from the successful development of a complete and mature "personality." At first glance this analogy may seem somewhat curious and slightly fanciful. Yet the analytical problems which led to the development of a psychological perspective for the study of the great figures of history, focusing on the individual personality interacting with his own external environment, are parallel to the analytical problems faced by the student of parties. Just as the Stimulus-Response epistemology which underpins the view of human personality as the sum of environmental forces impinging on it is unprovable in any human behavioural context, so too the view that a political party is an automatically regulated apparatus, performing tasks determined by the sum of the social, economic, and cultural forces impinging on it, is based on merely an asserted determinist framework.

In rejecting the Stimulus-Response formulation of the behavioural psychologists, Sigmund Freud, Harold Lasswell, Robert Lane, and others have substituted a Stimulus-Organism-Response model in which the Organism – the "persona" – interacts with the external environment to produce autonomous responses moulded, but not determined, by the external environment.[5] In recent years other social scientists, notably Amitai Etzioni, have also rejected a rigid determinist epistemology in favour of the view that human behaviour is, in part at least, autonomous and voluntarist.[6] If therefore one rejects a rigid determinism in the study of parties, then parties can be seen as autonomous institutions in a social space with an independent life in particular socio-cultural contexts. It is this whole life which can be dissected and analysed.

There are, of course, dangers in using such an analogy, in particular, the twin pitfalls of anthropomorphism and reification. In the first instance, it is possible, certainly, to compare a party's beginning to a birth, its elites to the brain, its supporters to muscles, and so on. Yet this is certainly pointless – a political party is not a human individual writ large. In making the analogy, one must also avoid giving the impression that the party, as an organic entity, is somehow devoid of individual human personalities. The party is not a Platonic form or an abstraction separate from the human personalities who give it life.

I begin, then, with the particular, in this instance the CCF/NDP. I also begin with an analogy which predicates a universal form – an analogy between the human personality with its unconscious Id, its natural form, and a political party seen to have a similar nature. I make the analogistic assumption that the phenomenal organizational structure of the party is derived from universal patterns of organizational process and political activity. The justification for this approach is not the production of some definition of the party Id or natural unconscious (in large measure this has not yet been successfully accomplished for "man-animal" by the Freudians or their imitators and competitors); instead, the justification is the insight that such an approach yields. More precisely, the justification rests on the usefulness of hypotheses generated from the analogy. If the hypotheses provide an insightful analysis of the CCF/NDP and of parties generally, then the analogy is worth while.

The development of any institution from sectarianism to secularism is typical and normal and parallels the development of the human personality from childhood (where one is, in a certain sense, incarcerated or confined) to adulthood (where one is potentially free). It is my hypothesis that political parties survive by integrating, though imperfectly, with the external world and that this integration can be described as a process of secularization similar to the development from sect to church propounded by Troeltsch in his massive study of Protestantism in Europe.[7] Further, this process of integration is characteristic, and from an analysis of the character of an individual party its response to external circumstances should be predictable. Thus, in this study the CCF/NDP "personality" has a character (consistency, order, form, structure) which can be described and analysed and which patterns the internal crises of the party and constrains the effect of external stimuli from the political milieu of Ontario.

To test this proposition more easily, it is helpful to associate with it the more obvious implications. If these implications can be shown to have validity, then the proposition itself is likely valid and it will be possible to apply this theoretical framework to the study of individual parties with a certain confidence. The more significant implications of this secularization hypothesis are as follows:

1 Changing party behaviour patterns are directly related to stages of party growth and development. Contemporary party practice is, in part, determined by the pattern of party growth.

2 The party program is most easily understood in symbolic rather than rational terms. Both particular proposals and the overall program are more closely related to party character than to electoral imperatives or ideological consistency.

3 Throughout the stages of party development the basic structure of internal governmental processes should remain fundamentally the same. Some formal structural changes will inevitably occur but they will be changes of style, not "personal" substance.

4 Party personality is formed by a wider set of environmental stimuli than those ordinarily associated with the political system. The mature party personality cannot be explained simply in terms of immediate political constraints.

5 The party's electoral record not only reflects the stages of party personality growth, but also, as an objective indication of how the party is perceived by its external world, informs the party's self-consciousness, and hence its "personality growth."

6 As the party develops over time and adjusts to the external world, there will be corresponding changes in its internal life in terms of factional dispute, the hegemony of elites, and so on. If such change does not occur, it would indicate that the party has not adjusted to the external world and, we should expect, has not "survived" in the special way indicated previously.

In a sense the secularization hypothesis is merely an inspiration for its corollary propositions. In another sense these propositions stand by themselves and illuminate the life processes of political parties and again in turn confirm the utility of the personality analogy.

Finally in considering the proposition that the party "individual" undergoes a process of integration with its milieu, one major implication is the establishment of a link between party behaviour and identifiable stages of development. It is important, therefore, to characterize analytically the particular development of the CCF/NDP of Ontario. It does not hurt, however, to keep in mind that the history of this party is not a bloodless one, that it has an intrinsic as well as a theoretical interest. Moreover, the drama of the history has a basis in reality which makes it a guide for analysis as well as a script for a modern morality play. The thesis/antithesis of victory and defeat and victory again translates for the student of parties as a concern about political development and about the temporal stages of that development. As Samuel Beer suggests:

There is no single meaning that must be adopted as the definition of the term development. The essential question is how useful any definition proves to be in organizing material and directing research. In common usage three notions are often associated with the idea. The principal one is the notion of directionality of trend in the historical process. Along with this go the notions that such directional change occurs in stages and that, with regard to causation, each stage is produced by the preceding stage. Several successive stages of an entity, each caused by the preceding stage, the whole process showing a trend – this is the distinctive pattern of historical process to which a concept of development calls attention as a possibility to be looked for and tested by research and theorizing.[8]

By identifying and examining in some detail the various stages of party development – stages, Beer tells us, which have some characteristic or principle attached to them[9] – an explanation for the differences observed between stages if evident is, at least, demanded. Moreover, since the concept of stage implies the notion of change (from one stage to another), of periods of stability and transition, of other periods of instability and revolution, of crises marking the transformation from one stage to another, and of a contemporary stage of development that is in part an accumulation of the elements in the preceding stages, it follows that the explanation demanded must inform us not only of the pattern of development, but also of the condition or "character" or "personality" of the party in a contemporary world.

2

The Setting: Political Culture and Ontario

It is a truism to state that the milieu in which the "person" of the CCF/NDP of Ontario lives is Ontario and not Canada. In this instance to state the obvious is a necessity. It is a mistake to examine the political, social, or economic life of Ontario and assume that conclusions drawn apply to Canada. The party has had its character shaped by its particular environment, in a broad sense, the Province of Ontario, in a narrower sense, the union class of Ontario.

There are a myriad of academic definitions of political culture. Typical is the one provided by Lucien Pye in the *International Encyclopedia of Social Sciences:* "Political culture is the set of attitudes, beliefs and sentiments, which give order and meaning to a political process and which provide the underlying assumptions and rules that govern behaviour in the political system. It encompasses both the political ideals and the operating norms of a polity. Political culture is thus the manifestation in aggregate form of the psychological and subjective dimension of politics."[1]

Two major problems emerge from such a definition. First is the difficulty of considering psychological phenomena in terms of collective entities. This problem is somewhat overcome by the acceptance of the analogy between the party "persona" and the human individual. The second, also of significance, is distinguishing attitudes, beliefs, and sentiments from actual behaviour. As Pye states elsewhere: "Should the concept [of political culture] apply only to subjective considerations, why does it also involve actual behaviour patterns? If the term is meant to include both psychological and behavioural patterns, then it would seem to come perilously close to being no more than a pretentious way of referring to political behaviour."[2] The difficulty is that underlying psychological attitudes or sentiments are often inferred from observed behaviour, and if the two are not analytically separated, then Pye's fear of academic pretentiousness is well founded. In fact in Pye's definition and in other definitions of political culture, the critical insight is the distinction made between attitudes and behaviour. In a very real sense the development of the concept is an attempt to understand behaviour, not simply observe it and describe it. Put another way, political culture is a technique for finding independent variables in a world of interstitiality, variables which can explain observed patterns of behaviour. An older scholarship was familiar with this quest as an attempt to analyse human nature and to then use the concept of human nature as an explanation for all manner of political and social phenomena. All the definitions essentially admit the need to explain observed behaviour by some identification of subjective underlying attitudes which in the aggregate predispose the collectivity to behave as it is observed to behave.

The distinction between subjective attitudes and objective observable behaviour is critical. Unhappily, political scientists have tended, with the development of relatively sophisticated survey research techniques, to attempt the discovery of these underlying subjective orientations by the simple device of asking people about their fundamental attitudes.[3] The logical difficulty here is clear. Inferences are drawn from respondents' answers to a variety of questions concerning the nature of the regime, their trust of the regime, their feelings of efficacy, their attachment to various symbols of state, and their fears concerning the various impositions of government. However, the answers may not reveal fundamental underlying attitudes, but rather may be the product of learned behavioural responses.

To overcome this problem, a number of political scientists in recent years have based the concept of political culture on a broader concept of culture itself, one inspired by the work of many anthropologists. In fact the early cultural theorists in political science were aware of conceptual developments in anthropology, particularly those developed by anthropologists interested in psychological orientations. Almond has written of his debt to the anthropologists in developing his concept for political science.[4]

In considering this broader definition of culture, anthropologists and other social scientists have been aware of two major streams in the analysis of a culture. Daniel Levine puts this most explicitly when he states:

What does the concept of culture mean in the social sciences today? Simplifying considerably, two major streams of thought may be identified in recent American scholarship: what are called here ideational and structural approaches. These differ on both substantive and methodological grounds. The ideational approach identifies culture largely with ideal patterns or salient public norms. Culture is viewed as an idealized vision of society, and the primary data of cultural analysis become ceremonial norms and values. Given these premises, it is understandable that ideational approaches focus on dominant value patterns, with variations seen in terms of deviance from the general norm. A structural approach takes a more comprehensive view, incorporating economic, social, and political factors as well as strictly normative ones. Furthermore, overt patterns of behaviour are brought into the sphere of culture. In this way, value patterns are explicitly related to social class and institutional position. Thus, following this approach, national cultures are not studied in terms of generalized public norms alone, for these may fail to reflect the operative norms guiding behaviour in concrete, institutionally defined situations. For, as Steward points out, "The culture of a nation is not simply a behavioral norm which may be ascertained by the observation of all or a significant sample of individuals. Different groups of individuals are substantially dissimilar in many respects. They have subcultures, which is a concept that has long been understood but surprisingly disregarded in social science."[5]

Leslie White defines culture this way: "By culture we mean an extrasomatic temporal continuum of things and events dependent upon symbolizing (keepsakes, fetishes, language). The components of culture are logical, sociological, attitudinal and technological."[6] Culture is dependent upon the symbolic faculty in man according to White; man and culture are inseparable because culture distinguishes man from the apes in the sense that while apes have behaviour that is observable, that behaviour is not caused by a fundamental principle described as culture.

This broader structural view of culture does, however, lead to a further reductionism, usually a technological reductionism. White, for example, argues that the agricultural revolution meant that the life-style attitudes of man changed when man was able to harness solar energy. This incredible technological advance is the sine qua non of a settled way of life so very different from that enjoyed by nomadic tribes. It leads to an agricultural society which develops a system characterized by a certain order and regulation and customs, and the maintenance of these customs or uniformities or culture is a product of theological or religious beliefs that exist in all civil societies. According to White, theology, therefore, is an instrument of state control or more broadly of the maintenance of settled order.[7] T.S. Eliot has argued that culture could not come into being or maintain itself without a religious basis, and by this he means that the attitudes or beliefs of people which permit a settled order to exist are essentially the product of a particular religious view – a weltanschauung.[8] Eliot, in some sense, suggests a religious reductionism rather than a technological one, but both are intimately tied to the anthropological notion of an objective culture.[9]

Leaving aside the metaphysical difficulties of reductionism, it is important to note that this structural view of culture is one that is bound up with the forms of objective observation and data. We are freed from simply asking people about their attitude because in addition to obtaining that kind of information we must also study, as Levine puts it, "economic systems, key organizations, patterns of association, the distribution of resources." Even in terms of an ideational approach to the study of culture, the range of phenomena includes "child socialization, articulated values, ceremonies, psycho-dynamics."[10] Besides the objective data about religions, business, and trade union groups, the range is even wider than Levine suggests and includes such things as geography and climate, social and economic history, political history, and, of course, prevailing ideological systems.

These phenomena can be quantitatively described and consequently culture can be more fully understood by using these data. Moreover, the need to describe culture fully, both political and social culture, exists because the differences between observed behavioural patterns of institutions and social entities remain to be explained. The concept of culture, by analytically distinguishing between attitude and behaviour, provides the basis for such an explanation by focusing on underlying attitudes as predisposing particular and different behaviours observed in individuals and social entities. The difficulty is to ensure that culture does not become a shorthand term for some kind of mystical first cause which in fact cannot ever be accurately described, but which must exist only to satisfy our desire for an explanation of behavioural differences. The temptation is always to reduce culture to its various components; the Marxist reduces everything to economic factors, others to technological or religious or sociological factors. Yet the concept is resistant to such reductionism because the web of interrelationships which it embraces transcends the various ideas and structures which inform the whole culture. Culture in fact is a kind of shorthand for a whole way of life and therefore must be empirically described. It cannot, however, be seen as a product of any one of the factors which permit us to describe it.

If the concept of culture is not easily reducible except through some "religious" position as Marxism, it becomes necessary to produce some synthesis of the social and economic factors which come together to make a particular culture. The ideational approach to culture which dominates political science – the equation of culture with the subjective attitudes which predispose particular behaviours – is, in a certain sense, an attempt at such a synthesis. Attitudes are assumed to arise from the combination of the other social and economic factors. Yet, we cannot distinguish attitudes from behaviour simply by asking people about their fundamental beliefs. There is some necessity, therefore, to go beyond this ideational approach to analyse the social and economic factors directly and to attempt some synthesis of them.

There are two methods of attempting such a synthesis. First and most simply is by comparison, that is, social and economic factors can be compared among social entities and collectivities. Just as one can compare and observe behavioural differences, so one can also compare cultural differences by making the analytical distinction between behaviour and culture. The differences among collective individuals in terms of such factors as geography, climate, economic conditions, and political history can be measured and described not simply as behavioural symptoms, but rather as behavioural causes. The political culture of France is to be understood by examining the factors which make up a culture within the context of a comparison with, for example, Britain, Germany, or Italy, so that the conditions which exist in France are seen to have a definition imposed by the differences observed. Second, it is possible to synthesize culture by adopting the view that culture yields particular behavioural patterns. By accepting this view, there is established a dialectic between the synthesis of social and economic conditions and the observed pattern of life which one finds in a particular social unit.

In Canadian studies such syntheses are often attempted, particularly in those works devoted to a particular province or provincial government, though invariably the methodology is not presented in such explicit terms.[11] Two attempts at providing a description of the political culture of Ontario, one by John Wilson and the other by François Pierre Gingras, make use of comparisons with other provinces and, in addition, describe a variety of social, economic, and political factors in some combination.[12] In terms of this view of political culture, a consensus is possible. Ontario may be seen in the period from 1932 to 1972 as a rapidly industrializing, urbanizing society and, in the latter years of this period, as a technologically sophisticated economy in which consumption and service industries are emphasized.[13] While experiencing this rapid social and economic change, Ontario has also experienced a very unsettled population, unsettled by immigration primarily from Western Europe and by internal migration from rural to urban areas. All was overlaid with the veneer of prosperity. It was, and still is, a situation in which one would expect an equally unsettled polity where shifting voter alliances yield a succession of different political regimes. In fact the most notable and dominant characteristic of Ontario politics in this century, certainly since the Second World War, has been the longevity of the Progressive Conservative party in provincial office.

The Political History of Ontario

In the late nineteenth century, after Confederation, Ontario gave its primary political allegiance to the Liberal reformers. Partisan affiliations were somewhat unclear in the early decades after 1867, but it is certain that the Conservatives as a party had relatively little impact in the province outside their strongholds of eastern Ontario and Toronto. In the last years of the century the Liberals under Oliver Mowat were in firm political control.[14]

By 1905 partisan lines in Ontario had solidified and this process meant the end of the Liberal/Reform domination of the province. Since 1905 the Conservative party has been out of office in Ontario for only two relatively short intervals – from 1919 to 1923 when the United Farmers of Ontario/Labour coalition held office and from 1934 to 1943 when Mitchell Hepburn's Liberals formed the government. Certainly since the formation of the CCF in the early 1930s the political history of Ontario has been primarily characterized by this one-party dominance in the legislature and, as table 1 indicates, for most of the

TABLE 1
Standings in the Ontario Legislative Assembly, 1934–1971

1934	
Liberal	66
Conservative	17
Liberal-Progressive	4
CCF	1
Independent	1
UFO	1

1937	
Liberal	63
Conservative	23
Liberal-Progressive	2
Independent Liberal	1
UFO	1
CCF	0

1943	
Progressive Conservative	38
CCF	34
Liberal	15
Labour Progressive	2
Independent Liberal	1

1945	
Progressive Conservative	66
Liberal	14
CCF	8
Labour Progressive	2

1948	
Progressive Conservative	53
CCF	21
Liberal	14
Labour Progressive	2

1951	
Progressive Conservative	79
Liberal	8
CCF	2
Labour Progressive	1

1955	
Progressive Conservative	84
Liberal	11
CCF	3

1959	
Progressive Conservative	71
Liberal	22
CCF	5

1963	
Progressive Conservative	77
Liberal	24
NDP	7

Continued on next page

1967		1971	
Progressive Conservative	69	Progressive Conservative	78
Liberal	28	Liberal	20
NDP	20	NDP	19

Source: *Canadian Parliamentary Guides*, 1935–72.

Note: In official records issued by the chief electoral officer of Ontario there is a designation Liberal-Labour. This term was first used in the election of 1945 when several trade unionists sympathetic to the Communist appeal for a coalition to defeat Drew, and therefore hostile to the CCF, stood as Liberal candidates under this name. In federal elections the term was first used in the Kenora–Rainy River riding from 1921. In Ontario those elected have always been included as full members of the Liberal caucus and they have not maintained a separate political organization from the Liberal party. The term has died out except in the Kenora–Rainy River area. Consequently I am ignoring the designation and adding those MPPs elected to the Liberal total.

period the Conservatives have enjoyed a substantial majority in the Legislative Assembly.

Yet this statistic, although undoubtedly important in terms of the political consciousness of the electorate inasmuch as it reflects the reality of the exercise of power, does not in itself provide a complete picture of the political realities of the province. Other data are also revealing. Table 2 shows the popular vote for each provincial general election from 1934 to 1971 divided among the parties. Table 3 again indicates the popular vote, but takes into account nonvoting as a preference to be recorded.

The statistics on the popular vote inform us that despite a Conservative monopoly of government power, other political parties have consistently received support from a significant proportion of the Ontario electorate. By analysing similar aggregate data, Dennis Wrong, writing in 1957, is able to conclude: "Ontario, then, has had a three-party system since 1943. It appears unlikely that the province will soon revert to the supposedly 'normal' two-party system in view of the firm basic support received by the CCF from organized labour."[15] John Wilson and David Hoffman make a similar inference from more recent data and conclude that Ontario indeed has had a three-party system, though they argue that it is one in transition and that at some future date the Liberals will be reduced to minor party status.[16]

TABLE 2
Popular Vote in Ontario General Elections, 1934–1971

1934		1951	
Liberal	51%	Progressive Conservative	48%
Conservative	40	Liberal	32
CCF	7	CCF	19
Other	2	Other	1

1937		1955	
Liberal	52%	Progressive Conservative	49%
Conservative	40	Liberal	33
CCF	5	CCF	17
Other	3	Other	1

1943		1959	
Progressive Conservative	36%	Progressive Conservative	46%
CCF	32	Liberal	37
Liberal	31	CCF	17
Other	1		

1945		1963	
Progressive Conservative	44%	Progressive Conservative	48%
Liberal	30	Liberal	35
CCF	22	NDP	16
Other	4	Other	1

1948		1967	
Progressive Conservative	41%	Progressive Conservative	42%
Liberal	30	Liberal	32
CCF	27	NDP	26
Other	2		

Continued on next page

1971	
Progressive Conservative	44%
Liberal	28
NDP	27
Other	1

Source: *Reports of the Chief Electoral Officer, Province of Ontario,* for the years cited.

I would argue that the aggregate data available yield two additional conclusions which are significant and which are not seriously impaired by the truism that individual preferences can only be inferred and never absolutely known from collective data. Just as the inference that popular vote totals reflect a viable three-party system in Ontario (an inference which, it must be noted, contradicts the simpler view that Ontario is essentially a one-party state) is readily made and almost irrefutable, so the data suggest the reality of other forms of a political behavioural structure.

First, there is significant evidence that CCF/NDP electoral gains, at least in terms of seats, have often been at the expense of the Conservatives rather than the Liberals. Others have suggested an opposite view. Wrong, for example, states: "While Liberal support is geographically scattered and socially heterogeneous, CCF strength is more homogeneous and is heavily concentrated in Toronto, Hamilton, the industrial areas in Northern Ontario and in several smaller industrial centres where the CCF has displaced the Liberals as the second party since the war."[17] It is true that in 1943 thirty of the thirty-four CCF gains were in Liberal seats – but then the Liberals had held most of the seats in the previous legislature. In 1948 the situation was reversed and of the sixteen CCF gains fifteen were in previously held Conservative ridings. Obviously a party is most likely to gain seats from the party with the most seats to lose. A more suitable election for evaluation of CCF/NDP gains is in 1967 when NDP gains are disproportionately made in ridings previously held by Progressive Conservatives. Even if we ignore newly created constituencies, of the eleven NDP gains, nine were from the Progressive Conservatives and two from the Liberals. Jack Granatstein, studying the South York federal by-election of 1942, concluded that the decisive factor in

TABLE 3
Percentage of the Total Electorate Favouring Individual Parties in
Ontario General Elections, 1943–1971

1943		1959	
Progressive Conservative	20.7	Progressive Conservative	27.2
CCF	18.3	Liberal	21.6
Liberal	17.9	CCF	9.8
Other	1.0	Other	0.3

1945		1963	
Progressive Conservative	31.6	Progressive Conservative	30.6
Liberal	21.2	Liberal	22.2
CCF	16.1	NDP	9.8
Other	2.6	Other	0.3

1948		1967	
Progressive Conservative	27.7	Progressive Conservative	27.7
Liberal	20.0	Liberal	20.8
CCF	17.8	NDP	17.0
Other	1.6	Other	0.1

1951		1971	
Progressive Conservative	31.3	Progressive Conservative	32.5
Liberal	20.3	Liberal	20.2
CCF	12.3	NDP	19.9
Other	0.6	Other	0.5

1955	
Progressive Conservative	29.4
Liberal	20.1
CCF	10.0
Other	1.1

Source: *Reports of the Chief Electoral Officer, Province of Ontario,* for the years cited.

Note: Those who do not vote also express a kind of political "choice." This table shows the support that each party obtained from all those eligible to vote, not just those who did vote.

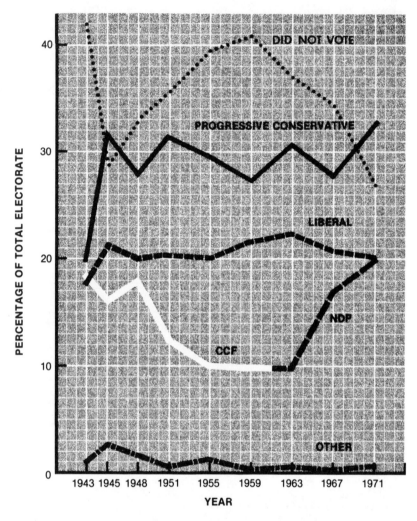

Percentage of the total electorate favouring individual parties in Ontario general elections, 1943–71. Data from *Reports of the Chief Electoral Officer, Province of Ontario.*

Conservative Arthur Meighen's defeat was not the fact that the Liberals failed to field a candidate and that the Liberal votes all went to the CCF, but rather that the traditional Conservative vote from the working-class sections of the constituency transferred heavily to Joseph Noseworthy, the CCF candidate.[18] Similarly in 1967 most NDP gains were in constituencies which had traditionally supported the Conservatives, but were predominately working-class areas (for example, Oshawa and the east end of Toronto). The view that CCF/NDP support has primarily come from the Liberals is attractive assuming an ideological spectrum with the Progressive Conservatives on the right, the Liberals in the middle, and the CCF/NDP on the left. The idea of this spectrum, however, is much too simple and the argument that CCF/NDP electoral appeal is not of this ideological kind is borne out by statistics recording party electoral gains.

Second, as the figure indicates, CCF/NDP support is at its lowest ebb when voting turnout is also lowest. As the CCF/NDP becomes able to provide an election machine that has some capability of bringing voters to the polls, such organization has a direct effect on the electoral result. The two exceptions to this general rule are in 1945 and 1971, election campaigns in which the people of Ontario were warned that the CCF and the NDP might well capture the government and that the results of such socialist victory would be disastrous. These "red scare" elections produced a higher than usual turnout, resulting in a lower vote for the CCF/NDP and a proportionately higher vote for the Conservative party. The Liberal vote stayed amazingly constant throughout the twenty-eight-year period.

A Liberal-Colonial Society

A number of observers in the Ontario political scene have accused political leaders in Ontario of the sin of blandness. The sin is particularly annoying to political journalists, many of whom have wondered in print about the camaraderie that pervades the Ontario legislature, a legislature that is made up of those who support the economic system – the Conservatives and the Liberals – and those who do not – the New Democrats. It is deceptively easy to characterize Ontario politics as being very different from the scandal-ridden type found in the United States or from the European type characterized by mass strikes and occasional political kidnappings. Politics in

Ontario is even seen to be very different from politics in other Canadian provinces where fistfights have occurred on the floor of legislatures. Yet to make this sweeping assertion would be to repeat the old mistake of assuming that the fashion of today is the truth of yesterday. In fact, since the formation of the CCF in Ontario, there have been several episodes of what can only be described as vicious political debate between the socialists and those who sought the destruction of the CCF/NDP and all its works.

Undoubtedly the most notable ideological battle took place during the joint federal and provincial election campaigns in 1945 when a series of antisocialist leaflets were published. Among the most important was an illustrated pamphlet entitled *Social Suicide!* by B.A. Trestrail.[19] This pamphlet offered five thousand dollar awards to those who could correctly answer "a simple test of skill" concerning the information contained therein. That information included such broadsides as

Goodby Democracy ... conclusive evidence of their [the CCF's] determination to stay in power is confirmed by the fact that their "new 19 Point Plan" falls far short of their programme of complete state socialism. In fact it is just one step toward their ultimate goal ... "But," you say, "that is nonsense. They can't stay in power unless we want them there. All we have to do is defeat them at the polls." That's what Germany thought. And here in Canada, even under a democratic government; even without the use of armed force, once a socialistic government had five years in which to pass on its controls on us, would you be willing to bet that your ballot would be of any value? I think not ... the fact remains that the party has already demonstrated in actual practice their readiness to use "strong-arm methods." At a political meeting in Lethbridge in the recent Alberta elections Mr. Landeou, a Social Credit candidate, was given five minutes by Mr. Coldwell, leader of the national CCF party, to retract a statement which offended Mr. Coldwell. Failing to heed this ultimatum Mr. Landeou was beaten up and forcibly ejected from the hall – not by the police, mind you, but by the CCF ushers – "storm troopers" of the future.

This startling pamphlet was written entirely in this excited style and painted a picture of socialism as a totalitarian, misguided, evil, and insane political doctrine which, in Canada, was controlled by two individuals: Frank Scott, denounced as an intellectual who had never met a payroll, and David Lewis, sneeringly referred to as a Polish Jew whose family changed their name.

The CCF reacted to this campaign with its own pamphlets but was clearly outgunned. It did show that Trestrail was not alone and that his previous campaigns had been sponsored by such corporate worthies as A.L. Ainsworth of the John Inglis Company, Oliver Betts of Canadian Breweries, R.A. Bryce of the National Trust Company, H.D. Burnes of the Bank of Nova Scotia, Edgar Burton of Simpsons, F.A. Gaby of BA Oil Company, H.T. Jaffray of the Imperial Bank, F.H. Marsh of the Bank of Toronto and Excelsior Life, Gordon McMillan of Algoma Steel and the Chartered Trust Company, R. Mitchell of the Royal Bank, J.G. Parker of Imperial Life, Robert Rae of the Dominion Bank, Clifford Sifton of the Sifton newspaper chain, H.M. Turner of Canadian General Electric, and S.M. Wedd of the Bank of Commerce. The CCF, however, could not afford to send such information to every home in Ontario but the antisocialist literature, with this significant financial backing, was in fact that widely available. In some sense E.B. ("Ted") Jolliffe, provincial leader of the CCF, was responding in kind by the use of dramatic language in his famous Gestapo speech, which will be related in chapter 3.

This hostility to the CCF/NDP which occasionally surfaced in the politics of the province, though less frequently after the 1940s, caused a considerable reaction in the party. For many the appropriate response to such antisocialist sentiments was an equally virulent attack on the inequities of capitalist institutions. This group favoured the polarization of politics in the province and pointed to the experience of social democrats in Britain and other European countries. Others, like Desmond Morton, argued strenuously against this view. Morton, in a witty circular sent to key members of the party leadership in 1970, stated:

Of course polarization has a crude fascination for the ideologues and extremists of both left and right in our own humble political spectrum. It entrances "Buck" Randall on one flank, the Waffle on the other. It has a magnificent "High Noon" quality about it, a John Wayne simplicity. Once the deed was done, neither side would ever have to compromise again. Both left and right can indulge in paroxysms of their respective kinds of nonsense. Instead of choosing between products which are drearily similar, the poor harried voter could choose between opposites which are appallingly distinct. The problem is that the entire strategy is nitwittery at its finest. It is the result of the kind of political self-abuse which occurs when ideologues talk only to themselves and their admirers and not to real people. For a political party, that kind of masturbation is suicidal.[20]

This debate had its ultimate catharsis in the leadership contest between Stephen Lewis, representing the forces favouring polarization, and Walter Pitman, representing those favouring accommodation. Its inevitable denouement came with the victorious Lewis's acceptance after 1971 of the arguments advanced by John Wilson and others that "the Ontario electorate is, fundamentally, both progressive and conservative."[21]

In a subsequent article published in a more scholarly setting Wilson argues that Ontario is in fact a "red tory" province;[22] that every government of Ontario, Liberal, Conservative, or United Farmers of Ontario (UFO), has consistently attempted to manage the province's affairs carefully and economically in order to introduce changes that are inevitably required by changing sociological circumstances. Every government contains those who long to preserve on older way of life alongside those who are eager for social and economic reform, and every government goes through periods of reformist activity and periods of rhetorical, if not actual, conservative reaction.

There is some question, however, whether the red tory label is the best one for this set of peculiar circumstances. Professor Alfred Bailey argues vigorously that Canada in a cultural sense is essentially a colonial society. As he states:

It is certain that Canada, even through the most recently developed phases of its existence, could have approached only remotely to the condition of being a "world in itself" like the great metropolitan centres of France and Great Britain which in early modern times became the foci of complex political-economic systems, centralized, differentiated and dynamic, in which mounting cultural pressures sporadically discharged in radiations that renewed the cultural modes prevailing in all the regions that paid tribute to them, and from which the dependent peoples' sense of the meaning of life was derived.

Canada was, and to a large extent, still is, in a non-political sense, an aggregation of such dependent regimes, and in consequence the most salient features of its culture have more closely represented a reflection of the existent modes of the metropolitan areas than a growth of that problematical internal soul for which Canadians have come to search, with a view to calling it their own.

In speaking of the Loyalists, Bailey argues:

There was, however, another handicap from which they suffered in a cultural sense, in addition to the attitude of dependence upon a distant mentor. They could not invoke moral and aesthetic sanctions which had been worked out in their "own" communities within their present territories. This, as has been said, is the paradox of the position in which all dependencies find themselves.

He goes on:

The fact that Haliburton's *The Clockmaker* exerted some influence on the literature of the United States and Great Britain, but contributed virtually nothing to later Canadian writing, is indicative of the folly of attempting to treat the culture of a country like Canada as though it were a discrete development, detachable from the North Atlantic context.[23]

The arguments Bailey advances apply not only to his native Maritime provinces, but also to Ontario where many Loyalists settled. Ontario is a colonial society in the cultural sense, as Bailey uses the term, and it could well be argued that the toryism that Wilson and others find in Ontario is simply colonialism; that is, the desire for order and settlement which pervades Ontario society is a desire dictated, indeed commanded, by the prevailing order of the metropolitical centres of Great Britain and the United States. There is no evidence that the Ontarians' notion of peace, order, and good government is in any way unique or indeed in any way self-generated. Peace, order, and good government certainly exist in the Ontario consciousness but the idea of what this is, is surely as dependent on London and later Washington as the words in the British North America Act were dependent on the law officers of the Crown at Westminster.

As for the red aspect of Ontario – its progressiveness – the manifestations of this progress are not socialist or communitarian or collectivist but rather liberal. The imperialist ideology of nineteenth-century Britain and of twentieth-century America is not toryism or even militarism but liberalism, the doctrine that man, free from the superstitious taint of original sin, will inevitably grow better and better if only he is provided with education and better drains. It is that impulse which lies behind the Ontario welfare state, whether borrowed in its particulars from Britain or the United States.

This is not to argue that the label of red tory is fundamentally wrong or without utility. It is to argue, however, that a more appropriate label for Ontario's political culture is liberal-colonial and that while no essential truth attaches itself to this formulation, it does convey a somewhat different perspective on Ontario culture, a perspective which allows one to go beyond the usual generalizations about the progressive-conservative nature of the province.

The Union Class Subculture

The liberal-colonial characterization of Ontario political culture has a special significance in considering the CCF/NDP's immediate environment. The link between the party and the trade unions is not merely formal or structural. Trade unions in Ontario, at least the industrial unions, are in part defined in terms of their relationship with this democratic socialist political party. The party, in turn, is in part defined by its relationship with these unions. The party is not simply linked to the unions, but is a part of the industrial union movement in the province. This relationship is not unique. It provides the fundamental principle of the British Labour party. That principle finds a congenial environment in Ontario as a consequence of the colonial nature of the society. A principle, a belief system, derived from British experience, even a socialist experience, is in part legitimate in Ontario because it is derivative.

The ideological tension found in some periods in Ontario, and already referred to, is itself not unique to Ontario. The debates in Ontario were paralleled by similar debates in other parts of the world, in particular Britain and Western Europe. Moreover the reaction of the CCF/NDP to this ideological tension was similar to reactions elsewhere – similar because a fundamental feature of Ontario's political culture was imported from Britain and the United States. That feature was the existence of an organized working class, organized in trade unions.

Now the industrial labour movement, that part of the labour movement most closely associated with CCF/NDP, was formally linked with the Congress of Industrial Organizations (CIO) in the United States. Yet, as Charles Millard, a CCF MPP and the first national director of the Steelworkers' union, points out: "It's a mistake to believe that we adopted our industrial unions from the States, because they in turn got it ready-made from Britain. Both John L. Lewis [the founder of the CIO and president of the United Mine Workers] and Phillip Murray [first president of the United Steelworkers of America] came out of the Mine Workers' union in Britain where they had industrial unions donkey years before the industrial union was revived in the CIO."[24] It was to these unions that the party turned for solace from the painful crises of ideological warfare. The CCF attempted to isolate itself from the harshness of the world it found in Ontario, not by retreating from that world, but by helping create a new world in conjunction with the rising industrial union movement. It attached itself to the culture associated with this new world, a culture more accurately described as union class rather than working class. The CCF focused its electoral energies in certain regions and these were not simply the regions in which it had done well in the 1943 elections, but rather the regions in which the industrial union movement was most powerful and most active.[25]

The trade union movement as a manifestation of working-class aspirations for a better life has significant and relatively deep roots in Ontario. The first union of printers was organized in the province as early as 1832 and the Toronto Typographical Union has continued from 1844 to the present. As Doug Hamilton, author of *Trade Unions in Canada*, a pamphlet published by the Ontario Federation of Labour, points out:

Almost from the beginning, Canadian unions had international affiliations. The first "outside unions" were British. The Amalgamated Society of Engineers established its first local in Canada in 1850, followed by three more in 1851 ... The Ironmolders [was] the first American union [to come to Canada] ... in 1861, followed by the Locomotive Engineers in 1864. The National Typographical Society, and the Cigarmakers came in 1865, the Knights of St. Crispin (shoemakers) in 1867 and the Railway Conductors in 1868.[26]

Hamilton was at some pains to show that not all unions had these international affiliations; however, all the early examples he gives are of unions established outside the province of Ontario.

Hamilton observes that the first real public impact of unions in Ontario was during the printers' strike in Toronto in 1872, a strike to promote the nine-hour day. Twenty-four union leaders were jailed on charges of criminal conspiracy, an action which resulted in the Trade Union Act which "freed trade unions from liability to prosecution as criminal conspiracies on the grounds that they were in restraint of trade." The act was passed by John A. Macdonald's Conservatives against the anguished opposition of George Brown, the Liberal leader and, not so incidentally, the publisher of the *Toronto Globe*. Following this official formal recognition of trade unions, the labour movement in Ontario began to grow. In 1883 the Toronto Trades and Labour Council called a meeting of twenty-one unions to establish a national labour body known as the Canadian Labour Congress, a title which would be revived again in 1956. In 1894 the federal government established Labour Day as a national holiday and in 1900 established the federal Department of Labour and published the first issue of the *Labour Gazette*, under the editorship of William Lyon Mackenzie King. In 1907 the Industrial Disputes Investigation Act was passed, and in 1919, while Winnipeg was in the throes of its General Strike, the Ontario government set up its own Department of Labour.

The labour movement was relatively quiescent in the province during the 1920s and in the early years of the Great Depression, but this introspective calm was quickly shattered with the movement into Canada of the new industrial unions from the United States. The first unions had been craft unions, that is, they were organized by skilled tradesmen for their own mutual protection. Many of these organizations were reluctant to admit unskilled workers, as the craft unions had a proud history going back to the old medieval guilds. In an age of mass production and geometric industrial growth this situation proved to be intolerable. In the United States John L. Lewis and others broke with the American Federation of Labor (AFL), which primarily represented the craft unions, over the issue. They founded the CIO and began to organize both unskilled and skilled workers in the major American industrial enterprises. As many of these enterprises, such as General Motors, were established in Ontario, it is hardly surprising that this renewed union activity quickly spilled over the border. It was as a result of a strike at the General Motors plant in Oshawa that Mitch Hepburn, the premier of Ontario, resolved to drive the CIO unions from the province. He inevitably failed, but provided the more radical union leaders, particularly socialists and Communists, with legitimate reason for opposing both established political parties in the province. In 1943 the new Canadian Congress of Labour (CCL), formed to provide a central labour federation for the CIO unions in Canada, endorsed the CCF as labour's political arm.

The labour movement, as table 4 indicates, grew very rapidly during the war years and the need to provide industrial peace for the war effort meant that governments were forced to give legal recognition to this new social force. Under the War Measures Act the federal government took the initiative with a series of orders-in-council on

TABLE 4
Trade Union Membership in Ontario,
1935–1945

1935	64,989	1941	132,556
1936	79,831	1942	180,380
1937	112,074	1943	211,970
1938	105,353	1944	210,592
1939	109,257	1945	204,399
1940	110,497		

Increase, 1935–1940: 70%
Increase, 1940–1945: 85%
Increase, 1935–1945: 315%

Source: Canada, Department of Labour, *Union Growth in Canada 1921–1967*.

industrial relations. The most important was PC 1003 of 17 February 1944, which provided rules for organizing and for collective bargaining and established machinery for handling the collective bargaining relationship between the employer and the union. It also set up a National Labour Relations Board with provincial and regional boards which established certification machinery and negotiating procedures for industrial disputes by employing conciliation officers and conciliation boards. At the same time the Ontario legislature passed the Labour Relations Act, establishing the Ontario Labour Court and later the Ontario Labour Relations Board which, however, operated under the aegis of the National Labour Relations Board during wartime. By 1947 the legislature had incorporated the major provisions of PC 1003 into the Ontario act and had established an orderly procedure for certification and collective bargaining in the province.

The labour movement was beset with a number of internal difficulties from the time of the war until the mid-1960s. First, many union leaders, particularly those with CCF affiliations, felt that they could no longer associate themselves with those unions led by members of the Communist party. In 1949 both the Trades and Labour Congress of Canada (TLC) and the CCL expelled the Communist unions and turned their jurisdictions over to other unions still inside the central labour bodies. A series of raids on these Communist-controlled unions then began, the most important of which was conducted by the United Steelworkers of America against the International Union of Mine, Mill, and Smelter Workers, a union based primarily in northern Ontario, in gold mines around Timmins and in nickel mines in Sudbury. In addition tension between the TLC and the CCL continued for some of this period although this stress was reduced as the craft union and industrial union forces in the United States moved towards a merger in the AFL-CIO. In 1956, following the American lead, the TLC and CCL merged to form the Canadian Labour Congress.[27]

Despite these tensions and despite a number of strikes and organizing campaigns the labour movement considered it had lost, the trade union movement as a whole continued to prosper and to be involved actively in the political and social life of the province, not only through the CCF/NDP, but by direct lobbying of the government for legislative reforms affecting working people. In particular trade unions were instrumental in obtaining a Human Rights Code and acts on loggers' safety, construction safety, pension benefits, and the minimum wage in 1963; on industrial safety, apprenticeship and trades qualification, and industrial standards in 1964; on the settlement by arbitration of labour disputes in hospitals in 1965; and on operating engineers in 1966.[28] By the mid-1960s the labour movement in Ontario had become influential, and although only about 33 per cent of the work force was enrolled, it did not see itself as a marginal social force,[29] nor was it treated as such by the government of the day, despite that government's unhappiness with the labour movement's formal political ties to an opposition party.

It should also be noted that the labour movement in Ontario operated with certain assumptions. E.R. Black and Alan Cairns have indicated that provincial governments as institutions have an impact on the political culture of the province and so create differing social and cultural elements among provinces.[30] So too union institutions have significant impact on the working-class culture, creating a union class subculture with, in the anthropological sense, a structure and a character. Larry Sefton, for some years the director of District 6 of the United Steelworkers, has stated that unionists are naturally conservative. They embrace a conservatism which arises from the need for an organic solidarity among members in the economic warfare which unions wage.[31] Richard Perlman and John Commons, in discussing labourism as the ideology of the American working class, have noted that trade unionists in North America are primarily concerned with pragmatic short-term economic gains. Being confident that those gains will eventually give them a significantly better life, they are therefore prepared to wait for the full flowering of that better life.[32]

One concludes that Ontario is a heterogeneous and diversified polity united, in the cultural sense, not by red toryism, but rather by what is more appropriately termed liberal-colonialism. It is at the same time tolerant of diversity and subcultural groupings of which the union class subculture is particularly significant. The union class subculture, in terms that Frank Parkin uses in referring to the English working class,[33] is a subculture alienated from the main cultural traditions of the province and yet, as in England, it is not a marginal culture, but rather one which, in part because of Ontario's colonial heritage, is seen as legitimate. The NDP need not retreat from the world to avoid the hostility of its ideological enemies in the province because it can re-create a different world which is at one and the same time part of the diversity of Ontario culture and self-sufficient within that culture.

PART TWO

The Maturing Party: Acquiring Stability

3

The Party in the World

In examining the history of the CCF/NDP in Ontario, we are driven to consider the fundamental nature of the party: the historical facts illuminate the problems of party survival. It should be noted, keeping in mind the analogy of the party as a human personality, that this is a kind of private or domestic history, a biography dealing not only with the great events of the party's lifetime but also with events which are peculiar to its domestic life and which have a real impact on it. For a political party an election is not only a public occurrence but also an intensely private one experienced uniquely by those involved.

In terms of this domestic history the party's development may be examined in temporal periods or stages. Five stages seem convenient and persuasive. The first may be characterized as the sectarian period from 1932 to 1942 when the new party wandered in the electoral wilderness. The second, from 1942 to 1951, is the period of socialist inevitability, of dizzying success and equally dizzying failure. This stage witnessed the emergence of a new generation of leaders. In the third stage from 1951 to 1964 the party sought respectability. In the fourth stage from 1964 to 1971 the party sought power, and in the fifth after 1971 the party coupled its quest for power with a quest for relevance.

The use of these stages of development is particularly apposite in terms of the analogy between the human personality and party life. Erik Erikson's adaptation of Freud's epistemology for the study of childhood development as a prototype of all human development provides, in this context, significant insights into party development.[1] Erikson himself argues that "each successive stage and crisis [in human development] has a special relation to one of the basic institutionalized endeavors of man for the simple reason that the human life cycle and human institutions have evolved together."[2] This link between human and institutional development is even more pronounced if one considers Erikson's views about the healthy personality.

There are many formulations of what constitutes a "healthy" personality in an adult. But if we take up only one – in this case Marie Jahoda's definition, according to which a healthy personality *actively masters* his environment, shows a certain *unity of personality* and is able to *perceive* the world and himself *correctly* – it is clear that all of these criteria are relative to the child's cognitive and social development. In fact, we may say that childhood is defined by their initial absence and by their gradual development in complex steps of increasing differentiation.[3]

For the institutional personality a like process could be said to produce such a "healthy" personality, a process readily labelled as secularization.

In considering human personality growth Erikson derives from this concept of a healthy personality the idea that growth is determined by the epigenetic principle. As he elaborates:

Somewhat generalized, this principle states that anything that grows has a ground plan, and that out of this ground plan the parts arise, each part having its time of special ascendancy, until all the parts have arisen to form a functioning whole ... Personality, therefore, can be said to develop according to steps predetermined in the human organisms' readiness to be driven toward, to be aware of, and to interact with a widening range of significant individuals and institutions.[4]

By analogy, the institutional personality develops according to certain predetermined patterns and not merely in response to environmental forces. In constructing an epigenetic diagram for the human personality, Erikson employs symbiotic polarities such as Trust vs Mistrust, Initiative vs Guilt, Apprenticeship vs Work Paralysis, Integrity vs Despair. Certain of these polarities form an epigenetic ladder of growth; others are residual categories which more precisely define the epigenetic poles. Taken together, in varying permutations and combinations, they provide a means of explaining an infinite variety of human growth patterns. Thus an individual in beginning his schooling may experience a genuine apprenticeship which provides him with a consciousness of his capacity for industry which in a later stage of development permits him to avoid despair as he accepts himself as an integrated personality.Another individual who fails to experience this sense of apprenticeship may in a later stage have a very different consciousness of himself as a "whole man."

Similarly, in considering party development as predetermined this is not to say that its pattern is inevitable. The characterizations of the successive stages of CCF/NDP development in Ontario imply the possibility of polar opposites. For example, the party did not have to seek respectability. It might well have sought notoriety by declaiming positions it knew to be unpopular. The seeds of such an attitude were certainly present in the party's sectarian period. There was nothing inevitable about the party's emergence from sectarian attitudes, and nothing inevitable about the emergence of a new generation of leaders who believed victory to be inevitable. It is certainly possible to believe in inevitable defeat. Some of the characterizations employed to describe the stages of CCF/NDP development may be directly linked to Erikson's epigenetic categories. For example, the quest for power from 1964 to 1970 has at its base a desire to pass on to the community the principles of democratic socialism and the fruits of NDP policies. For human individuals, as Erikson notes, "evolution has made man a teaching as well as a learning animal" and this leads to a generative stage of development in which there is "primarily a concern [for] establishing and guiding the next generation." The polar opposite is stagnation, a state in which there is "an obsessive need for pseudo-intimacy,"[5] and, again, the possibility of the party turning in on itself, becoming an obsessively closed world, was always a potential choice.

Others have also interpreted the history of the CCF/NDP in Ontario in terms of stages. Gerald Caplan implicitly presents two, possibly three, stages of development: the earliest lasting for a brief period in 1933 when the new party made some significant gains, the next stage when the party had little electoral support after the collapse of its alliance with the United Farmers of Ontario, and the final stage when the party became a significant electoral force after the South York by-election victory.[6] Leo Zakuta is quite explicit about the stages of CCF development; his chapter heads reveal them – "The Protest Movement, 1932–1942"; "Major Party: Ascent, 1942–1945"; "Major Party: Decline, 1945–1949"; "Minor Party, 1950–1961"[7] – and these stages form the basis for his hypothesis. My epigenetic developmental framework, different from either Caplan's or Zakuta's leads inevitably to different conclusions about the nature of the party. In particular three important differences emerge. First, the party remains conscious of itself as a major force in provincial politics even after the dramatic loss of seats in 1945. It is not until 1951 that the perception of inevitable victory is fundamentally altered. Second, the party does not revert to sectarianism in the 1950s but instead seeks to find a solution to its electoral difficulties. Third, although the formation of the New Democratic Party in 1961 is an important event in the party's history, it does not bring about a new stage in its development in Ontario. The 1961 date is convenient for historians but misleading for analysts of the growth of the CCF/NDP in Ontario. At the same time there is nothing magical about these dates; they have a logic which arises from the epigenetic analogy but they are not self-evidently true. What follows is an attempt to link the logic with the empirical reality.

1932–1942: The Political Sect

The Co-operative Commonwealth Federation was founded in Calgary, Alberta, on 1 August 1932. The new party was formed out of the desire, born of the Depression, to unite those varied political groups, socialist, labour, and farm, which more or less vaguely were conscious of themselves as part of the Canadian and international left. In the beginning the CCF was very much a federation of these heterogeneous groups, united only by a common desire to ameliorate the consequences of the Depression and by a mutual faith in the integrity of its first president (national leader), J.S. Woodsworth.[8] As Walter Young describes it:

The resolution setting out the purpose of the new federation groups and parties was moved by M.J. Coldwell on behalf of the "Labour Political Parties" ...

... the object of the new organization was to promote co-operation between the member organizations and "correlate" their political activities. The organizations in the federation were to be those whose purpose was "The establishment in Canada of a co-operative commonwealth in which the basic principle regulating production, distribution, and exchange will be the supplying of human needs instead of the making of profits."[9]

With but one exception, no delegates from Ontario were present at the conference. The exception was A.R. Mosher, a Nova Scotian, who as president of the Canadian Brotherhood of Railway Employees lived in Ottawa. Mosher, however, did almost nothing to promote the new party in Ontario,[10] and essentially the CCF was a creation of labour, socialist, and farm groups in the four western provinces.

Nevertheless CCF activity quickly began in Ontario after the Calgary meeting. The basis for the Ontario organization was initially a remnant of the Canadian Labour Party and the Independent Labour Party of Hamilton, who were joined by some doctrinaire members of the Socialist Party of Canada and by a handful of University of Toronto academics, most notably Professor Frank Underhill. The activists from these groups were sustained by two hopes: that they would be joined by the still-powerful United Farmers of Ontario, most of whose leadership was sympathetic to the CCF, and by the wilder hope that the ordinary people of Ontario, caught in the grip of the Depression, would quickly rally around the new political standard.[11]

The expectation that the UFO would join the new party seemed realistic. In 1918 the Trades and Labour Congress of Canada had sponsored a new political party, the Canadian Labour Party, in an early attempt to promote a significant electoral organization based on the trade union movement. The founding conference was held in Toronto and was attended by a number of people who were not trade unionists but were interested in reformist political activity. Among those present were E.C. Drury, who a year later became premier of Ontario in the Farmer-Labour government; J.J. Morrison, secretary of the United Farmers of Ontario; W.C. Good, later a UFO MPP; and Arthur Roebuck, a member of an independent Labour party in northern Ontario and later a prominent Liberal politician.[12] The result of this Farmer/Labour alliance was the formation in 1919 of a government under Drury, which included in the Cabinet two trade unionists. This government was badly defeated in the subsequent election in 1923,[13] but it left behind it the dream, particularly for trade unionists, of political co-operation between the labour movement and the farmers' organizations. That dream was very much alive in 1932 and it encouraged the belief in Ontario that the new CCF could become a potent political force.

This brief was further strengthened by the fact that, as Caplan points out, in the first year of the CCF's existence the party made remarkable strides in the province. Prodded by Agnes Macphail, Canada's first woman MP who was elected for the UFO from Grey

South in 1921 and re-elected in each successive general election, and by her protégé Elmore Philpott, a former Liberal, the UFO associated itself with the new party. Completing the "triple alliance" were Ontarians who joined the CCF through the CCF clubs, which grew rapidly in 1932 and 1933.

This initial success did not last. Caplan gives four reasons for the rapid decline.[14] First, the party suffered a series of electoral defeats both in Ontario and in the rest of Canada. Second, "irresponsible" statements of individual CCF members, some actually altered, others distorted, by the media, inhibited public acceptance of the party. Third, Caplan contends that there was a lack not only of a national organization, but also of any central leadership. "Woodsworth was accepted as national leader, [but] the multifarious groups within the party took literally the concept of the CCF as a federation rather than an integrated organism, and acted accordingly."[15] Finally, according to Caplan, the CCF failed to communicate its program to people in readily understood terms.

Equally important, however, is the fact that the "triple alliance," like its European namesake, was from the beginning an uneasy association. Members of the UFO were immediately alarmed by the Marxist rhetoric which characterized the statements of many of the socialists and trade unionists in the party and were readily offended by such practices as the use of the term "comrade" at party meetings. The trade unionists seemed to represent almost all parts of an ideological spectrum, though much divided amongst themselves, while many of the socialists were concerned that the unionists as new members of the party were not properly imbued with the revolutionary spirit.

The UFO was the first to leave. Alarmed by a call for a united front with the Communists and others, the Farmers decided to withdraw from the CCF early in 1934. By this point the CCF clubs had been thoroughly infiltrated with Communists and Marxists of more exotic persuasions. In desperation Woodsworth announced at the end of the 10 March meeting of the Provincial Council that the council was suspended and that the CCF in Ontario would be reorganized by the National Council. As Caplan writes: "That was all. In ten short minutes, much of the original CCF was destroyed. Leadership went as precipitately as structure. Agnes Macphail automatically ceased being a CCF member when the UFO withdrew its application."[16] A new constitutional structure was established in April and a more centralized but much smaller CCF was launched in the province. In this state of disillusionment it endured rather than lived through the remaining years of the decade.

It is not surprising given this unfortunate beginning that the party has been seen as essentially sectarian and isolated during this period. Electorally its record was dismal. In the provincial election of 1934 the party managed to win but one seat – by Sam Lawrence in Hamilton East. It garnered only 7 per cent of the popular vote and did not manage to come second in any other seat. In 1937 it held most of its popular vote, but Lawrence was defeated and the CCF came no better than third in any constituency. Federally the record was equally dismal. In 1935 and again in 1940 the party was unable to win a single seat in the province and came second in only one seat in 1935. It managed to win 8 per cent of the popular vote in 1935 but could muster only 4 per cent in 1940.

The lack of electoral appeal of the CCF may be partly explained by the presentation of its program. It alienated the party from many in society, not so much in terms of specific proposals, though some of these were undoubtedly frightening to many, but more so in terms of the style of presentation. The Regina Manifesto, adopted at the first national convention of the CCF held at Regina, Saskatchewan, in July 1933, contained such exhortations as "we aim to replace the present capitalist system with its inherent injustice and inhumanity, by a social order from which the domination and exploitation of one class by another will be eliminated ... no CCF government will rest content until it has eradicated capitalism and put into operation a full program of socialized planning which will lead to etablishment in Canada of the Co-operative Commonwealth."

Instead of the more modest proposals of the party concerning social welfare, a centrally planned economy, and immigration policy, these and other ringing declarations received considerable public attention. Instead of using the familiar examples of New Deal reforms in the United States, which in fact were similar to many CCF proposals, the party in Ontario attacked the New Deal and all its works. As the Ontario executive committee reported to its membership in 1936:

There is the complementary factor – the failure of all efforts to reform capitalism, to make it stable, while retaining its essential characteristics of private ownership and profit. The New Deal in the United States, the control measures in Britain, the more rigorous capitalistic regimes in Germany, Italy and Japan, all alike have failed to end unemployment, raise the standard of living or escape depressions. Some measure of recovery is apparent, but it is recovery for the profits of large corporations rather than recovery for the masses of farmers, workers and dependent middle classes.

In addition, in explaining the need for a socialist program, many in the CCF were fond of pointing to the Soviet Union as the model society for the future. Again, from the same executive committee report we find this interesting analysis:

The outstanding political factor in the world today is the economic success of the Union of Socialist Soviet Republics in Russia [sic]. No other long-term factor is so potent in its influence. Here is a nation that has, under workers and socialist government, become one of the greatest industrial powers in the world, that has attained a rate of industrial progress unknown before, and that has ended depressions, mass unemployment and capitalism. Within a decade, to quote Sidney and Beatrice Webb, "the USSR will have become the wealthiest country in the world and at the same time the community enjoying the greatest aggregate of individual freedom."

These sentiments did not have mass appeal. On occasion the CCF itself seemed to be calling for a degree of state control quite unacceptable to large elements of the Canadian and Ontario populations, and although the party very clearly eschewed the use of violence in obtaining power, at the same time spokesmen would occasionally insist that a CCF government would require thoroughgoing change. In this context one must consider this statement from the executive committee report:

In no sense is the socialism of the CCF mere reformism, mere gradualism, or a compromise with capitalism of any kind. A CCF Government attaining power must proceed promptly, drastically, thoroughly to liquidate the power of capitalist forces and secure for the socialist party in control of the organs of the state a most ample assurance that capitalist interests could not sabotage, weaken or overthrow socialism. The CCF must recognize and prepare for the most ruthless opposition to its activities before and after the attainment of power ... anyone who does not understand the nature of the struggle has no place in the CCF as a candidate, delegate, officer of a club or any other position of the most minimum importance. The CCF is on the uttermost Left in objective and understanding or it is nowhere.[17]

This declaration, drafted by an executive committee which for the most part represented moderate forces in the party, contained words which appealed only to those already inside the party while scaring away those outside it.

In terms of policy the CCF was unfortunate in the major issue of these years. That issue was Canada's entry into the Second World War, and the CCF was much divided over it. Woodsworth, a strict pacifist, a man of extraordinary moral courage, opposed all wars and rose in Parliament as the sole English-Canadian voice to speak against this one. The CCF National Council, though it did not repudiate him, did not follow his lead and passed a statement essentially favouring Canada's participation. Yet many in the party were unhappy with the council decision, and this unhappiness was communicated to those outside the party.[18] The CCF saved itself from the worst of public opprobrium by its formal stand but its apparent division on the issue meant that a formal position did not entirely rescue it from the wrath of patriotic English Canadians.

In addition to this lack of popular appeal, the Ontario CCF exhibited other characteristics of sectarian organizations. One was the requirement that its adherents, activists, and, certainly, its employees, exhibit a total dedication to the organization and sacrifice on its behalf. The executive committee report makes the point well: "As an illustration of what the services of the individuals giving full time to the CCF headquarters would cost if minimum wages were paid nine of the permanent staff, a wage bill of $8,840.00 would be required. Actually the maximum of all wage costs of the CCF Headquarters in the past year has been under $1,600.00."[19] The dedication of a number of individuals meant the party was able to enjoy a larger staff than it would have in later more affluent periods. Not until the 1960s did the party again have so many full-time employees.

Sectarian groups are also characterized by a disregard for community sensibilities. The use of the term "comrade" that the members from the small socialist groups and the more militant sections of the trade union movement insisted upon symbolically dissociated them from the UFO and in large measure forced the UFO to reconsider its commitment to the new federation. Another example was the party's habit of holding important meetings on Good Friday and Easter Sunday. In the 1930s Ontario was a self-consciously Christian community and many saw this practice as sacrilegious and offensive. Ironically this tendency to flout community values was exacerbated by the communities' treatment of the party as a sectarian group which held dangerous ideas. Incidents such as President Cody's banning of a CCF Club meeting at the University of Toronto at which Charles Millard was to have given a speech entitled "Hepburn Must Go" and two policemen's attempt to prevent a meeting of the Lithuanian CCF Club on the grounds that political meetings were illegal on Sundays obviously rankled. Even more traumatic was Premier Hepburn's attempt to have Frank Underhill and George Grube dismissed from their professorial posts at the University of Toronto largely because of their association with the CCF and the party's stance on rearmament and foreign policy. An influential part of the community tended to treat the CCF as an outcast and the CCF responded, at least in part, by behaving as such.[20]

That many CCFers, even at the end of this period, opposed effective electoral activity is surely evidence of a certain unworldliness. As Ted Jolliffe, first provincial leader of the Ontario CCF, states: "I knew people who were actually ashamed we won the South York by-election. They enjoyed being in the wilderness; they enjoyed their sense of virtue. Of course this is sectarianism gone mad."[21] The party had been formed as a vehicle for socialists to contest elections, presumably to contest them effectively. Yet as late as 1942 key figures in the Ontario party opposed all attempts to create an effective electoral machine. For example, several members of the provincial executive in the early 1940s strenuously opposed the creation of the post of provincial leader.[22] In the 1934 and 1937 elections the provincial president had acted as spokesman for the party but had not been able to devote much time to the task. Between 1934 and 1937 Sam Lawrence, as Member of the Provincial Parliament, had acted as party spokesman but after 1937 there was no one who could fill the role adequately. Lawrence himself raised the question of creating the post of provincial leader on 2 January 1942,[23] and later in the year a motion to that effect was carried by the provincial executive but not without considerable debate.[24]

Given these considerations it is not surprising that Caplan, Zakuta, and others have labelled the CCF of this period as sectarian and otherworldly. It bore an obvious and great resemblance not only to religious sects but also to political groups both of the left and of the right which were electorally unsuccessful but consisted of highly motivated individuals with a disregard for public opinion. Yet this label does not tell the whole story. While the CCF had many, if not all,

of the characteristics of a sectarian group, it exhibited other characteristics. Like a child, its personality contained the seeds of maturity; in
the midst of its sectarian phase the CCF contained elements to be found
later in the fully developed institution.

While it is true that the party had little electoral success, it did have
some and that should not be ignored. The election of one member to
the provincial assembly in 1934 seems a feeble record, but at the same
time it is an infinite improvement over the situation which existed for
other small groups with no representation. More important is the
success of a number of CCFers in municipal races. During this period
the mayors of Windsor, Hamilton, and Toronto were active party
members, and in the 1934 federal election the mayor of Toronto, James
Simpson, campaigned actively for the CCF in the mayor's official car.[25]

While a number of individuals were obviously dedicated to serving
the party to the exclusion of all other interests in life, undoubtedly the
result of a need for some kind of personal salvation which they hoped
to find in political activity, not every member of the party was so
dedicated nor was every dedicated member necessarily seeking such
salvation. Jolliffe contends that "party membership did not exist
exclusively of misfits as some scholars suggest ... it included doctors,
dentists, lawyers, veterinarians, trade unionists ... many of these
members, including some artists and writers, have become well
known since that time."[26] As well party members had connections
with other organizations in the society that counterbalanced the
tendency of some members to disregard community norms. Fred
Young, a former NDP MPP, recalls that many early CCFers were
members of the Fellowship for a Christian Social Order and other
religiously inspired study groups.[27] The fellowship consisted of
United and Anglican church adherents, and those churches, the
largest Protestant denominations in Ontario, were certainly established institutions.

Moreover those key CCFers who were unhappy with the prospect
of electoral success and opposed the party's participation in the South
York by-election, and the move to have a provincial leader, lost those
battles. By the end of the 1930s a new group of leaders emerged in the
Ontario CCF, a group which came to dominate the party over the next
decade and beyond. The group was comfortable in the dominant
political culture. It included Ted Jolliffe, a Rhodes scholar and a
lawyer who, like so many Canadian radicals, was the son of
missionary parents who served in China; Charles Millard, the

Canadian director of the Steel Workers' Organizing Committee and the most important figure in the CIO in Canada; Andrew Brewin, another lawyer, son of a prominent Anglican churchman with local ties to many of the social elite in Toronto; George Grube, a classics professor at Trinity College; and Agnes Macphail, who following her defeat in the 1940 federal election soon became active in the Ontario CCF, providing the party with its best-known political figure. Under the leadership of these individuals the CCF held a special meeting to consider the Rowell-Sirois Report on Dominion-Provincial Relations on 31 January 1941 and issued a statement that was wholly at variance with the idea that the party was a kind of opposition sectarian movement always anxious to condemn the works of the establishment. As the provincial executive minutes record: "Minor amendments were made and the report adopted as a whole with the exception of the section on Quebec, which, was felt, should not be passed upon until the Quebec delegates to the Eastern Canada Conference had been heard." Moreover the party began to consider the question of image and public relations in a more sophisticated way. Again, as the executive minutes record:

Brewin gave a resume of the various types of publicity being investigated by the [publicity] committee. They included polls of public opinion; establishment of a single source of official CCF news; propaganda for women to be carried on by women's groups; a core of letter-writers to the Press; articles in farm papers and small-town weeklies; articles in magazines and periodicals; personal contact with people influential in the journalistic world.[28]

The party was also moving into a closer relationship with the burgeoning industrial union movement. On 19 September 1941 the executive issued a press release condemning PC 7307 which prohibited strikes after a conciliation board had reported its findings on an industrial dispute, except when a government ballot of employees was conducted. On 3 October 1941 there was an expression of concern about Communist party attacks on union leaders, especially on Millard. On 1 December 1941 a large meeting organized specifically for trade unionists was held at Massey Hall in Toronto.

In other instances this "sectarian" group displayed the characteristics of a mature political party with active electoral ambitions. In 1942 the CCF nominated Noseworthy to oppose Meighen in the South York federal by-election, and later that year it created the post of provincial leader and elected Ted Jolliffe to fill it. It is also noteworthy that in South York the CCF campaigned effectively and with considerable organizational skill. The party adopted a zone-poll organization featuring a door-to-door campaign very similar to the by-election campaigns conducted by the NDP from the 1960s.[29] The party had three hundred regular canvassers who attempted to call on each home at least three times. There were one thousand workers to help on election day. Almost two thousand persons contributed money.[30] Moreover the CCF spent in excess of five thousand dollars on the campaign and accepted assistance, both overt and covert, from the Liberals, who did not field a candidate because former Prime Minister Meighen was running as Conservative party leader. Prime Minister King was clearly most anxious that Meighen be defeated and to this end the Liberals were prepared to assist Noseworthy's campaign.[31] Arthur Roebuck made a number of vitriolic speeches attacking Meighen, and the *Toronto Daily Star* controlled by Joseph Atkinson, usually a staunch supporter of the Liberal party, editorially defended the CCF decision to contest the by-election. The Liberals themselves contributed five hundred dollars to the campaign, the contribution being sent by Senator Norman Lambert, then in charge of the National Liberal Federation, to Andrew Brewin.[32] The National Liberal Federation also urged the Liberal organization in South York to assist the CCF campaign.[33]

Finally it might be noted that while the CCF was often treated as a sectarian organization by the community at large, this treatment did not always result in a defeat for the party or for individuals involved in the party. When Hepburn moved to have Underhill and Grube fired from their posts at the University of Toronto, he did not succeed. The substantial support received from the *Toronto Daily Star* and others in the South York by-election even in the face of great hostility from those institutions in which Conservatives were prominent also attests to this favourable treatment.

It is true that during this period the party was small,[34] electorally unsuccessful, and a number of individuals in it behaved as though they were utterly alienated from the society around them. Too much can be made of this. The membership was small but it was not minuscule. The party was electorally unsuccessful but not totally. Many in the party sought their own vision of the truth above all else, but by the end of this period many others sought their vision of truth through electoral politics.

1942–1951: The Pursuit of Inevitability

The second stage of the party's development began in victory. The CCF win of the South York by-election marked the transition to this stage and heralded a new potency in electoral campaigning. In the 1940 federal election the CCF had not carried a single polling subdivision and had received only 16 per cent of the votes cast in South York. In the 1942 by-election the CCF carried 93 of the 117 polls and received 58 per cent of the votes.

The following year provided even more encouragement. In September 1943 a national Gallup poll gave the CCF a narrow lead over the Liberals and the Conservatives: the CCF registered 29 per cent and the Liberals and Conservatives each received 28 per cent. The CCF slogan of "conscripting wealth" had proved popular, particularly against the backdrop of the 1942 referendum that released the federal government from its pledge not to impose conscription. There was considerable sentiment at this time for the view that the workers and ordinary people were doing their share to win the war but that capital and big business were shirking. The CCF began to see itself as the voice of the future and the inevitable victor in elections. This view was confirmed by the very strong showing of the party in the 1943 provincial election.

The CCF had been without representation in the provincial assembly since the last election in 1937. The life of the legislature had been extended beyond the normal five-year period and there was some feeling that no election should be held until the war was over. Premier Mitch Hepburn's retirement from political life, in combination with the events that led up to that retirement, threw the Liberal government into considerable disarray.[35] The new party leader and premier, Harry Nixon, decided that the only honourable course was to seek a fresh mandate from the people.[36] The people, however, cut the Liberal representation in the legislature from sixty-three to fifteen seats. The Conservatives won thirty-eight and the CCF thiry-four. Two Communists were elected under the label of the Labour Progressive party and one independent, for a total of ninety seats. In terms of popular vote the Conservatives won 36 per cent, the CCF 32, the Liberals 31, and others 1. Although the Conservatives had the most seats, the 1943 election was seen as a socialist triumph.

The year 1944 brought more exciting news for the CCF. In Saskatchewan the Liberal government called an election. Under the leadership of T.C. Douglas, who resigned his federal seat to become the Saskatchewan leader of the CCF, the party swept the province, capturing forty-seven of the fifty-two seats. The socialists were finally inside the gates of government and CCFers throughout the country rejoiced in the acquisition of power.

Flushed with these electoral successes and confident of further victories, CCFers in Toronto decided that the time was ripe for a takeover of city government. The City Council of Toronto and the Board of Education were controlled by Liberal and Conservative supporters who could usually be counted on to reject the proposals of the handful of CCFers who had achieved civic office. The CCF felt that local problems, such as the provision of milk in schools, were best solved by socialist policy and it was determined to elect a majority to the council. It decided, despite the nominal nonpartisanship of civic elections, that the most honest and straightforward way of doing this would be to run candidates under the party label. The result was disaster. Not a single CCFer was elected, and several who had previously been elected were defeated. After this shattering experience the party did not again run candidates for Toronto municipal office until 1969.

As a result of an advertisement placed by M.A. Sanderson in the *Toronto Globe and Mail* on 1 January 1944 in which certain members of the CCF were described as "Communist-controlled rubber stamps," a libel suit was initiated. The trial was a major event, presided over by Mr Justice Keiller MacKay (later lieutenant governor of Ontario) with a jury to decide the issue. The CCF was represented by J.R. Cartwright (later chief justice of Canada) and Andrew Brewin. In the case of fourteen plaintiffs the defendants were found not guilty of libel. Two other plaintiffs, George Grube and Eva Sanderson, were awarded token damages of one cent each. This decision did not help stem the flood of antisocialist propaganda.

Further disasters followed in 1945, a critical electoral year. The first event was the Grey North federal by-election in which General Andrew McNaughton, the Liberal minister of national defence, was seeking a parliamentary seat. After some initial hesitation, the CCF decided to contest the election and ran a prestigious candidate, Air Vice-Marshal Earl Godfrey, who gave the party high hopes for doing very well. Prestige was not enough, either for Godfrey or for McNaughton, as the Conservatives captured the seat; the Liberals ran second and the CCF third.

The real trauma occurred in June with provincial and federal elections only a week apart. The provincial election was held on 4 June. On 24 May Ted Jolliffe made his controversial Gestapo speech. Jolliffe had received detailed information from constable J.A. Rowe of the Ontario Provincial Police about a small branch of the force concerned with monitoring political activity, particularly that on the political left. Jolliffe had before him statements from an operative identified as D208, which included such statements as:

The CCF, during the last two years, has been financed and subsidized by the Communist-controlled CIO Labour Unions ... 32 [sic] of the CCF candidates nominated for the provincial house in the recent election [1943] are definitely known to have been members of the Communist and Communist-sponsored organizations in Ontario ... Messrs. Scott and Lewis reveal definitely [in the book *Make This Your Canada*] that the same methods to enforce the confiscation of Banks, Industry, Services and collectivization of farms as was carried out first in Russia as Communism and latterly in Italy and Germany as Fascism and National Socialism will be invoked by the Communist-controlled CCF.

The report ended with: "The Communist Party of Canada and its sympathizers will make every endeavor to hoodwink the people of Canada into electing a Communist-controlled Government and thus pave the way for a Soviet state in Canada."[37] Jolliffe knew that this report, and others like it, linking prominent CCFers with well-known members of the Communist party was sent directly to the attorney general and he assumed it was then passed on to the premier. He was incensed. Moreover he felt that if the public knew what was happening they would be as outraged as he and would turn on the government which had made such ill use of the Ontario Provincial Police.

Jolliffe decided to prepare a bombshell. Working closely with Lister Sinclair, a well-known Toronto broadcaster, he prepared a hard-hitting sensational speech. His opening words were:

Tonight, I want to tell you about what is probably the most infamous story in the history of Ontario; infamous and I warn you almost unbelievable, but every word of it true, and supported with affidavits which I have beside me right now! It is my duty to tell you that Colonel Drew is maintaining in Ontario, at this very minute, a secret political police, a paid government spy organization, a Gestapo, to try and collect, by secret spying, material that

Colonel Drew wants to use to try and keep himself in power. And Colonel Drew maintains his secret political police at the expense of the taxpayers of Ontario – paid out of *public funds!*

Jolliffe went on to charge that this secret force was headed by a man named Osborne-Dempster, who signed his reports D208, and that these reports were made to the commissioner, and the deputy commissioner of the provincial police and occasionally to Attorney General Leslie Blackwell or to Premier Drew. Jolliffe charged that a blacklist was kept: "Drew's blacklist of suspects doesn't just include labour leaders. It includes Ministers of the Gospel, teachers, professors, businessmen and housewives. You will notice that nobody is safe from suspicion by the twisted evil mind of Drew's professional spy." Finally he charged that the information gathered by Osborne-Dempster was made available to M.A. Sanderson, Gladstone Murray, and other "apologists" for big business who conducted the propaganda campaigns against socialism and the CCF in the mid-1940s. Jolliffe ended with this ringing declaration:

But the history of other countries is full of anti-democratic organizations created and supported by big business. Remember the Croix de Feu and the Cagoulard in France, the Blackshirts in England, the Falangists in Spain and similar gangs in Belgium and Holland and Norway, with their miserable Quislings. Remember too, the forces which helped Hitler to power and which supplied him with the finances and materials to build his war machine. When parties like the CCF, or the Labour Party of Britain or the Socialist Party of France and Trade Unions and farm organizations were collecting funds to help the German underground, big business in the same countries was making loans to Hitler and dealing with him as with a welcome customer. This is the pattern into which the story fits. It is the pattern of big business versus the common people. Today in Canada, big business is backing John Bracken and George Drew.[38]

By enlisting Sinclair's assistance in drafting the speech, Jolliffe clearly intended to cause a sensation. He succeeded. The resulting furore was so intense that the Drew government had no choice but to appoint a royal commission under Mr Justice LeBel to investigate the charges. The LeBel Commission was appointed only four days after Jolliffe's speech but it could not report its findings before the provincial election date. The CCF and Liberals made some halfhearted attempts to have the election postponed but the Conservatives argued that once the writs had been issued this would not be possible. The Conservatives also argued strenuously that Jolliffe's accusations were untrue and unfair.

Mr Justice LeBel had been appointed to determine the truth of the matter by holding a judicial inquiry; in large measure the real verdict was delivered, without benefit of any evidence, by the people of Ontario in the provincial election.[39] Jolliffe had made his charges, Drew had categorically denied them, and for many the victory of the Conservatives in the 1945 election vindicated Drew and condemned Jolliffe. To the ninety-seat assembly the Conservatives returned sixty-six members with 44 per cent of the vote, the Liberals fourteen members with 30 per cent of the vote, while the CCF was reduced to third-party status with only eight members and 22 per cent of the popular vote. Two Labour Progressives, A.A. McLeod and J.B. Salsberg, were returned.

In considering the extent of the effect of the Gestapo speech on the disastrous losses suffered by the CCF both in the provincial election and a week later in the federal election in which the party lost its only seat in the province, Caplan points to a Gallup poll taken before the radio broadcast which showed the CCF to have the support of 21 per cent of the electors of Ontario for a federal election and the fact that the party instead received 22 per cent of the popular vote in the provincial election.[40] Such hindsight, however, should not obscure the profound impact that these defeats had on the party itself. The party took the two election disasters to heart.

Many CCFers were persuaded that Jolliffe's speech was responsible for the debacle. Professor R.E.K. Pemberton, a classicist at the University of Western Ontario and a leading party activist in London, dealt fairly gently with the issue in a letter to George Grube, then president of the Ontario CCF. He suggested that the anti-CCF pamphlets, particularly *Social Suicide*, Trestrail's vicious masterpiece which was printed on paper said to be originally destined for the brassiere ads in the Simpsons' catalogue and which was sent to every Canadian home before the 1945 elections, would not have been so effective because of its extremely negative tone had it not been for the "intrusion" of the "Gestapo episode." He goes on to say: "For there is no shadow of doubt that the Gestapo business did do us harm, and plenty, and rightly."[41] Many shared this view.[42] Others were not so gentle. In an incredible speech at the 1945 provincial convention

Arthur Williams, a fiery Welsh orator who once worked in the same pit as Nye Bevan, a fact which he was fond of acquainting the world with, denounced Jolliffe for a full hour.[43] Others spoke in the same vein and the convention vented its spleen on Jolliffe by defeating his closest associate in the party, Andrew Brewin, for re-election as vice-president. Jolliffe himself was elected leader by acclamation, though he had lost his own seat in the election, but the dissatisfaction at this moment with Jolliffe's leadership was such that the Bernard Loebs and other party dissidents (known with a certain asperity as the Snake Islanders because they all gathered at the Loeb cottage on Snake Island, Muskoka) approached Charles Millard and asked him to oppose Jolliffe for leader. Since Jolliffe's opinions were considerably to the left of Millard's this was an extraordinary proposition. Millard declined the honour.[44]

Although 1945 was a difficult year for the CCF in Ontario, nonetheless it is not so clear that it signalled the party's decline, as Zakuta has suggested.[45] The party carried on. In 1946 it prepared a series of briefs and memoranda, the most important of which were an analysis of the Ontario government's proposals to the Dominion-Provincial Conference on Reconstruction, a program for housing, recommendations to the Royal Commission on Milk, recommendations to the Royal Commission on Forestry, and a detailed and comprehensive farm report. The party also played an active role in encouraging the trade unions to continue with recognition strikes, one of which, at Stelco in Hamilton, provided the basis for modern industrial bargaining in the province. A series of provincewide radio broadcasts was undertaken; details of the British Labour party's program were eagerly learned from a senior British cabinet minister, Herbert Morrison, who visited Toronto; and several study conferences were held, such as the Farmer-Worker conference in April. As well the leadership of the party essentially remained intact. Although Brewin was defeated for vice-president, this action was essentially symbolic because he was returned to the executive in another capacity and the following year became president of the Ontario CCF. And when Jolliffe was finally challenged for the leadership in 1946 by Lewis Duncan, a prominent newcomer to the party, Jolliffe was easily returned, obtaining more than two-thirds of the delegate votes.[46]

Similar activity continued through 1947 and 1948, and the CCF gained considerable attention for a number of its policies. Two had a wide impact. The first, a campaign to "buy from Britain," engendered a sentimental sympathy for the party. The second, the view that wartime price controls should be maintained during the reconstruction period, was favoured by many people and in October 1947 Jolliffe made a particularly effective speech on this policy.[47] In organizational terms the party was becoming more sophisticated. In addition to very active research and education committees, the party had an active women's committee and farm committee. All this activity culminated in the provincial election of 7 June 1948 in which the CCF again became the official opposition in Ontario. In this election the Conservatives returned fifty-three members with 41 per cent of the popular vote, the Liberals returned only fourteen members with 30 per cent of the vote, while the CCF managed to elect twenty-one members with 27 per cent of the vote. Two other MPPs were returned. On the next day Arthur Williams won a somewhat grander platform for his fiery oratorical skills with his election in the Oshawa federal by-election.

Throughout this period the CCF not only saw itself as a major party, but in many respects it was seen by others as such. It is true that for the national party the 1949 federal election was a grave disappointment, since the party dropped from 15.6 to 13.4 per cent of the popular vote and more significantly elected only thirteen MPs when it had elected twenty-eight in 1945. However, in Ontario the party's percentage of the popular vote actually increased and Noseworthy regained his South York seat (though Williams lost his in Oshawa). It was not until the humiliating results of the 1951 provincial election that the CCF in Ontario began to feel that the inevitability of socialism was not quite the same thing as the inevitability of a CCF victory.

Three important factors need to be considered, given the events of this period. The first concerns the leadership of the party. In considering the question of elitism in the British Labour party, Samuel Beer suggests that the period after the First World War saw the emergence of a "socialist generation" of individuals, both leaders and followers, who shared a common view. As he writes:

The party's purpose – what I have called Labour's orthodoxy – was rarely called into question either by the leadership or by any substantial section of the party. Throughout this period there was a broad consensus in the party on ideology, programme and strategy. Hence, the question that the elitist hypothesis poses – that is the question of power between leaders and party – hardly ever arose in a serious form ...

... the identity of purpose running from the commitments of 1918 to the manifesto of 1945 consisted not only in a fidelity to socialist ideology and gradualist strategy. It also involved the remarkable similarity of detail among the many statements of party programme.[48]

For the Ontario CCF the 1940s rather than the 1920s was the period of coming of age. And as with the British Labour party that coming of age affected the fundamental view of party purpose and party strategy of a large number of individuals. Thus what developed in the 1940s was a leadership which had a certain solidarity, a very real continuity, and a self-confidence that it could effect its program. It was a leadership that conducted the affairs of the party within a consensual framework in which the majority of party members shared the same basic values.

Second, this was the era of a new link with the trade union movement. The first formal acknowledgement of the relationship was made by the Canadian Congress of Labour in 1943 when in convention the CCL endorsed the CCF as labour's political arm. A number of leading trade unionists, most of them protégés of Charles Millard, the national director of the Steelworkers, held key positions in the party. Millard himself was an MPP from 1943 to 1945 and again from 1948 to 1951. While he was provincial leader, Jolliffe acted as counsel for the Steelworkers and other unions. The union link was firm and permanent.

Finally, it should be noted that the party displayed considerable sophistication in this period in dealing with the problems posed by political life. It ran a reasonably extensive educational program which served the purposes of reinforcing the consensus of the socialist generation and of providing new recruits in the movement with a sense of having mastered the mystery of the socialist alternative. The Ontario party, while it devoted much effort to issues of a purely provincial nature, was also capable of making its opinion known about the broader issues of the time. For example, it was very active in the fight to maintain price controls during the reconstruction period, it welcomed the Marshall Plan for postwar Europe with a reasonably detailed statement, and it was quick to denounce the Soviet takeover of Czechoslovakia in September 1948. Indeed, although the party was unable to create the cradle-to-grave counterculture that Guenther Roth describes,[49] it nonetheless made a significant attempt to be concerned with the whole man.

The party newspaper, the *CCF News*, certainly devoted much of its space to internal party announcements and commentary, but it also had articles on cooking and women's fashions (the Young CCF protest in 1947 against lowered hemlines caused a great deal of commentary from the press) and reviews of books, plays, and radio dramas. In the 23 October 1947 edition, for example, John MacKenzie (a pseudonym) urged the readers of the *CCF News* to forsake a steady diet of detective stories and romantic novels to discover Canadian poetry and prose. He suggested that the poetry of Frank Scott, P.K. Page, Patrick Anderson, and A.M. Klein would be rewarding and touted the novels of Hugh MacLennan, Gabrielle Roy, Morley Callaghan, and Sinclair Ross. With hints of the "socialist realism" views of European leftists, he stated: "In the tradition of realism springing from American writers such as Hemingway and Scott Fitzgerald, is, of course, Morley Callaghan of Toronto, who has done more and better writing than is commonly realised. Sinclair Ross of Winnipeg is a writer of cosmopolitan problems, his people are often big city people, who, for one reason or another, find themselves forced to live in small settlements." MacKenzie concluded by recommending Northrop Frye as a critic.

All these facts indicate a vigorous and lively organization which, despite some election setbacks, was confident of itself and of its destiny. It saw itself as a major party capable of taking over the reins of government as had its sister party in Saskatchewan (it had been re-elected in the 1948 election) and as had the Labour parties of Britain, New Zealand, and Australia.

1951–1964: The Quest for Respectability

The confidence did not last. If Zakuta is wrong in suggesting that the party was in decline after 1945, there is no question that he – and almost every other observer of the Ontario CCF – is right in noting that after 1951 the party was in sorry shape. The effect of the 1951 provincial election on party morale cannot be overestimated. It was a devastating shock. After 1948 the party had real hopes of continuing to make electoral gains. The election was held on 22 November 1951, and in a memo as late as 17 November the provincial campaign manager stated:

We're doing all right. Don't let the seeming lack of public interest disturb you, or fool you.

There is every indication that support for the CCF is coming up fast.

In fact, we appear to be making *more headway faster* than in 1948.

That's my considered view after getting reports from a dozen average ridings.

It may be a light vote ... but the CCF support is there ... do everything you can to get it out.[50]

In fact the CCF suffered a humiliating defeat, being reduced to only two seats in the ninety-seat assembly. Its share of the popular vote fell from 27 to 19 per cent. Ted Jolliffe was once again defeated in the constituency of York South.

The CCF was certainly reduced to minor party status. It could be ignored in the provincial legislature and its organization was in total disarray. Subsequent federal and provincial elections confirmed this status. It is interesting, therefore, to note that during this stage of the party's life it did not return to the sectarian habits of that earlier stage before 1942. Indeed what characterizes the party in this period is, not a retreat from the world which has rejected it, but rather a redoubling of efforts to achieve respectability. These efforts had three dimensions: the first was the party's desperate attempt to create a genuine organizational capacity; the second related to ideological divisions in the party and the factionalism which resulted from those divisions, as well as the concomitant concern of the party leadership that the CCF be utterly distinguished from the Communists and other Marxist groups; the third was the party's pursuit of a number of scandals which plagued the Conservative administration in Ontario.

Organizational Capacity

Linking the organizational capacity of the party with the search for respectability may seem curious. The CCF, however, saw its inability to publicly transmit its message as a grave weakness, one which in some sense shamed it. Jolliffe, as leader, had never been much concerned with organization.[51] He had focused on the work of the party in the legislature and had been very successful. Many measures ultimately adopted by the legislature had been first drafted by Jolliffe or by some other member of the CCF caucus. Jolliffe was such an expert on legislation that some years after he had left the Ontario legislature he was asked by Premier Leslie Frost to attend a cabinet meeting to discuss an important bill. As Jolliffe describes it:

It's typical of Frost that some years later, after I had left politics, he had a troublesome bill, which I had drafted originally for the veterinarians. The attitude of the minister of health was negative, the attitude of the attorney general was negative, and the minister of agriculture who was supposed to be sponsoring the bill was ambivalent about it. Well, Les Frost's method of dealing with that problem was to call me and say, "Look, Ted, how would you like to come around to the Cabinet on Tuesday morning and explain this damn bill. These fellows don't seem to understand it and I know you can explain it to them." So I went to the cabinet meeting – it's the only Ontario meeting I ever attended – and it was typical of Frost that after some fairly lengthy discussion in which several ministers participated ... Les said, "Well, boys, you've all heard Ted's explanation of this thing and it makes sense to me, so I think what we had better do is that Bill [Stewart] had better introduce it in the House tomorrow afternoon" – and that was it.[52]

After 1951 it was no longer possible for the CCF in Ontario to have any real legislative impact, and Jolliffe's neglect of party organization became an acute problem. Moreover this was a problem that was recognized by the party and alluded to, debated, and discussed in meeting after meeting and speech after speech. Typical of many is the speech by David Lewis at a meeting of the Provincial Council on 12 and 13 January 1952, which immediately followed the 1951 electoral disaster. A summary in the minutes states:

Enthusiasm could not be created synthetically, said Mr. Lewis. Our failure in the CCF to the extent there had been a failure, and in his opinion there had not been one, was only an organizational lack. In the last two or three years we have gone through a period of public apathy in politics which is a phenomenon throughout the world. People in the Western world are in a stunned state, through relative prosperity on the one hand and hopelessness in the world situation on the other. Every Socialist movement throughout the world has been affected. To the extent that there has been a failure, it has been on the part of our local organizations throughout the country and in this province. National, provincial and local organizations should concentrate on getting new members into the movement to revive enthusiasm and provide new workers in the movement.[53]

The need for some new arrangement was particularly urgent. Before the 1951 election the party had been aware that, for the most part, riding organizations throughout the province had deteriorated.[54] Over the summer an organizing program using university students had been established, and Fred Young, CCF organizer for the Maritime provinces, had been appointed to the Ontario staff in September 1951. After the election money was not available to continue even this skeleton arrangement, and the CCF in Ontario faced the prospect of literally having no full-time organizational capacity.

In this moment of crisis and imminent collapse the Ontario CCF had but two places to turn. There was, of course, the Saskatchewan CCF, which had been re-elected as the government in June 1948 and again in June 1952. The Saskatchewan party had a large membership, something in excess of thirty thousand members at a time when the Ontario CCF had less than ten thousand. More important, it held power. Throughout the 1950s the Ontario party relied on Saskatchewan for information about public policy alternatives and for reasonably detailed research on those alternatives. The Ontario provincial secretary (the chief full-time officer of the CCF), Ken Bryden, had been deputy minister of labour in Saskatchewan and was well acquainted with the leading personalities there. However, the Saskatchewan CCF had its own battles to fight and could ill afford to provide much material assistance to Ontario.

The Ontario CCF therefore looked primarily to the trade union movement and particularly to Charles Millard. Millard had always been a very active member of the CCF and had served as an officer of the provincial party on a number of occasions. He recognized the need of the CCF for significant financial assistance. As national director of the Steelworkers in Canada, however, he did not have complete authority over the expenditure of union funds; that authority lay with the international officers of the union in Pittsburgh and they were reluctant to subsidize directly a minor political party in Canada. Millard had attempted to obtain such a subsidy for some years but had been unsuccessful. Fate, however, played a hand. The president of the United Steelworkers of America, Phillip Murray (who was also president of the Congress of Industrial Organizations) died suddenly in 1952 and a new president had to be elected. Millard skilfully used his leverage as national director in Canada and as a very powerful member of the Steelworkers International Board to obtain an agreement for an informal subsidy. The new president, David J. MacDonald, who had been international secretary-treasurer of the union, agreed to add two individuals to the Steelworkers' staff in

Canada who would essentially act as CCF organizers. The two would be paid a regular staff representative salary and would be given other amenities, which included an automobile and an expense allowance. However, they would not be expected, in normal circumstances, to provide services for Steelworker locals or to do tasks which a regular staff representative would undertake. Instead they would organize for the CCF and would work under the direction of the Ontario provincial secretary. As soon as this agreement was reached, two organizers were quickly hired: Fred Young, who covered southern Ontario from Toronto, and C.C. ("Doc") Ames, who covered northern Ontario from Kirkland Lake.[55] As Ken Bryden put it: "It was really the Steelworkers who saved us from going out of business."[56] In addition other unions, particularly the United Automobile Workers, agreed to provide money to permit a leadership fund to be established which would allow the provincial leader, while not a member of the legislature, to work full time.[57]

In a sense, after 1951 the CCF became a kind of junior partner to the trade union movement, or at least to that section of the labour movement in which the Steelworkers, the Auto Workers, and other industrial unions were dominant. It was the new relationship which was so ably brokered by David Lewis and which in some measure gave Lewis the tremendous influence that he exercised in the CCF. Lewis was able to play this role particularly well because his law firm Jolliffe, Lewis, and Osler acted as legal counsel for the industrial unions.[58]

The long march back to electoral success and political influence had now begun in earnest but it was to prove a very long march indeed. The year 1953 saw two important events for the party. On 10 August a federal election was held in which the CCF share of the popular vote was reduced in Ontario. Joe Noseworthy, however, managed to retain his York South constituency. In November a special leadership convention was held at which Donald C. MacDonald, the national organizer and national treasurer, was elected the new provincial leader. He defeated Fred Young and Andrew Brewin for the post.

The new provincial leader immediately set out to rebuild the party organization. He was fortunately able to do so on a full-time basis, as he was provided with a salary of six thousand dollars a year from the special leadership fund donated by the unions. In addition he was provided with a small expense allowance and a car. MacDonald had the help of Ken Bryden, the full-time provincial secretary, and Fred

Young and Doc Ames, the two Steelworkers who were essentially full-time CCF organizers. There was as well an advisory committee to the leader established in December 1953, consisting of Bill Grummett (the CCF house leader), Ted Jolliffe, Andrew Brewin, David Lewis, Fred Young, Margaret ("Peg") Stewart (the provincial president), and Ken Bryden.

The first test for Don MacDonald came in 1955 with the September provincial election. The results were disappointing, as the party continued its downward slide in the popular vote from 19 per cent in 1951 to 17. However, there was some considerable consolation in that MacDonald regained the York South seat for the party and found himself in the legislature, together with Tommy Thomas, re-elected in Oshawa, and Reg Gisborn, elected in Hamilton East. Grummett, the former house leader, was defeated in his Cochrane South constituency. The result of the election was Conservatives eighty-four seats, Liberals eleven, and CCF three, in a slightly enlarged assembly, now boasting ninety-eight seats. It was a small gain for the CCF, but at least it was an improvement and it looked all the better now that the last remaining Communist member of the legislature had been defeated. There was naturally a certain disappointment after the election, but the party was not as demoralized and depressed as it had been after 1951.

Much of the credit for this buoyancy must go to the leader, Donald MacDonald. Zakuta speaks as though this buoyancy and enthusiasm were part of a role which the leaders of the party, particularly the provincial leader, were expected to play. He tells the story of the election-night gathering in MacDonald's home after the results had come in.

Their common lot – all but the provincial leader had lost – and the release from the wearying pressures of the campaign and from the almost unbearable suspense of election day all contributed to an atmosphere in which talk was spontaneous, lively and full of wry but exhilarating and comforting humour.

At 1:00 AM the Provincial Leader left the room to answer a long distance call. He returned and, after shouting over the hubbub for attention, excitedly exclaimed, "Who says we're licked? That call came from Kenora. They're starting in tomorrow to nominate a candidate and get set for the next election."

Someone asked, "How did they do?" "Badly," he replied, momentarily crestfallen.[59]

But MacDonald was not playing a role, for he had a naturally enthusiastic, irrepressible kind of personality and was an indefatigable campaigner. In reporting to the Provincial Council on his activities in 1954–5 he was able to announce:

During the past year he had attended 185 meetings as the main speaker plus a large number of others as a guest. He had given seven CBC broadcasts, ten broadcasts on other stations, had made five or six television appearances, had attended two conventions of the Ontario Farmers Union, one convention of the Ontario Federation of Agriculture, one convention of the Ontario Education Association, and had been at least once on all University campuses in Ontario except O.A.C. He had also spent a lot of time in the organization of his own riding of York South.[60]

The struggle continued. In early January 1956 the Provincial Council noted that the CCF should increase its organizational efforts (the constant cry), bring its program up to date, and present the program imaginatively. That same year saw the Winnipeg Declaration, a document designed to replace the Regina Manifesto as the statement of the party's philosophy. It was hoped that its more moderate language would appeal to a wider population. The party also was beginning to experiment with new campaigning techniques with television, and with survey research. There were some setbacks. On 31 March 1956 Joe Noseworthy died suddenly, creating a CCF vacancy in the House of Commons. As this was the only federal CCF seat in Ontario, there was considerable interest in the nomination. Two powerful candidates sought the party's nod: Ken Bryden, still provincial secretary, and William Sefton, a Steelworkers' staff representative and brother of Larry Sefton, district director of the Steelworkers' union, the district comprising Ontario, Manitoba, Saskatchewan, Alberta, and British Columbia. Sefton, to the distress of most of the CCF leadership, won the nomination. He then lost the by-election. This loss was particularly galling in 1956 because it was the year of the famous pipeline debate in Parliament in which the Conservatives and the CCF united in opposition to the Liberal government's invocation of closure. The unofficial leader of this combination was CCF MP Stanley Knowles, a master of the Commons Rule Book. The debate sparked interest in the national political scene for members of the Ontario party, and they lived in some hope that they could make considerable gains in the next federal election.

The federal election held in June 1957 was, however, another disappointment, although not to the same degree as the previous election. The party campaigned in large part on its forceful presence in Parliament and was rewarded in Ontario by three seats. The CCF popular vote in Ontario went from 11.4 to 12.6 per cent. Still the party was not completely happy with the results, as all its key figures were defeated. Those who won (Douglas Fisher in Port Arthur, Arnold Peters in Timiskaming, and Murdo Martin in Timmins) were all in northern Ontario and were all men with little connection to the leadership of the party.

In 1957 John Diefenbaker and the Conservative party astounded political observers by narrowly edging out the Liberals in the House of Commons. Standings were 111 Conservatives, 105 Liberals, 25 CCF, 19 Social Credit, and 5 others, for a total of 265 seats. The Liberals, who had formed the government since 1935, decided not to cling to office and Diefenbaker led a minority government. With the initiative in his hands Diefenbaker, after introducing some new legislation and mercilessly excoriating the Liberals for their political ineptitude and alleged mismanagement of the country, called a snap election for 31 March 1958. With his prophetlike campaign style and his exciting vision of the northern growth of Canada, Diefenbaker swept the boards. With 54 per cent of the popular vote the Conservatives elected 208 members. The Liberals were decimated, reduced to a bare 49 seats, while the CCF was almost completely routed, returning only 8 members. Among those suffering defeat were the leader, M.J. Coldwell, and the deputy leader, Stanley Knowles. Social Credit was eliminated from the House of Commons.

For some time the CCF seemed finished after this debacle. The party had prided itself on its performance in Parliament, particularly the work of MPs such as Coldwell and Knowles, and now it was not only reduced to a corporal's guard, but it was left with a fractious crew in the House. The story (no doubt apocryphal) is told that when those MPs met for the first time to elect their house leader, no one was elected on the first ballot because there was a tie for first place, each MP receiving one vote, presumably his own. Across the country the party received slightly less than 10 per cent of the popular vote and in Ontario it received only 10.6 per cent.

The party did not completely despair. In less than a month it was launched in a new direction. In April 1958 the Canadian Labour Congress (CLC) passed a resolution calling on the CCF and others to join it creating a new political force in the country.[61] The passage of this resolution was not an automatic response to the election defeat; it required considerable political effort, but it was a significant boost to CCF morale coming when it did.

When the Canadian Labour Congress had been brought into being in 1956 with the merger of the Trades and Labour Congress and the Canadian Congress of Labour, the craft unions in the TLC were the largest group in the new congress. As a result the industrial unions in the CCL, whose key leaders were mostly CCFers, had refrained from insisting that the CLC go on record as endorsing the CCF. They had hoped, of course, that they could bring the new congress to this position in four or five years. This timetable was rapidly accelerated following the March 31 election. With the help of some sympathetic officers of the old TLC unions, the industrial union forces were determined to have a resolution calling for a new political force passed at the April convention in order to preserve a social democratic party in Canada. Such an accomplishment was possible because most of the TLC leaders who were not members of the CCF were either Communist or, more usually, Liberal. Almost none were Conservative, and with a Conservative government in Ottawa the Liberal union leaders were prepared to consider new political arrangements.

Equally important to the success of this new party initiative was the election of officers at the 1958 convention. In 1956 the new congress had three full-time officers: a president, a secretary-treasurer, and an executive vice-president. The president, Claude Jodoin, was from the TLC; the secretary-treasurer, Donald MacDonald, was from the CCL; and the executive vice-president, Gordon Cushing, from the TLC. In 1958 Cushing had decided not to seek re-election as a congress officer in order to become assistant deputy minister of labour. As well the congress decided to create a second vice-presidential post, and joining Jodoin and MacDonald as full-time officers were Stanley Knowles and William Dodge. The balance had now shifted, and shifted in favour of CCL attitudes and co-operation with the CCF. Cushing, who was generally unsympathetic to the CCF, was gone. In his place were two committed CCFers. Dodge had been one of the most active members of the Quebec section of the party and had run for public office under the CCF label on several occasions. And as Horowitz points out,

The election of Knowles was especially significant. He was not a labour leader, but a CCF politician who had retained his membership in the ITU [International Typographical Union]. There could be no more emphatic demonstration that the CLC's formal non-partisanship was a thing of the past and that the CLC and the CCF had now entered into a very close partnership. Knowles' election also meant that there would be a full-time officer of the CLC who would devote the great bulk of his time and energy to the implementation of the new party resolution.[62]

The CLC initiative was particularly welcomed in the Ontario CCF, the more so because the resolution hinted at a new party which would be more broadly based than a party which was simply the product of a CLC/CCF merger. Later that year Donald C. MacDonald made an important speech in which he called on progressive Liberals to join the movement for a new party and presciently he ended his speech in French. The party was looking to the future, not the past. At the May council meeting of the Ontario CCF there was almost no discussion of the federal election disaster; instead there was a practical consideration of the advantages of concentrating the resources of the party in those seats it had the best chance of winning. In August, Stephen Lewis, David's eldest son, was appointed as an organizer and later Gordon Brigden was appointed as a part-time organizer in Toronto. By 1958 the University of Toronto CCF Club had become a large and influential group on that campus,[63] and other university clubs, such as the one at the University of Western Ontario, were beginning to gain a significant membership. Late in the year, on 20 December, MacDonald proposed that a CCF businessman's association be set up, a move which he hoped would assure small businessmen about the desirability of the CCF. At this time the party's economic thinking was particularly influenced by Kenneth Galbraith's *The Affluent Society*, a reformist, nonsocialist document,[64] which, it was hoped, would help the party to appeal to a broader base.

Attempts at integration continued. In January 1959 the CCF appointed an election committee consisting of George Grube as chairman, Donald C. MacDonald, Henry Weisbach, Marj Pinney, Ellen Camnitzer, and Ken Bryden. It was expected that the Ontario Federation of Labour (OFL) would appoint two additional members to the committee. However, by the end of February this was deemed to be inappropriate and instead the federation was asked to appoint six members so that the committee would be a large one with equal representation from the CCF and the labour movement. The OFL did so, appointing David Archer, Doug Hamilton, Morden Lazarus, Stewart Cooke, Cliff Pilkey, and Bill Sefton. All except Hamilton were active ccFers.

The provincial election which this committee had been established to oversee occurred on 11 June. The CLC assigned three of its staff to work as organizers full time, and in addition Cliff Scotton, the editor of the CLC magazine *Canadian Labour*, was assigned to organize the publicity campaign. Despite this help, the CCF did not make significant gains. The party campaigned against the Frost government by denouncing the scandals that had plagued the Cabinet over the past several years, castigated the Tories for their fiscal parsimony, and promised better hospitals, better roads, more schools, more scholarship assistance for universities, a public health insurance scheme, and other welfare state measures. In some ways the campaign is best summed up by the chorus of the CCF election ballad, sung to the tune of "Sixteen Tons."

They're in sixteen years and what have you got?
A heap of promises and Tory rot,
Political morals in a gruesome mess
Of highway scandals and natural gas.

The election results showed little change from those in 1955. With 46 per cent of the popular vote, down 3 per cent from 1955, the Conservatives won seventy-one seats. The Liberals, up 4 per cent to 37, doubled their seats with twenty-two, while the CCF held its vote at 17 per cent, winning two more seats for a total of five. Undoubtedly the greatest boost for the party was that Ken Bryden was elected in Toronto-Woodbine and was able to provide much-needed articulate assistance to MacDonald in the legislature.

With the election out of the way preparations for the new party intensified. Certain union leaders began to inject a more optimistic and aggressive note in the party's deliberations. At the August council meeting, led by Bill Sefton, they managed to have the council come close to repudiating its own formula that no steps be taken to contest a by-election in a weak riding unless some local initiative was present. In this instance council urged the executive to look carefully at the possibility of contesting a by-election in the eastern Ontario riding of Hastings-Frontenac. In another initiative Don MacDonald argued strenuously for an interest group approach to new party organizing. He suggested that for most people their concern about general political questions was not sufficient to motivate them to attend political meetings, but they would attend meetings related to their particular interests as businessmen, housewives, Italians, engineers, and so forth. A number of clubs along those lines were subsequently established, some of which attracted significant numbers of members. Young people were seen as particularly important to a new party, and the party executive endorsed a proposal to have an organizer spend at least a third of his time working with youth groups.[65] More important was the National Seminar on the New Party at which representatives from the larger provincial sections of the CCF were present. This seminar, held in Winnipeg in August 1959, considered possibilities for the new party organization and concluded that it would be desirable if "liberally minded Canadians" who had not previously been associated either with the CCF or with the trade union movement were to become involved. The idea of "founders clubs," through which this new group of people could participate in the creation of a new party, was first broached here.

The proposal to involve a new group of people was not universally acclaimed. Indeed, the whole new party initiative was greeted with suspicion by some sections of the CCF. Although the participants in the national seminar were mostly enthusiastic about these "founders clubs," that idea was, in fact, very badly received at a subsequent CCF National Council meeting, also held in Winnipeg.[66] Much of the opposition came from the British Columbia CCF, whose executive was concerned about the character of the people who might be invited to join the new party. Don MacDonald felt called upon to reply to this sentiment in a letter to Grace MacInnis, then president of the British Columbia CCF, on 2 September 1959. He wrote:

This brings me to the points in your letter which, quite frankly Grace, I find somewhat difficult to understand. For example, you say "we found it difficult to believe that Ontario or any other Province has large numbers of people who share the Socialist outlook and who are only waiting for some vehicle other than the CCF to make their entrance into political work". I feel quite confident in my own mind that simply is not the case in Ontario and from my knowledge of B.C. – admittedly some years out of date now – I cannot see how it is valid even for B.C. To illustrate my point for the Ontario picture: our membership now stands at its highest at any time since the end of the War. However, it is just over 10,000. During all these years we have never gotten fewer than roughly 300,000 and have gotten as high as 405,000 votes. I am convinced, and so are most of the Ontario leadership on the provincial and local levels that many more than 10,000 of the 300,000 who have consistently voted for the CCF can be persuaded to become members if we pursue the education and organization work to get them to sign on the dotted line. I find it difficult to believe that not a few tens of thousands of these people "share the Socialist outlook" as much as the majority of those people who have actually become members. Further, the prospect of a new party with a broader base and greater resources to do the job is just one more reason why they might be persuaded to come in now whereas they have stayed out, of course, simply because the CCF organization never got to them and asked them to come in.[67]

Even in Ontario, however, there was a certain discontent. At the October convention Douglas Fisher, MP for Port Arthur, publicly denounced the whole new party initiative and made it clear that his views were shared by Arnold Peters, MP from Timiskaming. Fisher then proceeded to run for the office of provincial president against Carrol Coburn of the United Auto Workers' staff, and Fisher received approximately a third of the delegate votes.[68] To make the division clear, it may be noted that all three MPs, Fisher, Peters, and Murdo Martin (Timmins), ran for one of the five vice-presidential posts. Martin, a supporter of the new party, was elected; the other two were defeated. Although there was opposition in the Ontario CCF, the leadership and the majority of the party were united in support of the idea.

Other problems were encountered at this time, particularly one which occurred when the press reported that Claude Jodoin, president of the Canadian Labour Congress, had declared that the CLC itself would not affiliate to the new party. Some pundits interpreted this statement as a backing away from the idea. In fact, given the constitutional structure of the labour movement in Canada, it would have been exceedingly difficult for the CLC as a central labour body to take this step (even the Trades Union Congress in Britain is not directly affiliated to the Labour party), and what Jodoin did was to point out the reality that affiliations would be the responsibility of individual unions. The Ontario executive hastily issued a statement clarifying this.[69]

Generally progress continued to be made in creating the new party. The National Committee for the New Party was formed in 1958 with equal representation from the CLC and the CCF.[70] Late in 1959 the committee appointed Desmond Sparham to head up on a full-time basis the development of New Party clubs, as the "founders clubs" became known. Because this was a national appointment, he was expected to work across Canada; however, since the initiative for New Party clubs was primarily MacDonald's, along with others in the Ontario leadership, he spent most of his time in Ontario, for the first while in Toronto. A subcommittee of the National Committee for the New Party was formed to consider the whole question of recruitment of "liberally minded" individuals and, in part, to oversee Sparham's work. The members of this subcommittee were Donald C. MacDonald (chairman), Thérèse Casgrain, Andrew Brewin, George Burt, Woodrow Lloyd, and Frank Scott. Sparham set to work to organize the clubs and achieved a certain immediate success, particularly in Toronto.

It is difficult from the records to gauge the real impact of this effort, since not everyone recruited to these clubs was in fact a liberally minded person waiting to see the light through this new organization. In some international union constitutions, local unions, not only in the United States but also in Canada, were forbidden formal association with a political party. In some areas therefore locals were urged to establish themselves as New Party clubs to circumvent this constitutional prohibition. In addition certain members of the CCF were urged to become involved in the clubs. MacDonald, for example, wrote a letter to a number of riding associations, asking for names of "middle-class types" who could be directed into the new party movement. Yet as Sparham points out in his final report, large numbers of new people did become involved through this device, and a number of very successful clubs consisting primarily of individuals who were not connected with the CCF and were not trade unionists were established.

Three major events in 1960 affected the Ontario CCF: the national convention of the CCF at which Hazen Argue was elected leader; federal by-elections in Peterborough and Niagara Falls; and the victory of the University of Toronto's CCF Club in that university's model parliament. The question of a national leader created a dilemma at the CCF convention in August 1969. After his personal defeat in the 1958 election, M.J. Coldwell decided not to seek re-election as national leader. He was then seventy years old. The party prevailed upon him to stay on as leader for another two years, but by 1960 his health was such that he felt he had to insist that he could no longer continue in the post. Who was to succeed him? The almost universal choice was Tommy Douglas, then premier of Saskatchewan, but Douglas did not want to leave Saskatchewan at this time (he had just won another general election in June). If there was any hope of luring him onto the national stage, it would have to be through the vehicle of the new party; however, the new party was not to be officially born until July 1961. The CCF national leadership concluded therefore that it would be best to leave the position vacant for a year until the founding of the new party. National executive members, primarily led by David Lewis and Stanley Knowles, proposed that, instead of electing a national leader, the convention should create the post of parliamentary leader which would be filled by Hazen Argue, the CCF house leader. Argue agreed, but other members of the parliamentary caucus were not so ready to accede to the wishes of the executive and persuaded Argue that he should not accept this half measure but instead should seek to be Coldwell's successor. On 1 August 1960, just before the convention, this group sent the following letter, on House of Commons stationery, to delegates and other key party members.

A certain group in the CCF wish to have the office of National Leader remain vacant, or have it filled by a figure-head until the official birth of the new party ...

We quarrel with no-one's desire to put pressure on each delegate but we ask that each of you who may have been lobbied by this "no leader for the CCF" to consider our theme: THE CCF NEEDS A NATIONAL LEADER – NOW!!

There is near unanimity that Premier Douglas would be the perfect CCF National Leader. But repeatedly Mr. Douglas has said that he cannot run because of previous responsibilities to the people of Saskatchewan. We must accept his decision.

But does this personal decision of Mr. Douglas mean we should delay a choice of leader until we die as a distinct entity? Well ... we have urged our present CCF House Leader, Hazen Argue, MP, to run for National Leader at next week's convention. (Hazen, of course, has always been a strong supporter of Tommy Douglas.) He agrees with us that it is imperative to have a National Leader. This for many reasons; but especially with an election possible in 1961.

We hope you will find it possible to agree with us that there should be a

Leader chosen now. We shall do our best at Regina to show you that Hazen is the man.

Yours sincerely,

H.W. Herridge, MP
Frank Howard, MP
Douglas Fisher, MP
Arnold Peters, MP[71]

At the convention the Lewis/Knowles proposal was rejected by the delegates and Argue was acclaimed national leader. The result was that despite the sentiment expressed in the letter about Argue's strong support for Tommy Douglas, once he became leader Argue decided he wanted to keep the job in the new party and he campaigned vigorously for it against Douglas. This intraparty warfare had important consequences, as it tended to shift some of the focus from the developing organizational thrust.

The federal by-elections were indeed an event. The party had been particularly hopeful in Niagara Falls. As Don MacDonald stated:

If we are able to persuade Mitchelson to stand in Niagara Falls, the enthusiasm will be high, not only because his reputation as a first-rate candidate has long since reached our people in Ottawa, but also because Liberal MPs from the Niagara Peninsula have privately intimated that they have no obvious candidate in sight, and therefore there is every likelihood that they will not be able to hold the seat. Of course, Peterborough can never be taken seriously.[72]

Ed Mitchelson was persuaded to run in Niagara Falls, and although in Peterborough the original choice as a first-class candidate, an insurance agent, decided not to run, a young attractive teacher, Walter Pitman, did agree. After learning that the first choice for candidate was out, MacDonald relentlessly pursued Pitman, and as he stated: "He [Pitman] professed to be flattered that he was approached to consider candidacy, stated flatly that he was interested, but wanted to think it over. I emphasized that under the circumstances of our organization at the moment, there would be no need to seek time off for the campaign for there is no prospect of winning, that the campaign would likely be all over by November."[73] It was correct that the election was all over by November, as the two by-elections were held 31 October 1960; it was not quite correct that there was no chance in Peterborough. In a startling electoral turn-around, Pitman, running under the New Party label, was returned. In the 1958 election the Conservative candidate had obtained 19,032 votes; the Liberal, 7,254; and the CCF, a mere 1,887. Two years later in the by-election Pitman received 13,208 votes, with the Conservatives running second with 10,240 votes and the Liberals third with 5,393. In Niagara Falls the Liberals held the seat with Judy LaMarsh, but Mitchelson came in a very respectable third under the New Party label.

The Peterborough result galvanized the new party forces and dealt those who would preserve the old CCF, or at least actively discourage the liberally minded and the New Party clubs, with a mortal blow. Writing of the Peterborough by-election, Walter Young argued that Pitman's victory was in no small measure the result of a modern and moderate image that the new party conveyed as opposed to the doctrinaire image of the old CCF.[74] This view was not uncommon in the Ontario CCF itself. Who could dispute that something extraordinary had happened – that in Peterborough in 1958 the party had finished an abysmal third and that under the New Party label and with a middle-class professional candidate it had come first. If the party could win Peterborough where two years before it had received a bare 7 per cent of the votes, could it not realistically and conceivably form a government in the country? Diefenbaker's swollen caucus was beginning to show wear, and with the Liberals still in considerable disarray the possibility existed that the new party could sweep to power. It was a heady victory, and the future consequences as seen by CCFers were even more heady.

There were still those who objected to the new party, but they found it more and more difficult to sustain those objections against the vision of instant victory which Peterborough seemed to portend. Instead these activists tended to rally around the Argue candidacy for federal leader and to give up the larger issue of the new party itself. As one MP wrote of the Argue campaign: "Hazen seems to have been able to rally every square peg, both in and around our movement, to his side – the Colin Camerons, the Dorothy Steeves, the Leo Nimsicks, the Cedric Coxs, the Pawleys from Winnipeg, the Bill Seftons and the Jack McVeys from Toronto, the Neil Reimers from the Oil Workers, the Doug Fishers and the Arnold Peters."[75] What aroused this MP's ire was a circular mailed in Vancouver from a

Herbert Kelly, claiming that the CCF national office had arranged a tour for Tommy Douglas but had refused to do the same for Hazen Argue, that Claude Jodoin had used his position as leader of the CLC to forbid the formation of unions of the unemployed, that provincial conventions of the CCF in Saskatchewan were called off to suit the national leadership, and that Owen Jones, president of the British Columbia CCF and a supporter of Tommy Douglas, ignored a picket of unemployed workers to attend a dinner in Kelowna honouring W.A.C. Bennett, the premier of the province.

Organizational work proceeded apace but with some complications. Before the new party was formed, organizations of the Ontario CCF in Toronto included the Ontario Committee for the New Party, the Ontario Federation of Labour, the National Committee for the New Party, the National CCF, the Toronto and District CCF Council, the Toronto Area Council for the New Party, the Council of New Party Clubs in Ontario, the Toronto Area Council for New Party Clubs, CCF riding associations, both federal and provincial, individual New Party clubs, the Young CCF, and New Party youth clubs. All these were officially constituted bodies and their existence meant immense complication. In terms of the nomination of candidates, Peg Stewart, the CCF provincial secretary, outlined some problems in a 1961 letter.

The point here is that while there is a very big job to be done by an area committee, if it results in an extra set of machinery being set up between the provincial body and the riding association, we will have cleavage instead of cooperation. I am thinking here specifically of the case of a Metro organizer going into Eglinton riding to meet with the Eglinton executive and tell the members what his plan was from the Metro committee point of view. It does not seem to me that the authority of the Metro committee extends that far without consultation. Or on the question of memberships. In the CCF memberships were the responsibility of the provincial sections. But for New Party Clubs the National Committee for the New Party had the authority. Because of a lack of staff the National Committee found it difficult to exercise this authority but clearly could not transfer it to the Ontario CCF where the staff was available, instead they had to consider transferring it to the Ontario Committee for the New Party which could then make use of the Ontario CCF staff.[76]

At the time of the writing of this letter it seemed that while the authority for individual or club memberships in New Party clubs remained with the National Committee for the New Party, the committee gave a firm undertaking that it would consult provincial bodies (of which there were several). Even if these provincial bodies were given the authority to act on an interim basis, the recognition of New Party clubs would still remain in the hands of the national committee. The party, at least in Ontario, found itself caught in a constitutional tangle.

Nevertheless all these little armies in step, or out, were marching towards the same goal – the founding convention of the new party, afterwards to be called the New Democratic Party, held in Ottawa from 31 July to 4 August 1961. The convention was a smashing success. As I. Norman Smith, associate editor of the *Ottawa Journal* and a newspaperman not noted for his sympathy with the left, stated:

This reporter looks back on the founding convention of the New Democratic Party with a strange kind of elation. It was a humdinger. The NDP is going to do things.

My elation is not that of a party supporter. It will neither surprise nor sadden them when I say I am not a party member, nor do I plan to be.

The feeling of warmth that ran through me as the convention hall throbbed with genuine fervour was an awareness that democracy was showing some life ...

... the convention to my eyes was not only larger than the older party's held, it had a greater zest to it. More of its members were between the ages of 20 and 40, a good age to be a participating democrat ...

... it seemed also that they worked harder, sat longer at their places, argued with more personal conviction ...

... "this is a well-organized meeting" said a non-party man to me, I think somewhat in self-defense for the old parties.[77]

Ramsay Cook, writing in *Saturday Night*, expressed similar sentiments:

From the first day of this extraordinarily well-organized meeting a division emerged between the moderates all the way from pragmatic, Fabian-like socialists to new party club representatives and trade union delegates, who were either left-wing liberals or practical social reformers who cared little for the subtleties of political philosophy ... the real leader of the moderates is the pragmatic Premier of Saskatchewan. Though the diminutive "cocky wee

Douglas" kept his own counsel during the first days of debate, there was never any doubt that he favoured the moderate socialist planks of the new party draft program.[78]

That program was handily carried and Douglas himself was easily elected over Hazen Argue as federal leader. The vote was 1,386 to 380.

If this founding convention was an inspirational success, it was, for the Ontario party, the provincial founding, held 7, 8, 9 October, which consummated the organizational marriage among the CCF, the labour movement, and the New Party club activists. The convention was a large one with 1,044 voting delegates.[79] By way of contrast, the last convention of the Ontario CCF in 1959 had 301 voting delegates. Despite the large size of the convention and the number of new people brought in by the New Party clubs, there were very few changes of substance between the practices of the New Democratic Party of Ontario and the practices of the CCF of Ontario. The key convention posts were in the hands of individuals who had long been active in the Ontario CCF. The convention chairmen were George Grube, who had chaired most Ontario CCF conventions, and David Archer, who in addition to being president of the Ontario Federation of Labour was also a long-time CCF activist. The Credentials Committee was headed by Henry Weisbach, the executive secretary of the OFL but also the past chairman of the CCF executive. The Constitution Committee was headed by Doc Ames, who, although a staff representative of the United Steelworkers, was essentially the northern Ontario CCF organizer. And even George Cadbury, chairman of the important Program and Resolutions Committee, though he looked the part of a liberally minded person come to join the new crusade, was in fact a long-time socialist who had served as the key economic adviser for the Saskatchewan CCF government.

The one important constitutional change which took place was that the full-time officer of the party, the secretary-treasurer, was elected from the convention as were the fifteen executive members at large. The CCF had used the Provincial Council for these elections. The holding of direct elections for all positions from the convention floor was a trade union practice, and despite some opposition from old-line CCFers, the trade unionists carried the day. On other matters very little changed. This was certainly true of the new party program. The convention adopted a report entitled "Planning for Abundance," which emphasized the importance of planning at all levels of government. It called for legislation to encourage trade unionism and collective bargaining without interfering with matters which belong at the bargaining table; for a new deal for the farmer by which was meant a better deal for the family farmer; and finally for public automobile insurance, a proposal which, though electorally attractive, was hardly revolutionary. Finally it should be noted that although the executive contained a number of new faces, it was still dominated by such key members of the Ontario CCF leadership as Donald C. MacDonald, Iona Samis, Peg Stewart, Carrol Coburn, Morden Lazarus, George Grube, and Olive Smith.

At the beginning of 1962 the mood of the party was still seemingly buoyant. The common view was that a real break had been made with the past, particularly with the electoral failures of the past, and that the party's prospects looked exceedingly bright. In Ottawa the federal office staff expanded and included a number of interesting and dynamic personalities. Among those working full time were Carl Hamilton, the federal secretary (later a lawyer and an alderman in Guelph); André L'Heureux, associate secretary (later a key figure in the Parti Québécois); Terry Grier, assistant secretary (subsequently vice-president at Ryerson Polytechnic in Toronto and MP from 1972 to 1974); Tommy Shoyama, research director (subsequently deputy minister of finance for Canada); and Stephen Lewis, director of organization (provincial leader of the NDP in Ontario from 1970 to 1978). The party also appointed a director of women's activities, created a special by-election fund, and made funds available for a full-time officer of the New Democratic Youth.

In Ontario vigorous preparations for an expected federal election were undertaken. In April a school for prospective candidates was discussed at the executive meeting. Later that month a joint meeting between officers of the NDP and of the Ontario Federation of Labour was held and a powerful election committee to take over the executive function during the election period was established. The committee included Ken Bryden, John Magder, Iona Samis, Henry Weisbach, Peg Stewart, Fred Young, and Stephen Lewis. The party girded itself for battle in the federal election campaign by directly challenging the Liberals to a debate. David Lewis and Andrew Brewin were picked to debate Walter Gordon and Mitchell Sharp. It also proceeded with plans for a giant election rally at the new O'Keefe Centre in Toronto.

Significant problems, however, arose. On 21 February 1962 Hazen

Argue, still NDP house leader, announced his decision to leave the New Democratic Party. In doing so he accused the NDP of betraying the principles of the old CCF and suggested that the party was controlled by union leaders. Argue's resignation came as a complete surprise and a real blow. He had spent the two days prior to his announcement attending a Provincial Council meeting of the Saskatchewan party. He participated vigorously in the debate, but when the meeting was over, he called a press conference and made his startling declaration. He then flew back to Ottawa (on the same plane as Tommy Douglas), returning to his office where he had had the foresight to change the locks. His closest friends in the party were shattered. Doug Fisher, Arnold Peters, and other issued strong statements disputing Argue's charges and portraying their author as foolish and misguided. A week later, after Argue joined the Liberal party, all his former friends ceased to have anything to do with him. There can be no doubt that the defection was a calamity. The charges about labour domination were clearly damaging. More important, the party was so shocked by this apostasy that its forward momentum was halted.

Other setbacks and pinpricks occurred. In the spring of 1962 the Canadian Chamber of Commerce announced that it would undertake an "operation freedom" project to warn Canadians of the dangers of socialism and remind them of the benefits of the market economy. To party activists, it smacked of the virulent antisocialist campaign of 1945. Fortunately for the party the times were not as they had been, and the Chamber of Commerce soon discovered that there was little support in the community for such a campaign. At the other end of the political spectrum the party was annoyed by the public endorsement it received from the Communist Party of Canada. The NDP, particularly with its new-found moderate, "liberally minded" image, was most anxious to have no connection at all with the Communist party, and it repudiated the endorsation. When the endorsation was repeated in advertisements during the 1962 election campaign, the NDP considered taking legal action.

The federal election was held on 18 June 1962. For the new party in Ontario the results were close to disastrous. After the Peterborough by-election it had high hopes – hopes which included becoming the government. After the founding convention party activists, even those of a pessimistic bent, were persuaded that at the very least the new party would make very substantial gains. If it could not be first, at least second, and if not second, a strong third with 40 or 50 Commons seats.[80] Given these hopes, the party was crushed. The Conservatives won 116 seats. They were the big losers in this election, down from 54 to 37 per cent of the popular vote and reduced to minority government status. The Liberals also received 37 per cent of the vote and won 100 seats. The NDP went up from the 10 per cent that the CCF had received in 1958 to 13 per cent and won 19 seats, but humiliatingly this did not even make them the third party, for Social Credit with 12 per cent of the vote captured 30 seats, 26 of them in Quebec where Réal Caouette had conducted a frenetic populist campaign which paid handsome electoral dividends. To complete the tragedy, Tommy Douglas, premier of Saskatchewan for seventeen years and running for the House of Commons from Regina, the capital of that province, was overwhelmingly defeated in his own seat.

The party, however, did not experience a collapse of morale as that which had followed the 1951 election. There was real pleasure in the fact that Toronto had returned three very strong members: David Lewis (York South), Andrew Brewin (Greenwood), and Reid Scott (Danforth). Lewis had been for many years the most powerful personality in the party and had a reputation as an extremely able debater. Brewin was also a member of the party oligarchy and a distinguished Toronto lawyer with a considerable reputation in the area of civil liberties, and Scott had been elected to the Ontario legislature in 1948 at the age of twenty-one, the youngest member to that date. The party had also elected Malcolm ("Vic") Macinnis in Cape Breton, Stanley Knowles was returned from Winnipeg North Centre, and a young labour lawyer, Tom Berger, was elected in Vancouver-Burrard. Yet when all was said and done, these were but glimmers of light in an extremely clouded sky.

In Ontario the repercussions of the election were quickly felt. On 7 July 1962 the executive decided to terminate the employment of four organizers for financial reasons. Retrenchment had begun, although in fact this initial move was reversed after strong appeals from Lewis, Brewin, and Bryden.[81]

The autumn of 1962 brought the Saskatchewan medicare crisis. In Saskatchewan the government (under Woodrow Lloyd, the new premier) had decided to introduce a compulsory universal medical insurance scheme to be run by the province. The doctors strenuously objected and, financed by the Canadian Medical Association and the American Medical Association, decided to resist the new program with every means at their disposal, including a doctors' strike.[82] Committees to support the doctors were formed with the acronyms KOD (Keep Our Doctors) and SOS (Save Our Saskatchewan). In this crisis the Ontario party did what it could. George Cadbury, David Lewis, and Frank Scott (from Montreal) acted as advisers to the government on constitutional and other issues. Stephen Lewis, John Brewin, and other young activists went to Saskatchewan to assist in the organizational efforts to counteract these pressure groups.

On the federal scene the New Democratic Party painfully turned to the agonizing task of keeping the new organization going after the dreams of the founding convention and the Peterborough by-election had been shattered. The feeling of many, particularly David Lewis, was that the full-time officers of the party had not been sufficiently energetic in taking advantage of the euphoria of the founding convention to create a first-class organization. They felt that the mistake of Jolliffe and others in the 1940s had been repeated, and the national leadership of the party, led by Lewis, decided that a shake-up was needed. The symbol of this toughminded belief was the resignation of Carl Hamilton as federal secretary.[83]

In Ontario a similar sacrifice was to be found, and in this instance it was Peg Stewart, the provincial secretary-treasurer. She had intended to run for one more term but was told that this would be impossible and that it would be better if she did not seek re-election. She complied.[84] In her place the provincial convention held in early October elected Jim Bury, a prominent trade unionist, a staff representative with the United Packinghouse Workers, and for a brief period a CCF MLA in British Columbia. In addition the executive was "toughened" by the election of such personalities as Andrew Brewin, Charles Millard, William Scandlan, and Stephen Lewis.

The Ontario NDP continued to maintain a reasonable staff of seven organizers by persuading key unions in promising areas to contribute a large portion of the organizers' salary each month. Finally at the end of 1962 Don MacDonald, in the wake of the federal election results, urged the party to switch its thinking to the provincial sphere, suggesting that it was there that significant gains could be made by the NDP. His suggestion echoed one made earlier by Pierre Trudeau in an article in *Social Purpose for Canada*, a book of essays written by leading socialist intellectuals in Canada to celebrate the founding of the NDP.[85]

The 1962 federal election had produced a minority government with the Conservatives retaining office. They relied for parliamentary support on the third party, Social Credit, which as a populist right-wing movement was more sympathetic to the Conservatives than to the Liberals. Unfortunately for the Conservatives, the Social Credit party was a house divided against itself. This was not surprising given the fact that its leader, Robert Thompson from Alberta, led a caucus whose deputy leader, Réal Caouette, was responsible for the election of twenty-six of the thirty members. In addition the Conservative government was slowly disintegrating from within and many of its members had lost any sense of purpose in remaining in office.[86] The issue which finally caused the defeat of the government was the proposal to place nuclear weapons on Canadian soil. The Conservative Cabinet was bitterly divided on this question, and when a nonconfidence motion was proposed, the prime minister was unable or unwilling to offer the Social Credit members the consideration they required in order to support the government once more. As a result a federal election took place on 8 April 1963.

The results of that election were even more demoralizing than those of 1962. This time Tommy Douglas was easily returned in the British Columbia seat that had been vacated for him and which he had won late in 1962 in a by-election; however, the new deputy leader of the party, David Lewis, was defeated in York South. The party ended up with only 17 seats and a slight decrease in its popular vote. The Liberals won 130 seats with 41 per cent of the popular vote, just shy of a majority; the Conservatives, 94 seats with 33 per cent of the popular vote; and Social Credit, 24 seats with 12 per cent of the vote. Diefenbaker resigned and the Liberals formed a government with Lester Pearson as prime minister.

It all looked bleak from the perspective of the Ontario NDP. Party members had generally believed that with the Liberals out of office events would follow the course they had in Britain, with the NDP playing the role of the Labour party in replacing a declining Liberal force. After 1963 this was not a likely scenario. As well the defeat of David Lewis was a sore blow. Lewis had immediately established himself as one of the most powerful parliamentary debaters and the party knew he would be missed. Indeed, Stanley Knowles proposed that Murdo Martin vacate his Timmins seat in favour of Lewis and run in the provincial election expected later in the year.[87]

There were some bright spots. Young and energetic Terry Grier, now the federal secretary, was able to provide a sense of direction and purpose to the federal office. A tour by a doctor and his wife from the British Labour party was arranged as an attempt to take some of the fear out of the party's medicare program. A number of young organizers were now available to the Ontario party, a full-time person to work on public relations was hired, and union affiliations were beginning to increase in the province. But there were also continuing difficulties. The party was rent with internal debates of a vitriolic and vicious nature, particularly in the youth section, and in 1963 ten members of the New Democratic Youth were expelled from the party because it was felt they had also joined the Trotskyist organization in Canada.[88]

The provincial election in 1963 was also something of a disappointment, although that disappointment was tempered by an increase in the number of seats won by the NDP. It was not a large increase: the party went from 5 seats in a 98-seat legislature to 7 in a 108-seat legislature and actually dropped from 17 to 16 per cent of the popular vote. The Conservatives easily retained their majority and the Liberals, down to 35 per cent of the vote, won 24 seats. Still there was something to be cheerful about if one was prepared to be cheerful about small victories. One member, Tommy Thomas in Oshawa, lost his seat but he was replaced by three new members: Ted Freeman from Fort William, who provided the party with a presence in northern Ontario; Fred Young, who was an excellent debater with a wide knowledge of public affairs; and Stephen Lewis, a brilliant parliamentary performer who at the age of twenty-six stunned the legislature with the eloquence and thoroughness of his maiden speech.

Yet these were definitely small victories and most in the party sensed this. Fred Young's election had been doubly welcome because he was able to resign as director of organization and his parliamentary salary was then available to hire other organizers. However, it was not easy to get a replacement. Marj Pinney was offered the job in October 1963 but she turned it down, perhaps not surprisingly, since after the election all the temporary organizers and two of the six permanent organizers were laid off. One indication of the party's doldrums was a note in the executive minutes that Stephen Lewis had been reduced to acting as an advertising agent for a planned NDP cookbook.[89]

More agony followed. Late in December 1963 the *Toronto Star* reported that three prominent New Democrats, Eamon Park, assistant to the national director of the Steelworkers and federal treasurer of the party; Murray Cotterill, public relations director of the Steel-workers; and Desmond Sparham, formerly the director of New Party clubs, had held talks with provincial Liberals on the question of some form of united action or perhaps even merger. The party reacted badly to these disclosures and on 11 January 1964 the executive sent a strong letter to the three "sinners," upbraiding them for taking part in such discussions. Park later replied in kind that he was not in favour of a merger but had every right to talk to whomever he wished and would continue to exercise that right. In the meantime, on 22 February, Ed Phillips, a party vice-president who had originally joined through the Engineers New Party Club, moved at a Provincial Council meeting that the party consider altering its image by adopting more moderate proposals. After considerable discussion the motion was tabled, but clearly this proposal was an outgrowth of the Park-Cotterill-Sparham talks held with John Wintermeyer, then Liberal leader, and that these talks in part came about because of a very real dissatisfaction on the part of a number of people about the progress the party had made to date.[90]

After this event, John Brewin, as editor of the party newspaper, *New Democrat*, wrote and published an article criticizing a prominent party member, Val Scott, twice the federal candidate in York Centre, the second largest constituency in the country, and the executive by motion forced Brewin to apologize to Scott. Scott repaid this gesture by suggesting that the party in Ontario might need a new leader and that Don MacDonald was not the man for the job.

The final blow came in early 1964. At the 11 April executive meeting George Cadbury, as president, proposed that a large social gathering be held to celebrate the expected victory in Saskatchewan – a gathering designed to boost sagging morale. Fortunately Cadbury's proposal was not adopted because after twenty years in power the CCF/NDP lost in Saskatchewan. The new premier, Ross Thatcher, was doubly hated in the NDP because he was ideologically an outspoken right-wing Liberal and yet had once been a CCF MP.

Some positive activity did continue. The executive authorized Andrew Brewin to negotiate the release from the armed forces of a young officer, Desmond Morton, who was anxious to serve as assistant provincial secretary. At the same time the executive discussed a program to canvass every member of the party to secure more membership renewals and more money. Most important the party geared up for two provincial by-elections in Windsor and Toronto.

Significantly, it was decided to make a major effort in the Toronto by-election to be held in the constituency of Riverdale.

The Riverdale by-election was the turning point for the Ontario NDP. In a very real sense the party, like a gambler, staked everything on this throw of the dice. The real possibility existed that unless something could be done to stem the feeling of demoralization that resulted from the electoral defeats and the incessant internal bickering, the NDP, at least in Ontario, would gradually wither away. It was hoped, therefore, that a victory in the Riverdale election would signal, not only to the people of Ontario but more importantly to the party membership, that the NDP, unlike the CCF, had considerable electoral clout. Given this feeling, the Ontario NDP did everything possible to win. Stephen Lewis and Marj Pinney were put in charge of the campaign. As soon as the election was called, they were able to make use of other full-time staff, who treated the by-election as the top priority. Considerable financial assistance was available, with $10,500 being spent on the campaign. A prestigious candidate was nominated in the person of James Renwick, formerly a corporation lawyer in the firm of Lang, Michener, Cranston, and Renwick. Renwick and his wife, Margaret, canvassed literally every house in the riding.[91] The election, held on 10 September 1964, gave Renwick 7,287 votes, the Conservatives (who had previously held the seat) 5,774, with 5,771 votes for Charles Templeton, who was seeking the leadership of the Ontario Liberal party.

The victory in Riverdale was much more important for the Ontario NDP than simply adding another member to the party's legislative caucus. That, in itself, was undoubtedly most welcome, the more so because Renwick as a lawyer added considerable expertise to a caucus which had not had a lawyer since Grummett's defeat in 1955. The real significance of the victory was that it gave the party a renewed confidence in its organizational capacity, for which it had strived since the trauma of 1951. The achievement of organizational capacity made the party more self-confident because it saw itself at last as a respectable political organization, respectable in the sense that it could compete with the other parties and, if circumstances were at all favourable, could beat them.

This self-confidence was increased when later that year the party won a federal by-election in the riding of Waterloo South with Max Saltsman as the candidate. Similar techniques to those used in Riverdale were employed and again they worked. Many more people became active in the Ontario party at this time, and it is important to note that many of these new activists (some of whom had been active before but had played only a minor role during the period of the doldrums) were individuals with considerable political experience or with real expertise in areas important in building and maintaining any organization. Generally 1964 was a satisfactory year, with two important by-election victories, with a renewed organizational thrust, and with a bit of reflected glory in the autumn victory of the British Labour party under Harold Wilson.

Factionalism

The second aspect of the quest for respectability that characterized the party during the period from 1951 to 1964 was bound up with an ongoing factionalism in the CCF/NDP. One of the chief concerns of the party at this time was to dissociate itself completely from the Communists in Canada. Both Walter Young and Gad Horowitz provide some considerable detail of this sentiment in the national party, particularly in terms of the trade union movement.[92] In large measure the urgency of this desire had its wellspring in Ontario where the battle between the CCFers and the Communists in the trade union movement had been intense and where the party was so eager for public respectability.

It is important to consider why the CCF/NDP became so obsessed with the need to dissociate itself from any form of communism. The intensity of this feeling was not always so great. Ted Jolliffe, in explaining the reasons for the 1951 defeat, suggests an answer.

The world situation has been unfavourable not only to us, but to our socialist comrades in other countries for several years. We received a lot of support between 1941 and 1945 for a strange reason, that of sympathy on the part of the public for Russia. Every time the Red Army won a battle our stock went up. Since then, the trend has been the other way. Our country has been enjoying unprecedented capitalist prosperity because of World Wars I and II and the world crisis since then. No other province has benefited from the past war as Ontario through industrial expansion. These things have influenced the public mood which in turn influences our party members. These factors are beyond our control.[93]

As Jolliffe states in outlining this Red Army thesis of CCF success and defeat, the world had changed since the Second World War. By 1952 it was in the grips of the cold war, and in the United States

Senators Joseph McCarthy and Richard Nixon and others were gaining considerable public support by suggesting that many public servants were secretly sympathetic to the Communist cause. There was an important movement towards a purge in American society of these suspect elements. The Korean War raised the spectre of "the yellow peril" and further implanted the fear of communism in the peoples of the Western world. Finally the Soviet Union had the atom bomb and was soon to have the hydrogen bomb. For many in the West, Armageddon was around the corner with Joseph Stalin starring as the Prince of Darkness.

In this atmosphere the CCF felt it had to tread warily. Early in 1952 the Ontario party decided it would have no dealings with the Canadian Peace Congress, an organization believed to a Communist party front but which included as its sponsors a number of prominent churchmen and other public figures. It began its activities by circulating a petition for peace. Most people, and certainly those who believe themselves to be progressive, are in favour of peace and against war and are prepared to sign a petition favouring peace. The Ontario CCF, however, feeling that this was a Communist-inspired organization did what it could to prevent its members from having anything to do with the petition and with the Canadian Peace Congress.[94] Moreover, the CCF publicly condemned North Korean aggression, though it called for an immediate armistice in Korea and the recognition of the People's Republic of China. In addition the party, while deploring any military buildup in Europe, firmly supported the NATO alliance, a stance which caused a good deal of internal dissent.[95]

In this context a major battle in the party took place over control of the Woodsworth Foundation, an independent research society associated with the party. For some time the foundation, which owned the building used as the Ontario CCF headquarters, located at 565 Jarvis Street in Toronto, had been controlled by individuals who were generally unhappy with the stance taken by the party leadership on questions such as the Korean War and the peace petition. The officers of the foundation included Frank Underhill, the chief author of the Regina Manifesto; Edith Fowke, a noted Canadian folklorist; Bernard and Alice Loeb; and Kay and Lou Morris. These individuals, all contributors to the *Canadian Forum* and other journals, consistently opposed the anti-Communist measures and caused the party leadership considerable embarrassment. It was then decided, primarily by David Lewis,[96] to administer a significant rebuke. Lewis encouraged a number of people, including many prominent trade unionists, to sign up as members of the foundation and to attend the annual meeting. Sufficient numbers did so, and when it came time for the elections, the old members of the executive were swept from office and the new people, all loyal to the party leadership, were installed in their place. Underhill and the others were furious and felt they had been very badly treated; Underhill vented his great displeasure in an extraordinarily vitriolic article in the *Canadian Forum*.[97]

The battle continued, most often over issues of symbolic importance. The party was usually pleased to have prominent spokesmen from the British Labour party come on a speaking tour of Canada. In 1952 those opposed to the party leadership proposed that Aneurin Bevan, the acknowledged leader of the Labour left, who had quit Clement Attlee's Cabinet in 1950 on an issue of principle, be invited. Bevan was a fiery speaker and obviously would attract many people to his meetings. After much debate the party decided at the end of 1952 that the national office should invite Attlee, not Bevan. If Attlee could not come, the invitation was to be extended to Jimmy Griffiths, who, appropriately, had been secretary of state for the colonies in the Attlee government.[98]

Also in 1954 fourteen party members, who were alleged to be members of the Trotskyist party as well, were expelled from the Ontario CCF. These expulsions created considerable controversy, as many party members believed that the CCF should tolerate all manner of views and that no one should ever be expelled. The leadership were of a different mind, and because most of the people on the executive were well known to each other, the executive and the council were able to act in a relatively unified fashion.. One of the fascinating realities of the party during this period was that a great many of those in leadership positions made it a kind of family affair, with spouses and sometimes older children very much involved in the party. At the 21 May 1956 council meeting, for example, the list of delegates included Miller and Peg Stewart, Andrew and Peggy Brewin, Francis and Mary Eady, and Eamon and Ann Park. Both spouses of other families were extremely active and included Linc and Marg Bishop, George and Gwynneth Grube, Ken and Marion Bryden, Don and Simone MacDonald, Boris and Karen Mather, Walter and Marj Mann, Morden and Margaret Lazarus, Dave and Doris Archer, David and Barbara Cass-Beggs, Tommy and Christine Thomas, and Reg and Mary Gisborn.

Perhaps the most important factional dispute at this time concerned the party's statement of fundamental principles. Socialists, and socialist parties generally, feel that it is necessary to have some document in which their principles are outlined to inspire party members and to assert before the world the truth as the party understands it. Religious movements have their creeds; parties, their manifestos. For the CCF this statement of principles was from 1933 the Regina Manifesto. But many were unhappy with the Regina Manifesto, believing that its language did not in fact convey the full truth about the CCF as a moderate democratic socialist party. As early as 1950 work was begun on a new statement of CCF principles, and in July 1951 the Ontario CCF executive held a lengthy discussion of a draft statement drawn up by David Lewis and Andrew Brewin.[99] However, manifestos, like creeds, are not changed without bitterness. The Regina Manifesto and its words had come to be seen as a kind of holy writ with which only those who would abandon the true principles of the party would dare to tamper. Nevertheless, after considerable agitation the leadership managed to persuade most members of the party that a new statement was needed and finally the national convention in 1956 promulated a new manifesto, the Winnipeg Declaration. The language of the Winnipeg Declaration was most circumspect.

Throughout the 1950s the party maintained its vigilance against the admission of Trotskyists, Communists, and other sectarians. The period of the formation of the NDP provided the Trotskyists with another chance to infiltrate the Ontario movement, since the control of New Party clubs was not well established. As a result, a number of individuals who the leadership believed had joined the League for Socialist Action, the name of the Trotskyist party in Canada, became members of the party, particularly as members of the youth section. As discussed previously, ten of them were expelled from the party in 1963. The leadership firmly, sometimes almost hysterically, repudiated any attempts by the Communists or others to associate themselves with the CCF/NDP and did what it could to make the people of Ontario aware of the party's basic anti-Communist position.

Scandal

Finally, during the period from 1951 to 1964 the intense desire for respectability led the party, and Donald C. MacDonald in particular, to emphasize the venal aspects of political life in Ontario and to attempt to persuade the people of Ontario that the Conservative government was essentially corrupt and scandal ridden. Three major scandals emerged during the period. A highways scandal in 1954 concerned the letting of contracts without a proper bidding procedure. MacDonald charged that this practice meant that friends of the government could be handsomely rewarded from the public treasury because the prices they charged need not be competitive. It is quite possible that this happened, although it is difficult to show that those awarded contracts were invariably Conservative party supporters and financial contributors. At that time political parties did not need to disclose their sources of funds.

A scandal involving Northern Ontario Natural Gas (NONG) was clearly an embarrassment for the Conservative government. Briefly, NONG was set up to build trunk pipelines off the Trans-Canada pipeline bringing oil from Alberta to supply the needs of communities in northern Ontario. A number of people, including two provincial cabinet ministers, had inside information about the location of these trunk pipelines and about the granting of licences to NONG. They and their friends used this information to make a handsome profit. MacDonald continually raised the whole question of the financing of this company in the legislature from 1955 on, and in 1959 it became certain that cabinet ministers were involved and that they had used information gained at the executive council table to enrich themselves and their friends. Leslie Frost's reaction as premier was to fire the two offending ministers and to call an election, asking the good people of Ontario to show their confidence in his firing by returning the government. The people of Ontario did exactly that.

Another scandal in 1956–7 concerned a development in the Township of Scarborough. MacDonald charged that Conservative members of the legislature had improperly voted on contracts to lay down water mains in this Toronto suburb. The Conservatives were furious at the charge and had MacDonald hauled before the Committee on Privileges and Elections. Andrew Brewin acted as MacDonald's counsel at the committee hearings. In the end the committee decided that no action should be taken against MacDonald, though it also concluded that the Conservative members had done nothing illegal.

Not everyone in the party was happy with MacDonald's emphasis on these scandals and on related matters.[100] Scandalmongering, however, did touch a deep chord both in the party and in the province. What MacDonald was doing was appealing to a strong puritanical presbyterian sense in Ontario and the indignation shown was part and parcel of the party's great need to feel respectable. Party members knew they were living in a sinful community, but it was a community that could, and must, be reformed by the righteo·is life of democratic socialism.

1964–1971: The Quest for Power

The victories in Riverdale and Waterloo South in a very real way transformed the Ontario New Democratic Party. The promise of the new party was, at least in large part, realized. The party had shown the province, and itself, that it could mobilize significant resources and that in some circumstances mobilization would lead to public success, that is, to an election victory. The party came to have a sense of its power to effect its desires, though in very circumscribed situations. Only a little elaboration of the personality analogy is needed to suggest that this sense of power is very similar to that which a young adult fresh from school or university has in terms of affecting things in his own life. The individual realizes that he can now rationally make plans capable of being consummated and that the ability to change the world, though limited, is still real.

The party then had come of age – it saw itself as a different kind of entity. By this stage the New Democratic Party was something other than the CCF, and as in the halycon days immediately before the formation of the new party, it again dreamt of power and indeed felt that it should actively seek that power. This is not to say that the concerns of earlier stages disappeared. As Beer states in speaking of developmental theory: "A third proposition that has sometimes been attached to the notion of development is the hypothesis of accumulation. The contention is that in each stage the modern polity has acquired certain features that have remained in succeeding stages. The developed modern polity in the present time, therefore, embodies accomplishments of previous eras as well as the present era of modernity."[101] The stages of the CCF/NDP history in Ontario are characterized by different principles and are not in themselves mutually exclusive. One stage anticipates another and the new stage itself has features of the older one. After 1964, though the NDP now sought power in a way different from before, it still sought respectability and was still characterized by the attitudes of the "socialist generation," that amalgam of intellectuals and trade union leaders from the 1940s.

Even after the by-election victories the Ontario NDP continued the attempts to enhance the party's organizational capacity. In late 1964 and throughout 1965 several programs were undertaken. First a booklet detailing the Riverdale campaign was published. As its author, Desmond Morton, put it in his report to the party as assistant provincial secretary: "To reinforce the invaluable morale effect of the Riverdale victory and to provide a textbook on detailed riding organization and canvassing [I] wrote and published ... *The Riverdale Story*. 2,000 copies sold within two months." The book was popular for some years. Then followed an every-member canvass, a testimonial dinner for Donald MacDonald, a contact canvass, a sign-making school, a public canvass in which it was hoped to obtain new members, and a campaign management school to train party workers in the techniques of electoral campaigning. At the same time, inspired by the prolific example of Morton, a stream of publications emerged from the provincial office. Before 1964 the NDP had produced only three pieces of literature: its program, its constitution, and a leaflet on medicare. Once Morton came on the scene, all this changed. After *The Riverdale Story* in November 1964 came *New Democrats Look at the New Canada Pension Plan* by Ken Bryden and Morton; *The Great Medicare Fight* by Donald C. MacDonald; a booklet entitled *Automation and Employment* by Morton; a pamphlet entitled *How a New Democratic Government Would Help Ontario's Independent Businessman* by Ted Freeman; a handbook for the riding association executives entitled *Part of a Team;* a procedural guide called *Make It a Motion;* a general booklet called *The New Democratic Way* by George Grube; a booklet of instruction for the contact canvass called *Getting to Know You;* and a small piece of catchy literature with an attached mail-in questionnaire designed for that same canvass. A number of mimeographed publications, including a short history of the party, also flowed from this never-ending stream. The provincial office continued to produce leaflets and booklets, though not with the same regularity, after Morton left the party's employ at the end of August 1965.[102]

In addition the Ontario NDP contested elections with renewed vigour. The first was a provincial by-election in Toronto Bracondale, a west central ethnic riding in the city. The party nominated Dr John Farina, a professor of sociology at the University of Toronto, and he made a respectable, if losing, showing. Then came a federal election late in 1965, called so that the Liberal party might at last achieve its majority. The results, although not spectacular for the Ontario NDP, were not displeasing either. In popular vote the party increased its standing in the country from 14 to 18 per cent, a not insignificant rise. It won twenty-one seats, nine of them in Ontario. More important it rejoiced in the return of David Lewis in York South, and it was delighted that its new MP from Hamilton, William Howe, was a medical doctor who favoured medicare. It was also most satisfied by the fact that a majority still eluded the Liberal party in Ottawa.

The party was pleased with its campaign. Not only had it done better than before (and there was always the consolation that proportional representation would have given it many more seats), but it had used better methods of campaigning. As Morton put it:

We set up our campaign last December [1964], we employed Regenstreif to make a survey and we followed the results of that survey in weighing the issues. We also practised concentration on seventy seats across the country and we employed a professional advertising agency which gave us excellent service. We also used imagination in producing our radio and T.V. time. All of this, by the standards of CCF campaigning, is marked progress, and I do not feel as do our fundamentalists, that we have betrayed ourselves in the progress.[103]

This more sophisticated organizational approach was repeated and indeed enhanced for the 1967 provincial election. John Wilson of the University of Waterloo and David Hoffman of York University carried out a major survey of voter attitudes. The results were analysed and the party adapted its campaign themes to the findings. Candidates were found to run in all 117 Ontario ridings – the first time in the history of the CCF/NDP that the party had fielded a full slate – and a real attempt was made to find attractive candidates in those ridings it thought it had some chance of winning.[104]

Other improvements were evident. In previous campaigns Mac-Donald had driven himself around the province, sometimes in the company of one or two newspapermen. This time a bus was hired so that the reporters could travel in a modicum of comfort. Relations with the press were handled by Macdonald's new special assistant, Terry Grier, who had left his post as federal secretary of the party to join the Ontario organization. While on tour MacDonald and Grier made the day-to-day decisions about the themes to expound in different parts of the province, but they stayed in daily contact with central headquarters, particularly with John Harney, the provincial secretary; Marion Bryden, caucus research director; and Ken Goldstein, the party public relations director. Goldstein was hard at work on a major campaign leaflet, designed to look like *Newsweek* magazine, with a picture of MacDonald on the cover. It had a major impact. The full-time organizers were all busy running key constituency campaigns. For example, Gordon Brigden, long-time organizer for the party, was assigned to run the campaign in High Park where Morton Shulman, former Conservative, millionaire, doctor, controversial Toronto coroner, and author of *How to Make a Million*, was the NDP candidate.[105]

The final results of the 1967 election were Progressive Conservatives sixty-nine seats, Liberals twenty-eight, and NDP twenty. While the results for the NDP might have been better, they were certainly good and the party was much elated by them. The downward trend in popular vote which had occurred since 1951 was finally halted and the party went from 16 to 26 per cent of the vote. With its twenty seats it became a significant and major force in the legislature.

Besides the search for better organizational capacity, other concerns evident in earlier stages of the party's development remained. The party was no longer much bothered by Communist endorsations, but it still had problems with its youth section and some Trotskyists in it. In 1967 a number of individuals were denied membership in the party. As for scandal, the party had the Prudential Finance collapse – the bankruptcy of a large investment company with charges of fraud surrounding it. Jim Renwick and other members of the party became much involved, and the party trumpeted about the immorality not only of the government for permitting it, but of the whole capitalist system for causing it.

Until 1966 the party in Ontario was still essentially in the hands of those who were part of the socialist generation, which had emerged in the 1940s. The president, George Cadbury, had worked in Saskatchewan. The secretary, Jim Bury, was a trade union official of the same generation. Other key members of the provincial executive included the legal counsel for the Steelworkers in Canada, the political education director of the Ontario Federation of Labour and former CCF provincial secretary, the research director in Canada for the United Auto Workers, two staff representatives with the United Steelworkers, the education director of the United Auto Workers, an education representative in Ontario for the Canadian Labour Congress, three MPS, the past president of the Ontario CCF (in 1945), and a staff representative with the United Packinghouse Workers. With the 1966 provincial convention a change to younger leaders began, but only slowly. Of the twenty-six members of the executive elected in 1966 eighteen were either trade union officials or key members of the party since the 1940s or both. The major change was the election of John Harney as provincial secretary. Harney was a relative newcomer to the party, having joined after the founding convention in 1961. He had been a federal candidate three times, in 1962, 1963, and 1965, and had been a member of the provincial executive from 1964. He was, however, very much a new face in this particular crowd, and though he was elected to the post by acclamation, was not unopposed.[106]

The real change came at the 1968 convention. Of the twenty-six members of the provincial executive only eleven were either trade union officials, CCF members from the 1940s, or both. Even then the break with the past was not as sharp as it seemed, since many of these younger executive members were in fact the products of the University of Toronto CCF Club from the late 1950s. They included John Brewin, the son of Andrew Brewin, and Stephen Lewis, the son of David Lewis. The members of this club were socialized into the party through familial links with the party leadership. There was, in other words, no fundamental break with the socialist generation nor indeed with the union foundation of that generation. If anything the party in Ontario became even more committed to the union connection. Members of the legislature and other party members publicly gave their support to several key strikes in the province in those years, strikes which were sometimes unpopular but which were critical for the unions. These included strikes at the *Oshawa Times* in 1966, Tilco in Peterborough in which several strikers went to jail, and Chelmsford School (school janitors here were forbidden by law to strike; the law was subsequently changed). In 1968 the party supported strikes at Proctor Silex and the *Peterborough Examiner*. In the following two years support was given to the Hanes Hosiery strike and to the campaign at the closed Dunlop Tire plant in Toronto to have workers reinstated and the plant reopened.

Yet what really characterized the party during this period was its new consciousness of gaining power in Ontario, since it had once again become a major force in the legislature. On the federal scene, the results of an election in 1968, though disappointing, were explainable in terms of Trudeaumania, and the Ontario party felt that it had not been disgraced. It lost only one seat, that held by Dr Howe, and the prevailing view was that he could have won had he been a little more regular in his attendance in the House of Commons.

In addition the party for the first time since the 1940s contested a municipal election in Toronto. Party members had always been active in municipal politics, but since the 1944 disaster the party had been loath to run candidates under the label. It did so in 1969 with a modicum of success. Three of the twenty-two aldermen elected ran under the party label: Reid Scott, who had retired as an MP in 1968; Karl Jaffray, a young Toronto lawyer; and Archie Chisholm, a long-time party activist and trade unionist.

In August 1969 a by-election in Middlesex South, a semi-rural constituency near London, Ontario, provided a further success for the party. The candidate was Kenneth C. Bolton, an Anglican archdeacon. The CCF/NDP had never done well in rural Ontario and it was anxious to make a breakthrough in this kind of constituency. The usual campaign techniques were followed, Stephen Lewis acted as campaign manager, and Bolton, almost handily, took the riding.

The victories of this period, however, were something less than satisfactory. The party was doing better electorally, not only in Ontario but throughout the country, than it had in those first grim years after the founding convention, and it was certainly doing much better than had the CCF. Nevertheless its victories were modest and fell short of the great dreams that had existed at the time of the founding of the new party and after the Riverdale by-election. It won power in Manitoba, and two years later regained the government in Saskatchewan, but it was a long way from its goal of federal power and still distant from the prize of office in Ontario.

Those who had constructed and built the machine grew restless. Here was all this political talent but the energy had to be expended in opposition or in infrequent by-elections. The party therefore turned in on itself, and the energy which had to be spent somewhere was spent in seeking compensation for the modesty of the public victories. And so, if the period is characterized by the electoral machine that works, it is also characterized by the machine working in the party to find new ways of promoting democratic socialism.[107] The questioning began and the questions focused on the provincial leader and the party program.

The party seemed relatively pleased after results of the 1967

Ontario election, and for many Don MacDonald seemed more secure in his leadership than he had previously been. The party, however, was changing. Jim Renwick, the victor in the Riverdale by-election and a relative newcomer to the party, decided that MacDonald's leadership was simply not inspiring enough for the party to ever win the government of Ontario and that he could provide that inspiration. He decided to challenge MacDonald at the 1968 convention. In the Ontario NDP the leader has the same constitutional position as any other officer of the party – that is, he must stand for election at every convention, held every two years. Although the leader is invariably acclaimed, a challenge can be mounted. Having made his decision, Renwick gave MacDonald a letter announcing his intention and a campaign was under way. MacDonald quickly rallied most of the key people in the constituencies and the trade union movement and had little trouble turning back Renwick's challenge, the final vote being 859 to 370. The seeds, however, had been sown and many in the party now began to feel that perhaps a new leader might be necessary for electoral success.

MacDonald was not the only party leader affected. Earlier in 1968 several key individuals in Ontario concluded that the federal party would do better, certainly in Ontario, with a leader other than Tommy Douglas. On 9 March 1968 John Brown and Walter Pitman, both MPPS, tentatively expressed this view on a news interview on television. Stephen Lewis flew to British Columbia to ask Douglas to consider stepping down in favour of David Lewis or some younger person such as Charles Taylor, either of whom he believed would have a more satisfactory image for urban voters. In 1967 the federal Conservatives had had a dramatic leadership convention at which John Diefenbaker was deposed and replaced by Robert Stanfield. The spring of 1968 saw the Liberals engaged in the same process, with Pierre Elliott Trudeau emerging as leader. Changing the guard was in the air and some New Democrats were afraid of being left behind in this new kind of political activity. This talk, however, was abruptly ended when the prime minister called an election for 25 June 1968. John Harney, one of those who had been in favour of a leadership change, expressed a new view in a letter dated 25 April to the federal secretary.

If anything, the mood was rather bullish on almost every point we discussed. The matter of the leadership was brought up by one of the members, but it was heartening to hear the executive express its wholehearted support for Tommy.

... One member of the executive suggested sending Tommy a telegram expressing our solid support but I was able to slap the idea down pointing out that there would be nothing more unnerving for Tommy than to receive a telegram of that kind. He's never had one and doesn't need one.[108]

The whole issue of the federal leadership was immediately on the agenda again, however, following Douglas's defeat in the 1968 election. Even after Douglas decided to contest the by-election in Nanaimo-Cowichan-The Islands, he made it clear that he did not intend to lead the party into another election. Indeed, on 15 March Douglas attended a meeting of the Ontario executive to discuss the strategy for calling a federal leadership convention at which a new leader would be elected.

For the provincial party the idea of a new leader continued to be mooted quietly. At first this seemed improbable, since Renwick had been soundly trounced by MacDonald and in 1969 the party had had a very real success in Middlesex South. MacDonald seemed to have very considerable support in the party and seemed to be electorally successful. There was one individual, however, who could mount an effective challenge – Stephen Lewis, eldest son of David Lewis, a brilliant performer in the legislature, and the organizer who had run the Middlesex South by-election. If anyone could claim more credit for the victory than MacDonald, it was Lewis. Moreover, Lewis, late in 1969, decided that he must become the new leader and that the basis for Renwick's challenge, that MacDonald could never lead the NDP to the government of Ontario, had in fact been right.[109] Lewis had supported Renwick and had nominated him at the 1968 convention. Lewis now laid his plans carefully, gaining considerable support in the caucus and then in the trade union movement, particularly the United Auto Workers, whose Canadian director, Dennis McDermott, decided early on that a change in leadership was desirable, provided Stephen Lewis was the new leader. Throughout the spring of 1970 pressure mounted on MacDonald as more and more members of the party indicated that they were not certain that he should stay. Lewis had not publicly announced his intention, but within the party there was little doubt that he would put his name before the 1970 convention. After considerable agonizing and wide-ranging in-depth survey of feeling within the party MacDonald decided that he had

had enough and announced that he would not be a candidate for the leadership again, thus opening the way for someone new.

Lewis did not succeed without opposition to the post, as a number of key members of the party leadership felt that he had grave electoral handicaps. They persuaded Walter Pitman, the MPP from Peterborough, to enter the contest. Lewis, however, by this time had very solid support from the trade union movement and he handily won the contest by a vote of 1,188 to 642.

Party leaders were not the only scapegoats for perceived electoral failures. Many were concerned that the basic party program was no longer exciting or relevant to the needs of the 1970s. At the federal convention in 1969 a new radical group emerged with the whimsical name of the Waffle, which began its campaign to change the party program, as do all good socialists, with a manifesto. The Waffle was particularly important in Ontario, since its leaders, Mel Watkins, an economics professor at the University of Toronto, and James Laxer, a graduate student in history at Queen's University, resided in that province. Most of the secondary Waffle leadership were also from Ontario.

Initially the Waffle was a very broad based group of younger people in the party who were concerned that the policy of the party had become somewhat outdated. The manifesto was signed by a number of key party notables. The insistence, however, by Laxer and Watkins that the whole direction of the party, not just in terms of its program but in terms of its leadership generally, must be changed meant that very quickly most of these others dissociated themselves from the group. The Waffle had a real impact by raising questions of party philosophy, which are considered in more detail in subsequent chapters. The Waffle in fact anticipated the next stage of party development, the quest for relevance, the seeking for some new meaning, some new raison d'être, for the party and for socialism generally.

1971 Onwards: The Quest for Relevance

In some sense the party's quest for relevance is a final stage. This is not to say that the Last Trumpet will sound or even that it is the final conflict. The Ontario NDP continues to evolve. This work, however, is essentially completed to 1972, with only a few references beyond that time. This arbitrary end point is justified both by the necessity of some end in any historical work and by the theory that by 1971 the party in Ontario has become mature: it is run by its professional cadre; it easily survives the conjunction of unfavourable electoral forces (even though it loses a few seats in the 1971 provincial election); and in this final stage it seeks relevance, that is, it seeks to self-consciously define itself without abandoning the core of what it has become. The repulsion of the Waffle group is not a climax but a catharsis; the Wafflers leave but the self-conscious search for a new role with the same personal identity continues.

Two things are important to note about this stage of development. Although the Waffle made a strong bid to take over the party and although it had much support in the constituencies, in the final analysis it lost. At the Provincial Council meeting in Orillia, Ontario, in June 1972 a resolution was passed demanding that the Waffle disband and that it cease to function as an organized group in the party. The Waffle leaders found this to be unacceptable and for the most part they withdrew. They were not expelled, but the effect of the resolution was the same. The Waffle was powerful because the party was searching for some new meaning, but it ultimately failed because the party was sufficiently settled in its habits, ideological, structural, and electoral, and though it might change these, it could not be easily changed by external pressure.

It must also be noted that in the four elections from 1971 to 1981 the party has maintained its status as a major force in the legislature and in the electoral politics of the province. The 1971 election was something of a setback for the party and particularly for those around Stephen Lewis. Nevertheless, the NDP emerged with nineteen seats and maintained its percentage of the popular vote. In 1975 it slightly increased its percentage of the popular vote to 29 and made a real breakthrough in seats, emerging with thirty-eight to become the official opposition in the legislature. In 1977 the party again maintained its popular vote and thirty-three seats in the legislature, though it lost its status as official opposition. Even in 1981, with a drop in the popular vote, the party won twenty-one seats and remained a significant force in the legislature and the province.

Federally in Ontario the party did not fare quite so well. In 1972 eleven MPs were returned from Ontario. Those returned included the leader, David Lewis, Ed Broadbent, Andrew Brewin, Terry Grier, and John Harney, but in 1974 Lewis, Grier, and Harney were defeated and the federal party found itself with a greatly reduced caucus though, for the first time, Ontario provided the bulk of the party's representation in the House of Commons. In 1979 six NDP MPS came from Ontario and in 1980, five.

Two important conclusions arise from this biographical sketch of the Ontario CCF/NDP. These conclusions, while they do not provide full evidential confirmation of the secularization hypothesis, are nevertheless a guide for a more probing analysis of the party's character. The themes explored in this domestic history suggest that an examination of stability and change in the party's ideology, structure, and processes of internal government is likely to be fruitful. The need for further analysis arises from the conclusion that there is a stage by stage development of the party "individual" akin to the development of the human individual. As Erikson describes that later development: "Each [stage] comes to its ascendance, meets its crisis, and finds its lasting solution ... toward the end of the stages mentioned."[110] A similar pattern of crises, solutions, and development has been the pattern of party life for the Ontario CCF/NDP.

Related to this view is the fact that throughout these stages of development there exists a recognizable pattern of consistent action. The observed changes from one stage to another do not indicate a radical or revolutionary break with the past, but rather provide evidence of a cumulative development in which the beliefs and activities of the past, if not always the lessons of the past, inform the present. The implications are important. If the party has a developing yet relatively consistent character, it would seem that as an "individual" it is not simply at the mercy of the forces about it; it is not a mere product of its socio-cultural environment. The changes which mark the party's development through the stages are, at least in part, the result of a collective effort of will. The energy in creating the New Democratic Party after 1958 or the decision to invest critical resources in the Riverdale by-election makes a difference to the party's fundamental life. This is not to say that the right strategy or decision has allowed the Ontario CCF/NDP to control events. Indeed, the massive effort to create a new party in 1961 did not, in Ontario, pay any real dividends before 1964. The party, like any individual, cannot "command the tide" or will itself into power. It can, however, help shape events; it can by its decisions make a difference in its public life, and an analysis of these decisions is vital for our purpose.

Finally, this epigenetic model of party development comes alive in considering the character of the party elite. The large number of husbands and wives participating in the executives and councils of the party suggests an intimacy in the collective group which is considerable. More important, the generational transfer of power in the middle 1960s from the socialist generation to a younger group of leaders takes place almost as an inheritance from one to the other. A very significant proportion of these younger leaders were once active in the University of Toronto CCF Club. Many of the leading personalities in that group were in fact sons and daughters of party leaders from the socialist generation. The socialization of this new group of leaders was, therefore, in very large measure conducted within the bonds of strong biological family units. The integrity of the party personality is undoubtedly strengthened by the operation of this familial intergenerational transmission of values.

4

Party Structure

In an important sense the institutional "persona" of the party is manifest in the formal constitutional arrangements. Just as the program defines a party for the external world, the processes of internal government define it, at least in part, for its members. The idea of the party as an integrated personality suggests that in these formal aspects of its life a real continuity should exist. The alternative is the party as an empty vessel to be filled by the political fashions of the age. Changes in the formal arrangements are, nonetheless, inevitable and ubiquitous. Constitutional amendments are passed at every convention. The administrative and organizational structure expands and contracts. The formal link with the trade unions undergoes a formal metamorphosis by the creation of the New Democratic Party in 1961. Yet in the midst of these changes, there exists a fundamental continuity of formal procedures.

When the CCF was first established, it was a federation which brought together a number of autonomous groups, large and small, for the study of socialism and for a variety of forms of political action. As a 1942 report to the Provincial Council put it:

Each group sets its own fees, based on the ability of its members to pay, and the nature and costs of the activities in which it is engaged. All clubs paid a uniform per capita fee to the central office monthly. Several clubs might ... exist in one geographical area, such as a city ward or a federal riding. The reasons for their separate existence have been special group interests and sometimes a sharp difference of opinion on certain fundamental principles. Though, in general, clubs drew their membership from a limited geographical area, the fact that many clubs came into existence because of special group interests or as an expression of a particular attitude (e.g., pro or con united front) resulted in many cases in a geographical scatter among the membership, so that one club might have members in several ridings (this in large urban centres only).[1]

In 1938 the first constituency associations came into being. In a number of ridings key individuals felt that the club structure was too cumbersome and unwieldy to be used effectively in election campaigning and that the most efficient unit of organization would be the constituency. As the 1942 report states: "The unit of organization was set as the federal constituency. (In Toronto it might have been either the city ward, the provincial riding or the federal riding.) For uniformity throughout the province in rural as well as urban districts, only one of the two latter was suitable. The choice of the federal riding as the unit was largely arbitrary."[2] The choice of the federal riding was no doubt arbitrary, but it is also significant that it constitutes a statement of the most pressing and important interests of members of the CCF in this period.

After the South York by-election in 1942, it was recognized that "the influx of new and unsolicited members in South York is much more easily handled under the constituency association set up than the club type of organization. For this reason, among others, the club type of organization, even where it has been very successful, is tending to break down and to be replaced by the constituency association."[3] The constitution of the CCF (Ontario section) at this time therefore recognized three forms of membership. As article III stated:

Section 1 – affiliation with the organization shall be open to:
(a) Political groups all of whose members subscribe to the principles and programme of the CCF and who are willing to adhere strictly to its constitution;
(b) Economic and cultural groups, such as trade union and farmers' organizations, which have decided to give general support to the CCF;
(c) Individuals who subscribe to the principles and programme of the CCF and are willing to adhere strictly to its constitution.
Section 2 – political groups shall affiliate as to all their members. For the purpose of paying dues, economical or cultural groups may affiliate as to all or part of their membership, provided that their representation at the annual convention shall be fixed by reference to that part of their membership for which they have affiliated [sic].

Although the membership clause included both clubs and constituency associations in the political groupings, by 1942 the association had become more important because many had joined the party as individuals and therefore related to the association rather than to a particular club. At this early date provision was also made in the constitution for trade unions and other groups to affiliate to the party and for their members to be considered members of the CCF. It is important to note that the constitution provides these economic and cultural organizations (essentially trade unions) the privilege of affiliating only a part of their membership. A union could therefore make provisions for those of its members who belonged to other political organizations, Liberal, Conservative, or Communist, and could support the CCF without forcing each and every one of its members to belong as affiliated members of the party.

In its early stages membership in the CCF therefore was closed and exclusive: that is, to become a CCFer, it was necessary to belong to one of the federated organizations or a CCF club. These organizations and clubs were autonomous and could (and often did) exclude individuals with whom they ideologically disagreed. Once past this sectarian phase, however, the party quickly adopted a constitution which permitted an open membership. Individuals could join provided they subscribed to the principles of the party, but they need not take any test. Moreover political groups which had to affiliate all their membership to the party could accept only individuals who agreed to abide by the principles and program of the CCF. Finally the constitution permitted trade unionists and other members of economic and cultural groups to join the party. It did so by recognizing the right of individuals in those groups to opt out of this membership. The CCF thereby implicitly accepted the principle that membership in the party should be in one way or another an individual decision. Once an individual made his decision, there should be no bar to membership status. Although initially some of the organizations affiliated to the CCF adopted the Leninist principle of exclusivity, that principle was quickly abandoned by the CCF through constitutional change and by a new emphasis on the constituency association as the primary unit of the administrative structure.

As with any organization with more than several hundred members, the members themselves could not all participate in conducting the business of the organization or all decide its program and policies. A pyramidical representative structure was established to accomplish these ends. It is useful to observe that although initially the organizations affiliated to the CCF were considered to be essentially autonomous, the provincial CCF was considered to have its own business separate from that of the federated organizations and clubs and therefore it had, in the Austinian sense,[4] a kind of sovereignty. The seat of this sovereign power was the provincial convention, an annual meeting attended by delegates from the constituent organizations and clubs. By 1942 the basis of representation laid down by the constitution was as follows. Each unit was to receive two delegates for the first twenty-five members and thereafter one delegate for each additional twenty-five or major portion thereof. The constitution went on to lay down rules for determining the membership of a given unit. In addition candidates running in federal and provincial elections were entitled to be at conventions.

Not all the business of the party could be transacted at such an annual gathering, and consequently a smaller body, the Provincial Council, was elected by the convention to conduct the business of the CCF between meetings of the convention. Originally the council consisted of a president, a vice-president, and twelve members at large. By 1942 it was expanded to include a president, two vice-presidents, and nineteen other members, all elected at the provincial convention. In addition a secretary and a treasurer were chosen by the Provincial Council as administrative officers responsible to the council. The practice of the party at the time was to elect the secretary from among the members at large. The secretary, therefore, would not only be an administrative officer but a full voting member of the council. The treasurer was selected from outside the council, and though he would attend meetings of the council and the executive committee, he would not have a vote.

Although the council was a relatively small body with only twenty-two voting members, it was found necessary to have an even smaller group meet more regularly to conduct the business of the party between meetings of the council. This group was known as the executive committee and was established under the by-laws of the organization. It consisted of the president, vice-presidents, and seven other members of the council. Inevitably the secretary was included.

There were three other key sections of the 1942 constitution. The first concerned discipline. Article VIII states: "Individual members shall be disciplined by the governing body of the club or group to which they belong, with the right of appeal to the provincial council; or by the provincial council, with the right of appeal to the provincial convention." Although local clubs were given some authority here, clearly the most important body was the Provincial Council which could set aside the acts of the clubs and which could be checked only by the convention. Moreover article v, entitled "Duties and Powers of the Provincial Council," in addition to stating that the council shall have the power to direct the affairs of the CCF in Ontario went on to detail the council's control over discipline. It gave the council power to accept or reject any application of a group or individual and the power to expel or discipline in some other way any group or individual who "does not conform to the principles, policy and constitution and laws of the organization, or who does not function with a reasonable degree of efficiency, or who persistently fails, neglects or refuses to cooperate in a project for the advancement of the CCF which has been authorized and directed by the provincial council." In short, it had now become possible to join the CCF directly, and the federated organizations and clubs could no longer offer tests and other impediments to bar members. At the same time the CCF itself, through the Provincial Council, was given sweeping powers to ensure that members, both groups and individuals, were acceptable to the council in terms of their political beliefs.

Second, the by-laws contained a section which ensured that all members would belong to a constituency organization. Each constituency would elect an official who was directly responsible for liaison with the provincial organization and was also responsible to the council and the executive for the actions taken by the constituency, particularly those taken in elections. Finally, two sections of the by-law dealt with the electoral machinery, one for municipal elections, and one for provincial and federal elections. The most important point here is that all candidates selected by constituency nominating meetings needed the endorsation of the Provincial Council which had the right to refuse endorsation if it felt that to be necessary. Thus, this early constitution of the party provided a representative structure by which party members could control the executive and at the same time provided the executive and council with very significant powers to control the actions of the membership or, that is to say, the actions of individual members or significant groupings of members who might wish to lead the party in a different direction than that ordained by the leadership.

This basic structure continued throughout the history of the CCF until 1961, although by the mid-1950s the form of the constitution had undergone a number of modifications. Essentially, however, the democratic principles underpinning the constitution continued. The logic of the establishment of an open membership by the encouragement of constituency associations as the primary form of organization was extended, and in its later years the CCF had two categories of membership: individual membership, open to "persons who have agreed to subscribe to the principles and policies of the CCF as set out in decisions of the national and provincial conventions," and affiliated membership, open to "economic organizations, such as trade unions, farmers' organizations, cooperative societies, cultural or educational organizations, who have applied for affiliation and whose affiliation has been accepted."[5] Clubs of special interests and of like-minded individuals had not been abolished but after 1947 they no longer had direct representation at conventions, thus ensuring the primacy of the constituency association as the key local organizational unit.

The same pyramidical structure of control also remained but with modifications. The provincial convention was still seen as the seat of sovereignty in the party, with a Provincial Council constituted to conduct the business of the party between conventions and an executive constituted to conduct the party business between council meetings. By 1955 the council had grown to include seven officers (the president, the provincial leader, and five vice-presidents), the immediate past president, two members elected to the National Council of the party by the provincial convention, four or five members of the National Council who resided in Ontario and who were elected by the national convention, twenty members at large elected by the provincial convention, one member from each constituency with more than fifty members (twenty-five members in all from rural constituencies), two members from the CCF youth movement, the chairman of the provincial women's conference, and chairmen elected by the annual trade union and farm conferences. Potential membership of the council had grown from twenty-two in 1942 to one hundred twenty-five. In actual fact the membership was somewhat smaller, since many rural constituencies were not entitled to a council delegate because they lacked sufficient members or because they lacked an organization sufficiently strong to ensure that a council member would attend the majority of meetings. The membership of council was more in the neighbourhood of seventy to eighty, and of those forty or fifty usually attended meetings. Because the council had become a much more unwieldy body, the executive committee seemed proportionately more significant in the party and was now dignified by inclusion in the constitution rather than in the by-laws. It consisted of the seven officers and twelve other members of the Provincial Council elected by the council.[6]

Perhaps unconsciously imitating the British North America Act, which failed to mention the office of prime minister, the CCF constitution failed to mention the office of provincial secretary, the party's full-time executive officer at this time. The old practice remained of electing the secretary from among the members at large elected by the convention. A new group, the table officers also emerged at this time, though it was not mentioned in the constitution. The table officers, who were the officers of the council, took to meeting by themselves to conduct the routine business of the party between meetings of the executive and particularly to advise the secretary on the administration of the party.[7]

Two other critical elements of the 1955 constitution concern discipline, of local organizations and of individual members, and control of the nomination process for public office. In terms of control of local organizations, article VII, section 6, states: "Each constituency association may adopt its own constitution and regulations subject to approval of the provincial council." In terms of the discipline of individual members, constituency associations retained the right enjoyed by the clubs and other federated organizations to suspend or expel a member and this continued to be subject to appeal to the Provincial Council. The council itself continued to have the right to accept or reject membership applications and to expel or suspend from membership or affiliation individuals or groups "who (or which) act(s) contrary to the fundamental principles and policies of the CCF." By 1955 there was no longer any automatic appeal of disciplinary actions to the provincial convention, although the convention as the supreme governing body of the party could initiate such a review if it so desired. In terms of the control of nominations, the constitution set out the general procedure to be followed in nominating candidates for municipal, provincial, and federal public office and included the provision that "any person selected as a candidate by a nominating convention must be endorsed by the provincial council and the council has the right to refuse this endorsation."

The fact that this basic constitutional structure continued through-out the history of the CCF, however, does not mean that the party was not concerned with its constitution or that debate over provisions of that document did not occur. A number of important constitutional questions can be identified, and the formation of the new party in 1961 focused attention on many of them and brought the constitutional debate to a head. The most important issues follow.

The first concerned the status of provincial organizations. The decision to form a new party was essentially a decision to form one political party in all of Canada. The temper of the times in the late 1950s and early 1960s, coupled with the strong centralist traditions in the CCF and in the labour movement, ensured that this would be done. On 8 August 1958 a top-level CLC/CCF subcommittee formed to discuss the structure of the new party decided that it must operate under the assumption that "under a federal system of government there should be provincial organizations as well as the national organization. The question that arises is what is the status of these provincial organizations? Are they to be creatures of the national party or are they to have some other status?"[8] In the end, despite these centralist traditions, the federal constitution of the party declared in article x: "Each province of Canada shall have a fully autonomous provincial party, provided its constitution is not in conflict with the constitution of the federal party." Theoretically the provincial parties are creatures of the federal party. Practically speaking the provision calling for autonomy provided a constitutional justification for the growing provincial party initiatives, particularly in Ontario.[9]

Debate over membership concerned the question of individual membership and the level of the party to which individual members ought to belong. Should the national organization control membership or should the provincial organizations? In the CCF the provincial organizations had done so by establishing machinery for screening members and disciplining them. The architects of the new party agreed that a similar situation should continue. A more complicated and important problem concerned affiliated members. The new party was a formal initiative of the CCF and of the Canadian Labour Congress, Canada's central labour body, acting on behalf of its affiliated unions. In some sense therefore the new party was to be a labour party, a party in which the trade union movement was actively involved, not simply through the initiatives of those members politically eager to have the new party succeed, but on a constitutional basis in which trade union organizations would have a formal relationship with the political party. A number of questions concerning this formal relationship arose, the most basic of which was its establishment or, rather, the formula for bringing it about. Essentially the CLC/CCF subcommittee considered two alternatives. The first was the formula found in the British Labour party. As the minutes of the meeting of the subcommittee record:

One possible approach is to follow, at least in general terms, the procedure of the British Labour Party. Under this system we would have:
(a) individual members who would pay a specified membership fee and would be organized in constituency associations and clubs;
affiliated organizations, trade unions, farm organizations etc., which would pay a specified per capita fee in respect of all their members other than those who might "contract out."

The implication of this formula is to make organizations themselves, rather than individual trade unionists or farmers, members of the party and to provide a system in which the union organizations affiliated to the party act in concert. For example, in the British Labour party the heads of the large trade unions cast the votes for all their members affiliated to the party on the grounds that the organization itself, rather than individual trade unionists, has affiliated. This structure also implies that there are in a sense two basic divisions in the party: the constituencies act by themselves without trade union participation; the unions act by themselves without constituency participation; and they only come together to consider political and other questions in convention. The other alternative was designated as the individual membership formula. As the minutes of the subcommittee explain:

An alternative to the formula just described [the British Labour party formula] would be one under which there would be no basic distinction between the members of affiliated organizations and the individual members of the party. The way this would work would be that an affiliated organization would pay a per capita fee in respect of all its members (other than those who contract out) and each member of the affiliate would thereupon be entitled to be a member of the constituency in which he lives without payment of any further fees.[10]

Essentially the second formula was adopted in Ontario, although not without a certain controversy.

The idea of affiliation, particularly affiliation by trade unions, was not new in 1958. The national CCF had had provision for such affiliation since the late 1930s. The first union to affiliate was the United Mine Workers, District 26, in Nova Scotia in 1938. The Ontario CCF had as a supplement to its constitution a resolution on trade union affiliation which provided that a union, either a local union or a union in respect of its membership in the Province of Ontario, could affiliate to the CCF by paying per capita dues of two cents per member per month. Affiliated unions would thereby become entitled to limited representation at CCF conventions and at constituency meetings and nominating conventions. A number of local unions had taken advantage of this provision, particularly local unions of the Steelworkers and Packinghouse Workers. Leaders of the CCF therefore favoured this particular scheme. It avoided the problems of block voting at conventions which the British Labour party model implied, and also avoided giving affiliated members the same representation at conventions or constituency meetings when they paid significantly less in dues and seemed less committed to the party than those who signed as individual members.

The individual membership formula favoured by the CLC/CCF subcommittee proposed to treat individual members and affiliated members equally at constituency meetings and particularly at nominating conventions. As the minutes record: "There would be no problem as to the relative status of members of affiliated organizations and individual members of the party because all members of affiliates would be (or at any rate could be) individual party members."[11] The minutes go on, however, to record that even though affiliated organizations would have a kind of indirect representation at conventions because their members could participate in constituency associations, it was seen as desirable to provide some direct representation for the organization which would be paying out substantial sums of money in affiliate dues. For the Ontario NDP this provision would in effect continue the practice of the Ontario CCF of providing reduced representation for affiliated organizations at conventions, but would make a very significant change by providing equal representation for affiliated members and individual members at constituency meetings and nominating conventions. This led to a third controversy.

Donald C. MacDonald, then Ontario CCF leader and a member of the National Committee for the New Party and the Ontario Committee for the New Party, expressed strong reservations about this scheme in a letter to David Archer, president of the Ontario Federation of Labour and chairman of the Constitutional Subcommittee of the Ontario Committee for the New Party. As he stated:

My initial worry regarding the proposal that all members of affiliated organizations be granted voting rights at a riding nominating convention stemmed from the fact that this is a reversal of what has generally been understood in the whole planning for the new party since the Winnipeg Seminar. Certainly, it had been my understanding that while affiliated organizations should be given delegate representation at riding nominating conventions – and I would favour that representation beyond the most generous basis deemed advisable and, further, that affiliated organizations should also have delegate representation on the riding executive so that coordination of activities would be on a continuing basis – rather than just at nominating conventions – it had never been understood that every affiliate member would have full voting rights in the choice of candidate ...

... the decision which we accepted at the OCNP [to treat affiliate members as full members] is not only a very far reaching one, but at variance with the whole new party development. My guess is that the overwhelming majority in the CCF support the view that affiliated members should be given voting rights at nominating conventions only when they had taken out full membership in the party, and at least a significant minority in the trade union movement do likewise ...

... second, the granting of full voting rights to every affiliate member will destroy the image of a broadly based party, involving all sectors of the community at the riding level. It will bolster the fears of those within the party that it is dominated by labour, and will give our opponent convincing evidence with which to clobber us from the outside.[12]

Others, particularly key trade union leaders, felt that affiliations to the CCF had not proved to be successful; most unions had not affiliated and the majority of local unions even in the Steelworkers and Packinghouse Workers, the unions which felt most strongly committed to political action, remained unaffiliated. There had to be some tangible change from the situation that existed in the CCF. In the final analysis the unions agreed to reject the British Labour party option and to adopt an affiliation procedure almost identical with that which operated in the CCF, with the significant change that affiliated members at the constituency level would be equal to individual members. The operative part of the constitutional resolution passed at the founding convention of the Ontario NDP in 1961 was as follows: "Members of affiliated organizations are entitled to attend and vote at constituency meetings and nominating conventions providing their names are registered with the constituency secretary. No such member will be entitled to vote at a nominating convention, unless he has been registered for at least thirty days. Such members may not vote in the election of constituency association delegates to provincial or federal conventions of the New Democratic Party."[13] The reason for this last directive was to placate CCFers who felt that affiliated members would be given dual representation if they could vote for constituency delegates to party conventions in the constituency and then, unlike individual members, turn around and vote for delegates from their union. On the key point, however, affiliated members were to be treated the same as individual members in the constituency associations even though their financial contribution of 60 cents a year was significantly less than the $2.50 a year paid by individuals. In practice most affiliated members did not bother to register with the constituency secretary and the constituencies continued to be dominated by individual members. Those trade unionists particularly keen on political action joined the NDP as individual members.

Another major constitutional question was the relationship of the new party with the central labour bodies (at the national level, the Canadian Labour Congress; in Ontario, the Ontario Federation of Labour and the various local labour councils). The CLC, in taking the initiative to form the new party by its resolution, was clearly a full partner in the negotiations towards the founding convention. When Stanley Knowles, the veteran MP from Winnipeg North Centre from 1942 to 1958, lost his seat in the Diefenbaker landslide, he was almost immediately thereafter elected an executive vice-president of the congress and was assigned duties primarily concerned with the formation of the new party. Knowles became the chairman of the National Committee for the New Party and continued to be a vice-president of the CCF while a CLC officer. Because the congress, however, is an organization made up of affiliated unions, it became apparent that the CLC could not speak for all its affiliates on the matter and that any attempt to affiliate the whole congress to the new party could cause very severe ructions in the labour movement itself.[14] Thus once the CLC decided that it could not affiliate itself but only urge its own affiliates to do so, its constitutional creatures, the provincial federations of labour and the local labour councils, followed suit. In the Ontario NDP constitution, therefore, they are given a kind of honorary status. Each local labour council is entitled to one delegate at provincial conventions, the OFL to two delegates, and both have the right to send resolutions to provincial conventions.

One of the few general constitutional questions in which the CCFers found themselves on opposite sides from most of the trade unionists concerned the method of selecting the provincial secretary. The CCF followed the European, rather than the American, tradition and named the secretary, rather than the president, as its full-time key officer. For the national CCF the secretary was undoubtedly the most important officer of the party, particularly during the tenure of David Lewis from 1938 to 1950.[15] In Ontario no provincial secretary was as dominant as Lewis was on the national scene and, therefore, the office did not achieve the same prestige there. For a period of time, as noted, the office was not mentioned in the constitution.

By 1961 it was clear that the secretary (or secretary-treasurer, as the position was called in 1961–2; the two offices were split at the 1962 convention) was its most important administrative official and that the office provided its holder with a certain amount of power. The trade unionists, who had experienced such power in their own organizations, felt that the secretary should be elected by the whole convention, that is, by that party body with the greatest trade union representation. In the same way that most industrial unions worked, the secretary would come to dominate the administrative side of the party and they wanted as much say as possible about who was chosen. The CCF leadership, on the other hand, felt that the secretary was in some sense an employee of the party and that the matter of employment was best left to a smaller body, the Provincial Council, as it had been in the CCF. Indeed, as Dean McHenry notes, in Saskatchewan the secretary was chosen by the executive because of that view.[16] Trade unionists, however, were not agreeable and insisted that the whole convention elect the secretary along with the other officers. This was done.

Another controversy concerned the status of the Provincial Council. Some of its members were elected by the convention itself but most were from each federal constituency association. At the formation of the new party the main question concerned representation from the trade unions. It was decided not to provide much representation for the unions on this body; the unions did not fight for such representation and others did not insist upon it. In fact the youth section of the party with eight members had better representation than did the trade unions. Formally the affiliated trade unions were entitled to only one member for each national or international union with a significant membership in the province. In effect this meant that the unions had six or seven union officers on the council, with four or five other trade unionists selected from the convention as officers or members of the executive. The full membership of the council in 1961 consisted of the provincial executive; two members elected by the provincial caucus; two members elected from the federal caucus representing Ontario constituencies; one delegate from each provincial constituency association; eight members from the New Democratic Youth, and representatives from national or international unions with over five thousand members affiliated in Ontario.

It was not until 1970 that significant change was made. In that year it was decided that constituency associations should have a weighted membership so that every constituency would get one representative for the first three hundred members and an additional representative for every further three hundred members or "major fraction thereof." In addition the constitution made it mandatory for these constituency delegates to be members of the executive of their association. At the same time area councils were given representation on the Provincial Council in the form of their president and vice-president. Most important, union representation was very much increased by a new formula which stated that "one member from each affiliated local or grouping of affiliated unions with a paid-up affiliated membership in Ontario of 500 or more" was to be on the council. This greatly increased union representation was to have significant consequences when the Provincial Council came to concern itself with the question of the Waffle group within the party.

At the time of the founding convention of the Ontario party, the main controversy involving the council and the provincial executive concerned the composition of the executive itself. In the CCF the executive had consisted of table officers elected by the convention and of members at large elected, not by the convention, but by the council. This gave the council the ability to choose the majority of members of the executive. Again, CCF activists favoured continuing this system within the NDP, while the trade unionists favoured the system of direct election from the convention floor itself for all members of the executive. Led by Bill Sefton, who also led the fight for

the election of the secretary, the labour movement argued strenuously that election of the whole executive by the convention was more
democratic, since the convention was a more representative body of
the whole party. Because arguments postulating improved democracy
are bound to have a considerable weight in a nonestablishment party,
the trade union view carried the day. The executive, therefore,
consisted of the Provincial Council officers; fifteen members elected
by the convention, no more than five of whom were to be Members of
Parliament or Members of the Legislative Assembly at the time of their
nomination; and two members elected by the convention to represent
the Ontario party on the federal council. In 1968 the convention
added two members elected by the convention of the Ontario Young
New Democrats.

Finally, it should be noted that after 1962 the officers of the
provincial party numbered nine: the leader, the president, five
vice-presidents, the secretary, and the treasurer. Until 1966 the table
officers and two members of the executive elected to sit with them
conducted party business between meetings of the executive. After
1966 this "inner Cabinet" came to be known as the administrative
group, or Administrative Committee, and consisted of the leader, the
president, the secretary, the treasurer, one vice-president, and the
chairmen of the executive standing committees (the Election Planning
Committee, the Publicity Committee, and the Membership and
Organization Committee), who could be either vice-presidents or
members at large on the executive. After 1970 all the vice-presidents
were invited to attend and vote at meetings of the Administrative
Committee.

What is notable about this structure is the tendency for the final
decisions to be taken by a smaller and smaller group of key
individuals. Although they may have been overruled by the more
representative bodies at the base of the pyramid, they effectively set
the agenda for the executive, the council, the convention, and,
ultimately, the party by taking the initiative for making decisions and
recommending these to the more representative bodies. This structure lent itself to oligarchical control.

There was relatively little controversy over the role of constituency
associations. The 1955 CCF constitution stated that "each constituency
association has the authority to do all it deems necessary in order
that its purposes shall be fulfilled." Its actions were subject to the
provisions of the CCF constitution and the decisions of national and

provincial conventions and of the Provincial Council. No such statement granting autonomy graced the NDP constitution, and it was clear that constituencies were seen as convenient administrative devices to ensure that election campaigns could be waged efficiently. The old principle of "club" autonomy had finally been expunged.

Finally, one of the most vexing problems for the party was the question of discipline. With the constitutional withering away of the clubs, the party, as a mass membership party based on social democratic models in Europe, sought to enrol as many individuals and groups as possible. At the same time the older tradition of the party as a band of like-minded individuals continued, and was strengthened, by the deeply felt need that a socialist party in Canada must dissociate itself from totalitarian strategies and, therefore, from the Communist party and other Marxist-Leninist groups, particularly Trotskyists. As a result it was seen as necessary to give the council and other organizations the power to expel or suspend individual members or to refuse an application for membership from individuals or groups.[17] Such provisions in the CCF constitution have been noted, and they continued in the New Democratic Party. Many in the party were unhappy with these sweeping powers and their maintenance was somewhat controversial.

While there were a number of constitutional changes throughout the history of the CCF/NDP from the 1930s until 1971, in fact these changes were not, after 1942, fundamental. Even before 1942 the basic outlines of the party structure existed and continued intact. Constitutional issues that arose after 1942 were important, but they did not change the nature of the party's formal arrangements. Indeed, the only fundamental change was one not enshrined in the constitution; it concerned the relative strengths of the federal party and the provincial party. In the 1960s there was a shift of emphasis and a shift of the focus of power from the federal to the provincial level.

The CCF was a centralist-oriented party and, as such, its own internal structure reflected this bias. Particularly for the Ontario CCF the relationship with the national party while David Lewis was secretary was "quite close,"and the provincial party was well represented on the national executive and the National Council. "It was ... easier for us [Ontario] to attend meetings in Ottawa than it was for other provinces."[18] This close relationship between Ontario and Ottawa is not unfamiliar to students of Canadian federalism, and there was little doubt that in the CCF the national party was dominant. As Jolliffe points out:

Indeed we had a lot of highly impractical people who didn't understand politics at all. We used to say, in an airy way, "I'm not interested in provincial politics but I do want to see J.S. Woodsworth or M.J. Coldwell ... with a large group in Ottawa, to get something done ... Provinces don't matter and I'm not interested." Some of us had to spend a lot of time, or waste a lot of time, trying to educate these people to an understanding that the CCF would never be a powerful federal force unless it had the support of powerful provincial organizations ... unfortunately a good education and high intellectual attainment give no assurance of sound political judgment, and I can remember some arguments with some university professors in our membership who thought the provincial campaign should be written off; it's a waste of time. After all, Mitch Hepburn had said that the legislature was no more than a glorified county council and these people tended to agree with him.

Jolliffe himself states that he was "far more interested in federal than provincial affairs. I can quite honestly say that I went into the provincial field from a sense of duty, and not because my major interest was there, just as, I think, Tommy Douglas returned to Saskatchewan from a sense of duty rather than with any great enthusiasm to be a provincial leader."[19]

Don MacDonald expressed similar views about his own interest in federal politics, recalling that he had come to the Ontario CCF leadership from a post with the national party and that after he had resigned the Ontario NDP leadership, he was elected as the party's federal president.[20] Stephen Lewis recalls that when he first sought election to the provincial legislature in 1963, he was in his own mind more interested in federal than in provincial politics.[21] Other members of the Ontario party hierarchy had similar sentiments.[22]

Yet there was a significant change in the early 1960s. George Cadbury, president of the Ontario NDP during that period, states flatly: "I do think that there was ... quite a big shift of thinking, of the priorities, a change from the old days, and while I would have said that when we started in 1961 there wasn't anybody who would have said that the federal party is more important than the provincial party or vice versa, by 1965 there were a lot of people who said that the provincial party is more important than the federal party."[23] Others have reflected on this shift of power. Don MacDonald explains it simply as the party "accommodating itself to the realities of Canada."[24] Because the provinces had become more important in the 1960s, the provincial sections of the NDP no longer saw themselves as sections of the party but as autonomous organizations. As a result resources were concentrated in the larger provinces, particularly in Ontario and Saskatchewan. The federal office was reduced during this period and key people like Terry Grier moved from a full-time role at the federal level to one at the provincial. In short, although the party's constitutional structure remained remarkably faithful to its origin, nonetheless the party, at least in part, adapted itself to the wider environment with its growing emphasis on provincial power.

5

Party Ideas

For that generation of political scientists who were primarily concerned with analyses of the legal formalities associated with the modern state, the political party was a problem. It was known to be important but was nonetheless rarely acknowledged in state constitutions and other fundamental legislation. This generation wished to ignore the political party, but it recognized that to do so was to mask the reality of political life. The party, therefore, was usually explained in terms of its own formalities – its constitution and its program.

Generally party constitutions are uninteresting and uninformative, and the suspicion undoubtedly lurked in the minds of these scholars that just as the existence of parties meant that the state did not operate according to its own formal rules, so it was likely that political activity within the parties did not correspond to the formal rules enshrined in the constitutions debated and passed by party congresses. It was tempting, therefore, to deal with parties in terms of their programs and in terms of the ideological underpinnings of those programs.[1]

The questions that followed focused on the parties' stances on the issues of the day, on their alternatives for managing public policy, and on their adoption of policies associated with such broad ideological perspectives as socialism, liberalism, communism, and capitalism. Does the party tend to collectivist solutions? If so, does it favour the nationalization of the coal industry? Does it favour an aggressive foreign policy with a large standing army? Does it wish to redistribute the wealth of the country? These were the kinds of questions asked about parties and the answers in large measure provided the definition and analysis of any individual party. Nor is this approach unreasonable. Fundamentally a party may be seen as a partisan organization and its partisanship is most easily identified in the terms of its program – both its immediate program and its underlying philosophical views.

Moreover, it is unwise to abandon this focus on program simply because in recent years social scientists have had access to information about the basis of party support, about the character of organizational structure, and about a myriad of other facets of political activity which permit a somewhat broader understanding of party life. The party program is still the most public manifestation of a party's reason for existence, and though we may cynically or scientifically note other motives, there is no sense in ignoring this obvious one. The notion that a party exists to bring about the incarnation of its cherished ideals and fond solutions to public problems may seem old-fashioned and unnecessarily formal but it is not without some basis in reality. Equally important is the fact that much of the literature on parties is concerned with these kinds of questions and provides a framework in which concepts such as the left, the right, socialism, communism, liberalism, conservatism, fascism have some substantive meaning. The CCF/NDP in Ontario therefore may be analysed within the framework of these concepts.

More important, it is necessary to analyse the party's program and ideology in considering the proposition of a characteristic process of adjustment to external reality as the sine qua non of party survival. A major implication of the secularization thesis is a pronounced relationship between party program and the party's fundamental development rather than a relationship in which the program is dictated by rational electoral considerations, or by ideological ones. One expects that the important programmatic concerns of the CCF/NDP of Ontario are symbolically attached to the party's self-conscious view of itself at any given stage of development and are not merely the manifestation of electoral calculation or ideological logic.

This view runs counter to the conventional wisdom which considers the Ontario CCF/NDP program in terms of a right-left continuum. For students of the CCF/NDP the most pervasive hypothesis associated with party program and ideology has been that of a "rightward drift." The party over the years has been seen not only to have gradually moderated its approach to the political issues of the day, but indeed to have altered its fundamental conception of itself as an instrument of social change. This view has it that the CCF began as a political group strongly committed to fundamental change in society and to collectivist solutions to public problems and that these twin commitments have gradually been diluted to the point where the NDP proposes very little that is fundamentally different from policies advocated by the Liberal and Progressive Conservative parties in Canada.[2] Even more starkly the CCF was originally seen as a left-wing party opposed by right-wing parties, the Liberals and Conservatives, but gradually the CCF/NDP has become less left wing and more right wing just as gradually the Liberals and to a lesser extent the Conservatives have become less right wing and more left wing to the point where it would seem fair to say that the three parties meet at some middle kingdom along this continuum. This has meant that gradually the CCF/NDP has been seen to drift to the right, or to use Louis St Laurent's gentle gibe, the party became a group of "Liberals in a hurry." Similar, if less gentle, sentiments have been expressed by many members of the CCF/NDP who, for the most part, have deplored this drift to the right.[3]

CCF/NDP Socialism

The literature on democratic socialism gives us some notion of the left-right continuum but provides little precision: indeed, there have been violent disagreements about substantive meaning.[4] There is some agreement that a left-right scale exists but little agreement about where parties and people should be placed on that scale and about substance at any particular point on the scale.

To examine the view that the CCF/NDP in Ontario has drifted rightward, it is necessary to consider the ideological strains present in the party. Fundamentally the party is a democratic socialist party similar to the British Labour party, the German Social Democratic party, the Australian Labour party, the French Socialist party, and a multitude of other democratic socialist parties associated with each other in the Socialist International. It is generally, or at least popularly, considered to be a left-wing party inasmuch as it advocates a more collectivist society in which the state provides many social services and ensures that those services are available by exercising considerable control over the economy. If this seems vague, perhaps it is easier to define the party, not in terms of what it is, but in terms of what it is not. It is not, for example, a party which advocates the complete collectivization of society in the sense that the state would control all or almost all aspects of economic life. Instead it believes in a mixed economy in which there is both public and private ownership in various forms; yet it is unhappy with the present mix in the economic system and therefore with the present society. It rejects the view that poverty is always with us and believes the free market tends not to equilibrium but rather to the domination of society by a small economic elite.

Certainly the party is left wing and socialist, but in what way is this so and which of the many socialist traditions have primarily influenced the Ontario CCF/NDP? Essentially four socialist traditions, Fabianism, Christian socialism (or the social gospel as it is called in Canada), Marxism, and labourism have had a profound impact on the CCF/NDP in Ontario. A fifth, that of the American new left, has had a more marginal influence.

That the party was greatly influenced by Fabianism and by the writings of members of the Fabian Society is hardly surprising. Canada began as a British colony and in large measure the CCF began as a colony of the British Labour party. Moreover it is not surprising that from this British Labour party connection the most important element would be that of the intellectual Fabians. The CCF began before the rise of the industrial unions and at a time when craft unions were usually hostile to socialist theories. Most of the craft unions in Canada were in fact "international," part of a larger American-based organization, and were hostile to socialism. Initially the CCF had very little support from the trade unionists. It did, however, have intellectual support. One of the key founding groups of the party was the League for Social Reconstruction (LSR). Many of the early leaders of the party saw themselves as intellectuals of one sort or another and first came in contact with the CCF by attending meetings of the league. The league itself played a vital role in the formation of the party. The Regina Manifesto was drafted by members of the league, in particular Frank Underhill who penned the final version. The league also undertook the massive task of analysing the Canadian economy and social system in attempting to provide alternative solutions. Active members of the league, Eugene Forsey, King Gordon, Leonard Marsh, J.F. Parkinson, Frank Scott, Graham Spry, and Frank Underhill, were the primary authors of this effort. In the preface to *Social Planning for Canada*, the result of the analysis, they acknowledge the assistance of others, including Alexander Brady of the Political Economy Department, University of Toronto; Humphrey Carver, later the operating head of Central Mortgage and Housing Corporation; George Grube of the University of Toronto;

and Professor K.W. Taylor, also of the University of Toronto and later deputy minister of finance of Canada. The book was immensely influential with the CCF, for it served as the reference work in speech making and letter writing. The solutions advanced in the book, it must be noted, owe much to Fabian proposals. Indeed, the LSR was in large measure inspired by the example of the Fabian Society.[5]

Some members of the CCF were more directly inspired by the Fabian Society in terms of their own socialist education. Andrew Brewin, for example, recalls that the first socialist book he read was George Bernard Shaw's *An Intelligent Woman's Guide to Socialism and Capitalism*, which he found most persuasive and which convinced him that the CCF was needed in Canada.[6]

What was it that distinguished the Fabians from other socialist groups? The Fabians enjoyed two major distinctions: their program and their peculiar view of appropriate political tactics for a socialist party. Three features were particularly important in defining their program. First was the strong view that capitalism is immoral. This belief is not, it should be emphasized, the same as that held by Marxists that capitalism is contradictory and hence inevitably wasteful nor is it even the view that capitalism is simply outmoded and old-fashioned. Instead the Fabians rather interestingly made use of religious images to describe the capitalist system and to denounce it as fundamentally wrong. Shaw was fond of pointing out that man, including the working man, in the capitalist state "are in the lump detestable."[7] Counterposed to this immoral society, R.H. Tawney suggested a new society of friends which, like the Quaker society, would be egalitarian and loving.[8] The Fabians first wished to reform a fundamentally corrupt society and with it fundamentally corrupt human beings, thus suggesting that Shaw, the Webbs, and other Fabian intellectuals, like the British Labour party, owed a great deal, if not to Christian theology, at least to Christian imagery.

Second, the most striking point about the Fabian program was its eclecticism. Fabians advocated any number of measures, many unrelated except in the vaguest sense. They advocated greater social security, usually interpreted as pensions and other kinds of direct payments. They favoured direct taxation and fair shares by which, some of them at least, meant unemployment insurance. Many Fabians were particularly concerned with local government – the gas and water socialists – and favoured public ownership of essential municipal services. Others were concerned with education and the moulding of childrens' characters and the need to create an education system in which the old class values of England would be socialized out of existence in favour of more egalitarian values. In more recent years Fabians have written of poverty in the Third World, regional planning and national planning, problems of the welfare state, and the dilemma of trade union power.[9] The list of ideas was almost endless but their presentation was incoherent and often resembling in form, if not in spirit, the quadrennial platforms of the Democratic party in the United States.

The third characteristic of the Fabian program, and almost an inevitable characteristic in the modern world, was the view that the new faith for man had to be a rationalist scientific one. The Fabians believed in planning as a panacea for all social ills. This touching faith in science was not unique to the Fabians. It is the hallmark of all liberals, that is, of all those who believe that man can create his own paradise. It provides the fundamental ideological link between the liberals and the Fabians.

In large measure the Fabians were famous for their tactical contributions to the socialist canon. The society, in a display of late nineteenth-century obscurantism, named itself after the famous Roman general Fabius Cunctator who adopted the guerrilla policy of avoiding a frontal attack on the Carthaginian army in favour of a slow wearing down of the enemy by worrying his weaker flanks. The Fabians transposed capitalism for General Hannibal and urged a similar strategy of avoiding a potentially fatal frontal assault.

This delicate tactical policy had several implications, and the Fabians made all of them manifest. Perhaps the most fundamental was the recognition of the need for socialist elites. Essentially the Fabians were paternalist in their outlook. They rejected the view that the broad mass of people would inevitably overthrow the existing order by sheer weight of numbers. They believed that more subtle methods were necessary, and by definition those methods required an intelligent and enlightened leadership, a leadership that had to be educated and therefore, at least for England of the early twentieth century, middle class rather than working class. At the same time the Fabian strategy also implied a democratic polity and Fabianism certainly implied a democratic premise. The strategy of attacking the weak link clearly could work only if the state was so structured to permit such attacks. Though elitist the Fabians embraced liberal democracy.

Finally, the Fabians tactically emphasized institutions; that is, as Shaw stated, they were out to "make socialism not socialists." There was to be no cataclysmic conversion of the masses but rather a slow penetration of institutions, which for the Fabians were the real building blocks of a society. This middle-class idealism should not be mistaken for liberalism because in a very real sense it grew out of an organic or tory view of society, which no doubt sprang from the middle-class Victorian awe of the monarchy. The point is that it was middle-class idealism and that the values that supported the Fabian notion of strategy were tory, while the values that supported their program were liberal. It was a neat combination but it was not one that could be mistaken for Marxism.

If Fabianism was the revealed doctrine from the land of truth, then it fell on soil fertilized by the doctrines of Christian socialism, or as it was called in Canada, the social gospel. Canada, particularly Ontario, is often described as an English microcosm. This is hardly surprising, since Ontario was colonized by the English and since Canada until 1931 (perhaps even until 1982) was legally a colonial state. But Canada was not, despite this status, simply a copy of English society. Those who immigrated to Canada from Britain were generally poor and therefore disproportionately from the Celtic fringe, particularly Scotland, and also from the English west country. In religious affiliation Ontario was very unlike England. The Church of England in Canada had fewer members in Ontario than the Methodists and the Presbyterians had before 1926 and continued to fall far short of United Church membership after union. This fact was important in terms of the CCF appeal and ideological commitment. In England the Methodists had always been associated with the poorer classes in society and to some extent with the emerging trade union movement – hence, the gibe "Socialism owes more to Methodism than to Marx." Although E.P. Thompson in *The Making of the English Working Class* points out that the influence of Methodism has been exaggerated, it was nonetheless real and in Canada, settled by Methodists and Presbyterians, it was not even exaggerated.[10]

Richard Allen lovingly details the extraordinary influence exercised by clergymen of various denominations who preached the "social gospel." These were men like A.E. Smith, later a member of the Communist party, who, as Allan suggests, "in the place of redemption of sinful man by Christ's sacrifice ... preached of a social redemption whereby men's ills would be overcome by fruitful work and equitable distribution. Poverty seemed to be the greatest evil and profiteering the greatest sin."[11] Others, without necessarily abandoning the notion of redemption through faith or by grace, similarly argued for a new society in which the goods of the world would be more equitably distributed.

As Allen points out, the ideas underpinning social gospel were not unique to Canada, and its theology was better developed in England, Germany, and the United States. However, because of the importance of Methodism in Canada and because of the evangelical influence in both the Presbyterian and the Anglican churches, religious leaders, once seized of these views, were able to communicate them effectively to large numbers of people. In real measure reformism in Canada from the 1890s to the 1930s was associated in largest part with the churches and through that vehicle penetrated the full community. This was as true in Ontario as it was in Western Canada, and it provided the CCF, if not with a ready-made constituency, at least with a cadre of leaders. An extraordinary proportion of the early leadership were clergymen. J.S. Woodsworth, Bill Irvine, Tommy Douglas, Stanley Knowles, and Fred Young are examples. Others, like Andrew Brewin,[12] recalled joining the party in part as a response to what they felt was a Christian imperative. Religion, particularly this evangelical Protestant social religion, was a part of the very fabric of Ontario society, and from the beginning the CCF was associated with this powerful religious impulse.

Inevitably Marxist thought has an influence on any political movement on the left and certainly on any that is self-consciously socialist. For the CCF this was particularly true in British Columbia where a number of founding groups there and elsewhere in the western provinces were consciously Marxist.[13] In Ontario Marxist views were not so significant, although some of the smaller socialist societies fancied themselves Marxist. After the first years they counted for little in the party. Nevertheless, because of the influence of Marxism in Western Canada and because the Marxist tradition in Ontario was never completely obliterated, it must be seen as one of the ideological strains in the Ontario CCF/NDP. In particular the view that the triumph of socialism is inevitable and that one must simply wait for history to unfold as it should was very much a part of early CCF thinking.[14] Faith in the state as the antidote for all social evils, a doctrine held by many CCFers, is also Marxist, though it comes by way of 1930s Stalinist thought – an inspiration for many on the left who had a real admiration and hope for the Soviet Union.[15]

A more important ideological impulse in the Ontario CCF/NDP certainly from 1940 onwards could be labelled labourism. In one sense labourism is the philosophical, or at least analytical, rationalization of trade union activity. Fundamentally labourism rejects the Marxist notion of inevitability and replaces it with a self-help strategy of demanding more. It acknowledges that the demand for more is unlikely to prove very fruitful if made in "Oliver Twist" fashion by one or a few weak individuals but that it will succeed if made in concert by a large group. The effect, however, is not a new order or a revolution but rather the amelioration of the condition endured by working people. Labourism implies that social change is slow and accomplished through unified action taken at some cost. It also implies the proverb, Half a loaf is better than none. Trade unionists in Ontario accepted this philosophy, often unconsciously, because early struggles taught them that the revolution was not inevitable. As a philosophy it can be found in its most developed form in the writings of two American academics, Richard Perlman and John R. Commons, both students of the American labour movement.[16]

Finally, it should be noted that the 1960s and 1970s Ontario NDP has been influenced, as always, by ideological currents fashionable elsewhere but particularly in the United States. Throughout the 1960s these fashions were most usually grouped under the label of new left thought, which basically provided an interpretation of much older socialist ideas of the utopian variety. Essentially four doctrines promoted by the new left influenced the Ontario NDP. First was the belief in confrontation politics. Two great American protest movements of the 1960s – the civil rights movement and the campaign to end the war in Vietnam – advanced and practised direct action, often illegal action, to gain their point. They used techniques such as sit-ins, demonstrations, both peaceful and not so peaceful, and a deliberate flouting of laws they believed to be unjust. Terry Grier explains how this view had its impact in the Ontario NDP.

There began to emerge a very primitive theory or version of the theory of confrontation politics: that the legislature and the parliamentary process were largely sterile and that the real battle was out in the streets ... and at this time you had the growth of the new left and its importation into Canada via the mechanism of the anti-Vietnam movement so that people in the party who ten years ago might have taken a different route to challenge or question the leadership in the latter 1960s were building on the confrontation theory, and to some extent of course it seems to me the ideology of what later became the organized Waffle movement is an ideology of confrontation – not of creativity but of confrontation.[17]

Both in Canada and in the United States the new left preached a distrust of institutions. The very exercise of power was seen as corrupting, a statement as true for the establishment of the Congress of the United States as for that of the Ontario New Democratic Party. Theirs was a kind of anarchist impulse, a view that the state, and institutions generally, inhibit the naturally co-operative inclination of man and that for liberty there must be only voluntary spontaneous conceptions of social organization.

The second feature of the 1960s new left was the impulse to go back to the land. Throughout North America large numbers of young people tried their hand at communal farming, away, so they hoped, from the contradictions of industrial capitalism. This Arcadian view of the world, a view held by many nineteenth-century socialists who established similar communities, sometimes with a religious base as well as a socialist one, was one that in large part equated industrial capitalism with urban living.

Third, because they distrusted the state and large-scale organization, the new left favoured small-scale economic enterprises and believed that they should be controlled by those who worked in them. This idea of worker control clearly related to Douglas Cole's guild socialism and was certainly a different vision of the order of society from that traditionally held by socialists who believed in central economic planning.

Finally, the new left rejected institutions, believing that fundamental social change would occur only when individuals were converted to better ways of behaviour and thought. Progressive changes in institutions could follow only these fundamental changes in individual beliefs. Again, this was a common theme of the early utopian socialists and one whose echoes had some influence on the Ontario New Democratic Party.

It is difficult to construct a rational left-right continuum from such ideological eclecticism. Certainly the policies of the party in any era may be compared with those of another era and differences, if any, may be noted, but there is no universal left-right scale upon which those differences can be marked. To some socialists this is undoubtedly an ultimate failure.

As noted, students of the CCF/NDP and members of the party often allude to a growing moderation, a change from the more doctrinaire or more left-wing approach to one that is less doctrinaire or right wing. Zakuta for example suggests:

Thus, as it neared the 1960s, the CCF seemed to be turning into a liberal reform party. Although it insisted, especially to its members, that its fundamental objectives had not altered, its ideological efforts to establish a new modus vivendi followed three main lines: one, a revision of its official doctrine towards greater tolerance of private enterprise, two, a heavier emphasis on specific, limited reforms and three, a heightened concern about explaining the role of a minor reform party to its members and the public.[18]

Zakuta points to the concern of many party members in 1956 that the attempt to replace the Regina Manifesto with the Winnipeg Declaration was clearly an effort to move the party to the right, while Desmond Morton has detailed similar charges by members of the Waffle group in the late 1960s and early 1970s.[19]

Those who recognize the metaphysical difficulties of constructing a left-right continuum suggest that at the very least there has been a change in the kind of rhetoric employed by the party. It is also argued that this rhetorical change is the manifestation of an underlying ideological change. The view exists that at some point there was a golden age of socialism in Canada, or at least a silver age, when the party avoided fundamental compromise, when it spoke more plainly about its socialist goals. Those who hold this position are particularly fond of quoting the notorious "bookend" passages from the Regina Manifesto:

We aim to replace the present capitalist system with its inherent injustice and inhumanity by a social order from which the domination and exploitation of one class by another may be eliminated ... we believe that these evils can be removed only in a planned and socialized economy in which our natural resources and the principal means of production and distribution are owned, controlled and operated by the people ...

No CCF government will rest content until it has eradicated capitalism and put into operation a full program of socialized planning which will lead to the establishment in Canada of the co-operative Commonwealth.

There are two difficulties with this view. First, there is evidence that even in terms of rhetoric the CCF/NDP in Ontario has not changed much, if at all, over the years. The whole of the Regina Manifesto is not a very strident document and the whole of more recent NDP publications and platforms are not without some colourful phrases. The preamble clauses to resolutions presented to and often passed by conventions more than occasionally resort to exhortation in vigorous language. As leader, Stephen Lewis was noted for colourful language and for his devastating characterizations of opponents. Dissident groups in the party have presented resolutions which, if they have not been passed, have received considerable publicity. For example, an economic resolution presented to the 1970 convention included such sentences as "Only by replacing a government controlled by profit seekers with a government controlled by the people can we make the preservation of our natural environment and the refashioning of our urban environment for human habitation attainable goals" and "Our colonial condition makes necessary an anti-imperialist struggle, if we are to achieve socialism and therefore independence."[20] It is not easy, therefore, to show that there has been a rhetorical shift from left to right since the formation of the CCF. Undoubtedly different phraseology has become dominant in recent years; but that is true of any attempt at English prosody in Canada and certainly not unique to the literary efforts of the CCF/NDP in Ontario. Terry Grier observed: "If you compare the kinds of rhetoric in which the party leaders engaged twenty years ago with what's being said now, I think you would have a hard time demonstrating a visible move to the right. We still attack the corporations, we still talk about profit exploitation, and in rhetorical terms I really don't see any substance to the argument."[21]

Second, even if it were true that the party in the 1970s used rhetoric very different from what it used twenty or thirty years ago, that fact in itself would not provide an explanation for a changing ideological perspective over the life of the CCF/NDP in Ontario. Fashions in phraseology change and what may sound militant or shocking in 1971 may have been perfectly commonplace in 1935. It is interesting to note that those who most strongly attacked the Winnipeg Declaration for its lack of vigour were often the very same people who had attacked the Regina Manifesto for similar sins. As Ken Bryden recalled:

You had this so-called left-wing group ... the guys who think there was a golden age when there were true socialists ... when men weren't made of the mortal clay they are made of now. Anybody who was around at the time of

Regina and Calgary knows of course they were the same human clay, and in fact the people who were supposed to have led us to the left were the men who wrote the documents of the time. J.S. Woodsworth has been completely misrepresented as being representative of them; he was fighting their counterparts of the day tooth and nail much more vigorously than anyone else. It was Woodsworth, for example, more than anybody who resisted the idea of popular front. He was absolutely adamant about it ...

... From the very beginning it was never a Marxist party, never was anything resembling a Marxist party. It was a democratic socialist party similar to the Labour party but not the same because Canada is a different country from Britain, definitely Fabian in its outlook. That's what it was in Calgary, that's what it was in Regina, and what it is now ... my God, the Regina Manifesto as a document among so-called left wingers had absolutely no status in its day. It was only long after this that it was seen as the revealed truth.[22]

If the conventional wisdom that the party drifted to the right is somewhat weak, how can the party's ideological development be described and analysed? To answer this it is necessary to consider the meaning of ideology. Clifford Geertz suggests that "ideology is a response to strain." More specifically he contends:

It is, in turn, the attempt of ideologies to render otherwise incomprehensible social situations meaningful, to so construe them as to make it possible to act purposefully within them, that accounts both for the ideologies highly figurative nature and for the intensity with which, once accepted, they are held ...

... Whatever else ideologies may be – projections of unacknowledged fears, disguises for ulterior motives, phatic expressions of group solidarity – they are, most distinctively, maps of problematic social reality and matrices for the creation of collective consciousness.[23]

Adopting this broad interactionist view of ideology, one could say that the ideological shift of the Ontario CCF/NDP is best described as one of big T truth to, in part, small f fashion. The eclectic socialism adopted by the CCF at its founding was clearly in large measure a response to the economic strains of the Depression, which were very important in Canada and most definitely felt in the western provinces where the CCF had its initial successes. To deal with these social strains the CCF imported an ideology, an ideology indebted to a variety of intellectual traditions, but one nonetheless perceived as a whole, which, if applied to Canada, would relieve the strains of the Depression. This socialist ideology was primarily concerned with the structure of the economy and with the need to construct a system of social services (pensions, hospital insurance, medical insurance) to the end that no one should live or die in poverty. Socialism, even the eclectic and amorphous socialism of the early CCF, was perceived as the "truthful" means of ensuring that poverty was eradicated and that the economic system was efficiently and appropriately restructured to the end of a better society. It is fascinating to note that the specific panaceas offered by the party have changed almost not a whit since the formation of the party in the 1930s. The fundamental policies of the party, those put forward by the League for Social Reconstruction in *Social Planning for Canada*, have essentially been reiterated in platform after platform of the CCF/NDP in Ontario. There has been almost no significant change, except that as the province has constitutionally come to occupy a larger place in the government of the people of Ontario, so the policy of the NDP has come to reflect that fact. In terms of economic and social policy (that is, educational, labour, and cultural policies) the CCF/NDP in Ontario has been extremely constant.

The party, however, did not continue to say in the 1960s and 1970s what it had said in the 1930s. It was not so much that the rhetoric was different but that the policy concerns of the party were different. The issues which have symbolically engaged the party over the last twenty or thirty years have, with one exception, not been those of central socialist concern. The Ontario party has focused on such issues as the granting of liquor licences for cocktail lounges and beverage rooms; the problem of permitting margarine to compete with butter; the difficulties encountered by changing the hydroelectric power of Ontario from twenty-five to sixty cycles; the question of Canada's participation in NATO; the question of extending public assistance to Roman Catholic high schools; the problem of controlling resource industries; and the controversy over abortion on demand. It was these issues, and others similar in nature, that have caught the attention of the party and have fundamentally divided the party.

Such issues have become foremost because as the party has matured, it has become more aware of its environment and hence of the strains in that environment. Perceiving itself to be a socialist party, that is, a party with a fundamentally different orientation to the state from that commonly held in western society and certainly from that espoused by its political rivals, the CCF/NDP requires its own symbols of its ideology, which are provided by these strains. If Geertz is right stating that ideology renders incomprehensible social situations meaningful, then it seems clear that such situations demand ideological symbols as a prophylactic to social, cultural, and psychological strain. After the Depression years the strain in Ontario society, or at least the immediate strains, were rather different from those in the early 1930s. In any society, of course, significant strains will arise from a lack of resources or from a maldistribution of resources. Such strains continue in Ontario to this day. However, other strains of more immediate social and cultural concern arise, which are often related to economic problems but occasionally are independent of them. The CCF/NDP in becoming mature, in becoming aware of its environment, responded to those strains by attempting to provide solutions to specific problems. A mature party therefore responds to issues different from those in its infancy but that does not mean it has changed its ideology or that its ideology has become more right wing or left wing, whatever that may mean in some platonic universe. Instead it means that the issues that exercise the party are culturally more significant than they would have been if the party had simply concerned itself with a restatement of its fundamental truths. From this, two hypotheses emerge: that the fundamental policies of the party have not changed since its formation and that the party has been more divided over "cultural" issues than over fundamental economic doctrine.

To provide a useful test of this view it is helpful to examine in some detail the party program over time as it has been presented to the public. The program itself is conveniently categorized under four main headings: economy and the state, welfare policy, labour policy, and education and cultural policies. It would be necessarily tedious, however, to examine in the detail needed all aspects of the party program in attempting to analyse this viewpoint. The particular policies concerned with the economy and the state are obviously the most central, perhaps to any political party, but certainly to a democratic socialist party, and are the policies generally referred to in considering the question of a rightward drift.[24] Consequently I ignore the other areas except to say that the original economist tradition of the party which was primarily concerned with a level of financing for various services has to a large extent given way to broader concerns about the administration of justice, electoral reform, legislative reform, ethical standards of behaviour in government, expansion of cultural and recreational facilities, and consumer protection. At the same time the general thrust of views expressed concerning labour or education or welfare administration in *Social Planning for Canada* has remained remarkably similar in all versions of the party platforms. The need to show this in detail is not so compelling, since there is little controversy on this question. Controversy does arise in terms of those policies dealing with the economy and the state.

Economic Policy

For greater clarity I reverse the usual chronological order and consider the economic program of the party as it developed in 1971. Bellamy-like, it is possible to look backwards and compare this mature policy with the CCF program of the late 1940s and then with the exhortations of the League for Social Reconstruction as set out in *Social Planning for Canada*. It is to be hoped that this retrospective look will provide a sharper delineation of the differences in emphasis that have arisen as the party has matured and, most important, of the essential similarities that have continued in terms of fundamental doctrine.

The program of a party is certainly the most convenient source of party doctrine, ideology, and promises, but it does not constitute the whole of the officially recognized party policy. The CCF/NDP in Ontario like many democratic socialist parties prides itself on its internal democracy. What this means in terms of party policy is that officially the party insists that all policies be laid down by delegates in convention who vote yes or no on the resolutions presented to them. Any resolution passed by the convention therefore becomes a part of the policy corpus of the party in Ontario. Moreover party apologists never tire of pointing out that while the Liberals and Conservatives also hold conventions at which policy is discussed, the leaders of these parties do not agree to always follow such policies and indeed feel free to promulgate new ones for any given situation.

Since resolutions are submitted to a provincial convention by several bodies, basically constituency associations, affiliated trade unions, the youth section, and the executive and council, it is possible that many are contradictory, some of which are passed almost simultaneously, that many are trivial, and that others are outdated. In short the totality of past resolutions presents certain impediments to the presentation by the party of a coherent attractive electoral platform. A program is drafted to overcome such impediments. Essentially a small committee or occasionally one person is designated to put the past resolutions into some order and to write a set of coherent proposals based on them in attractive prose, which in many instances may avoid the actual language employed in the convention decision. The 1971 program is such a document and is primarily the work of Desmond Morton, who actually shares the copyright with the New Democratic Party of Ontario. The program is not simply a collation of the resolutions passed by the convention nor is it simply a booklet of opinion; it is in fact the official version of convention policy decisions and as such reflects the party's considered view of public policy questions.

The 1971 program, described as a program "adopted and amended at the October 1970 provincial convention of the New Democratic Party of Ontario,"[25] and as the third edition of the New Democratic Party program for Ontario, is a relatively minor revision of the second edition published in 1967, also written primarily by Morton. This program in turn is substantially based on the first edition published in 1962 after the Ontario founding convention.

Although most policies have some economic aspect to them, I am concerned here with the central economic issues for the CCF/NDP in 1971: the questions of managing the economy through central planning, of public and private or co-operative ownership, and of the management of resources. In terms of central economic planning the program had five major aspects. First, it declared its faith in planning and it adumbrated the great transformation which could be achieved by such planning.

The New Democratic Party is the only party that offers genuine democratic economic and social planning. Starting with the needs of the people and giving them priority over profits as a criterion for investment and action, and arriving at final decisions by a fully democratic process, New Democratic planning will reflect the real interests of the people of Ontario – not just those of the few who share or hold high managerial positions ...

... the guiding principle of planning will be that the well-being and freedom of the individual is paramount. It will involve continuous co-operation between the government and the people in their capacities both as consumers and as producers.

And planning would accomplish much. According to the program it would:

One ... meet the needs of the people of Ontario and raise their standard of living; two, produce a steady and continuous rate of growth which will help achieve and maintain full employment of manpower and resources; three ... conserve and replenish Ontario's great natural wealth; four ... achieve a just and rational balance in the allocation of the wealth produced in the province to public and private purposes; five ... distribute that wealth in such a way as to ensure every individual and his family a decent standard of living and an opportunity to develop ... to the full; six ... foster Canadian independence by developing a strong and diversified Ontario economy.

Second, the program went on to indicate definitely the methods to be used by the new planners. Because of the interest in economic independence for Canada in 1971, these methods and means were cast as tools for the achievement of such independence. In fact, as we shall see in comparing them with earlier programs, they would achieve much more. The 1971 program reads:

Ontario can play her part in reasserting Canadian control over our economy by: 1. Establishing a provincial development corporation to actively develop resources, and secondary industry, and to stimulate new enterprises through crown corporations or in conjunction with co-operative and private ventures; 2. Mobilizing investment capital by requisitioning a proportion of the funds now in the hands of financial institutions and corporations and planning overall investment patterns so that capital goes into the most socially productive operations. Reliance on foreign capital would be greatly decreased in this way; 3. Stopping incentive grants to foreign based corporations, giving them instead to Canadian enterprises in turn for an equity interest so that the people share in any profits; 4. Establishing a take-over review board which would examine proposals for take-overs by foreign interests and work out methods of retaining Canadian control and/or protecting Canadian interests; 5. Amending the corporations and securities laws to provide for full disclosure of the operations of foreign controlled subsidiaries; 6. Setting limits on the degree of foreign ownership and provincially incorporated companies according to the needs of each industry and activity and the implications of foreign ownership in each industry. Since planning in Canada cannot be fully effective except on a federal provincial basis, a New Democratic Government in Ontario will co-operate whole-heartedly in any planning that may be undertaken in the interests of the people by the federal government.

Setting aside the more rhetorical aspects of this approach – those aspects solely concerned with the American economic menace – it should be noted that this was a relatively sophisticated program which called for a good deal of state intervention in the economy. The government would use public funds to stimulate the growth of some industries and thus retard the growth of others. Most important it would have the power to establish crown corporations, that is, public enterprises owned by the government and in the final analysis controlled by the government. It would also have the very important power of obtaining new capital by requisition. Banks, life insurance companies, and other financial institutions were to turn over a portion of the savings they held in trust to the government or to a government agency for investment. The government, in other words, could direct pools of savings to those enterprises or industries it favoured. And finally, the series of proposals directly dealing with foreign ownership meant that the government could establish agencies with the power to obtain information about the most intimate details of corporation life and to use that information for its own purposes – in this instance inhibiting foreign ownership. However, these powers of inquiry and disclosure could certainly have other consequences. The economy then was envisaged as a mixed economy in which the government, if it did not always act as the senior partner, was certainly capable of so doing.

Third, the program called for participation by the public in this planning process. "An Ontario planning council, fully representative of the municipalities, industry, labour, agriculture, consumers and other major groups, will be established. The government and the central planning organization will consult it regularly, testing performance and proposals from council members." The NDP was anxious to dispel the notion that this new central planning mechanism and these new powers would be exercised by faceless bureaucrats with no reference to public opinion.

Fourth, in a separate section the program made it clear that the government, in the final analysis, would use public investment, and other sources of investment which it came to control, as a means of establishing public policy priorities. This was implied in the section on Canadian control but because it was so important it was reiterated separately.

Finally, the program stated that this central planning would be made to conform to normal democratic practice.

The provincial cabinet will be the nerve centre of the planning process. A central planning organization will be established with adequate staff, under the direction of the Prime Minister.[26]

... With its advice and assistance the cabinet will continuously review the province's resources and needs, and will draw up, revise and carry out its plans in the light of such a review ...

... Both short and long term plans will be submitted regularly to the legislature with full opportunity for debate. The budgets of the province and of the various crown agencies and enterprises will reflect the decisions that are taken. These budgets will be key planning instruments. This will ensure not only that all plans will be subject to approval by the peoples' elected representatives but also that the public will be fully informed.

In other words this new planning agency would be under the control of the Cabinet, which would submit to the legislature the advice from the planning agency that it wished to adopt. The aim here was to reassure those who might feel that the introduction of central planning would create a new form of government.

The program also contained a long section on resources, which had two main features. First, the party recognized that resources were controlled and in the final analysis owned by the province and argued that resources – water, mineral, forest, or energy – were in fact leased from the province by private companies. The NDP essentially advocated that the government on behalf of the people should get a greater share of the return on these "leases." It argued that private companies have exploited these resources, and it hoped to redress this balance. Second, by recognizing that the system of resource exploitation utilizing private companies would continue, the NDP did not advocate either complete public ownership or complete private ownership. However, the party did declare that "to prevent continued sell-out of energy resources, the New Democratic Party advocates the nationalization of the energy resource industries of Ontario not now in public ownership." This proposal, however, was only a minor withdrawal from the position that there should be a mixed economy, one in fact that was repudiated by Stephen Lewis immediately after his election as leader in 1970. The repudiation was confirmed by resolution of the Provincial Council.

Is there more blood and thunder in the CCF program, as the conventional wisdom would have it? The CCF program is reasonably constant from the 1940s to 1961 and is based primarily on documents written in the 1940s. This program, known as the first-term program, was so called because it included those measures which would be carried out in a four- or five-year term of office. Recognizing that in a democratic polity socialism could not be fully achieved in one term of office, social democratic parties distinguished between a long-term program to achieve that end and a first-term program to achieve more immediate goals. The advantage for the party leadership was that the more outlandish proposals passed at conventions could be safely relegated to the long-term program and never printed except in resolutions books which, when possible, were hidden from public view. The more attractive proposals passed by convention were included in the first-term program, which was used by the CCF for the purposes of elections and internal party education.

Perhaps the best statement of CCF views on economic policy is found in a paper entitled *Planning the Public's Business*, which was part of a lecture series in 1948 on this first-term program. Ted Jolliffe, its author, quotes from the program what he calls the "keystone" section on the economy. It is worth repeating:

A CCF government will establish a planning board under the direction of the cabinet to advise on a program of social ownership and public development in coordination with regional and community planning. The board will survey the natural resources, industrial potential and essential services of the province. It will be particularly instructed to study the fields of mining and production of base metals, petroleum products, food processing, farm implements, the liquor industry and the production of building materials with a view to bringing them under social ownership.

More specifically the first-term program of the CCF promised to encourage the development of co-operatives; to set up a housing administration with sufficient power to order priorities in the field of housing; to enact legislation to permit municipalities to own the means of distribution (not production) for essential goods and services such as milk, bread, and fuel; to establish a forest resources commission with the aim of "bringing to an end the wasteful exploitation of our forests for private profit" but with an implied recognition that private individuals would still be involved with the cutting and marketing of timber; to set up a public automobile insurance plan; and, finally, to bring all highway bus transportation under public ownership. Jolliffe goes on to state:

From what has been quoted it will be apparent: 1. that the Ontario CCF undertakes to implement certain measures of socialization, not necessarily the most urgent or the most important, in its first-term; 2. that the Ontario CCF definitely has in mind certain other measures of socialization, yet defers making commitments thereon until further enquiry can be made by the board on behalf of the first-term CCF government; and 3. that planning on the scale envisaged by the Ontario CCF will probably open further avenues of socialization which may not now seem practicable.

In commenting on the first-term program, Jolliffe puts forward a number of caveats, two of which are most important. First,

in the earlier days of socialist activity there was sometimes a tendency to advocate the socialization of anything that seemed to be available, without much thought being given to the proper place or priority of a particular enterprise in a program of socialization. This is not a sound approach. There are some enterprises which it would be a mistake to socialize early in the day, for the simple reason that they would not function successfully in a capitalist environment.

He was warning members of the party that capitalism would continue for a good long period and that public enterprises would necessarily operate within a capitalist framework. Planning the economy was considerably more important than nationalizing industries, though they were obviously not mutually exclusive. Second, in discussing the planning board, which was clearly the central economic agency for a CCF government, he makes the point that

there is a very clear and important distinction between the government, or the cabinet on the one hand, and the planning board on the other hand. One, the cabinet is responsible: (a) for constitutional purposes to the members of the legislature and to the electorate; (b) for party purposes to the provincial council and to the annual convention of the CCF. Two, the planning board is responsible to the appropriate minister and to the cabinet. That is not the only responsibility of the planning board. And it will have not only the assistance of a technical staff. It will also have the duty of enlisting the help and cooperation of all manner of democratic groups throughout the province.

In other words, the planning done by the CCF would be undertaken within the normal constitutional framework and only after significant consultation with various groups within the province. A final caution was important. Jolliffe made the obvious point, although we shall see it has not always been obvious to social democrats in this country, that Canada was a federal country and that a socialist government, either in Ottawa or in one of the provinces, had to seek the cooperation of the other level of government if its plans were to be fully implemented.

In the course of this 1948 commentary on the Ontario CCF first-term program, Jolliffe referred several times to *Social Planning for Canada* written by the League for Social Reconstruction in 1935.[27] These were not perfunctory references, given the debt which the CCF continued to owe to this long socialist "tract." Part 2 of *Social Planning for Canada* is entitled "What Socialist Planning Really Means," and a number of critical points were made. In the first place the authors justified the need for planning essentially in terms of the breakdown of the market system – fairly evident in 1932 – and in terms of a hope for greater efficiency that could result from such central planning. The authors went on to make five major points on the CCF/NDP approach to the economy. They began by asserting that the fundamental constitutional structure of Canada would continue with socialist planning. Although they were unhappy with the federal nature of the Cabinet in Ottawa and proposed certain changes to that body, the authors generally were constitutional conservatives. As they declare:

In the planned state, the final authority of government is to rest, as it does theoretically today, in Parliament. More specifically, this means that the nation's primary executive is the cabinet, subject only to the established democratic convention that it shall have the confidence of the House of Commons. Also though important and far-reaching changes are required in the functioning of departments, executive and legislature, the ultimate responsibility of Parliament to public opinion is not questioned or denied. Indeed, the prime assumption upon which this book is based is that it is possible for a democracy to control economic policy intelligently; not the abolition, but the improvement, of the functioning of democratic government is the purpose of the reforms proposed.[28]

The authors proceeded to their central proposal of a national planning commission. As they state:

The planning commission is primarily a thinking body. It is not a representative body, seeking to give representation to different parts of Canada or to specific interests. It seeks primarily, if not solely, to provide an economic general staff to investigate and hammer out a concerted economic policy ... the Commission is specifically a body for investigating, for studying, and proposing a continuing plan for economic development. When its policies and proposals are formulated after consultation with its auxiliary organs, they are submitted to the Cabinet for consideration, Parliament for enactment, and finally to departments, state corporations or government commissions, for execution.[29]

This National Planning Commission was the indispensable tool for directing the economy to the desired ends of a better and more humane state.

As well, the authors proposed that certain industries should be socialized, that is, should become publicly owned. They argued that "a substantial part of productive activity must be socialized if planning is to have any fundamental and durable effects." The authors hinted that in some distant future all industrial activity would have a significant public component or would be in a certain sense socialized, but they firmly rejected the view that this could come about in the foreseeable future. They suggested instead that criteria be applied: "Assuming that socialization is to be undertaken step-by-step, the question as to which industry should be taken over first can be answered by reference to four tests. One, is it a key industry? Two, is it operated under conditions of monopoly? Three, is it seriously inefficient? Four, does it control important natural resources?"[30] The argument was that if it was a key industry, a good case could be made for socialization, and if it was a natural monopoly, such as hydroelectric power or telephone systems, an even better case could be made. The LSR authors also believed, interestingly, that if the industry was inefficient it should be socialized so that the goods and services of the industry would be more easily available and the economy would itself be more efficient. The resource industries, however, were those for which a case for socialization could be most easily made.

Again, it should be noted that in proposing socialization the LSR did not submit that all industries become government departments. Instead the authors suggested that either holding companies be set up under state control to bring whole industries under unified direction or that state trusts be set up which would be run by a small group of three to five expert trustees selected by an appointments commissioner. State trusts clearly resembled the modern crown corporation and the authors in fact used a similar rationale of "constant competitive comparison to maintain efficiency" for establishing public enterprise in this form.[31]

The authors conclude:

It should be pointed out once more that there is room in a socialist economy, just as there has been room in a capitalist economy, for many different types of industrial structure. Some of these will survive in the unsocialized fringe of economic activity, but many will persist among the socialized trades themselves. Socialism is not an inelastic method of running business through government departments administered from Ottawa by politicians or hidebound civil servants. It implies simply public ownership, production for the general good instead of for a private profit, and the placing of ultimate authority in the hands of the state instead of in the hands of private shareholders. This is all compatible with local and individual initiative in industry and a considerable amount of independence in operation. It is also compatible with varied types of organization according to the needs of particular trades, ranging from farmers' cooperatives to joint stock companies as we have already shown.[32]

In other words, despite its utopian vision of a completely socialized economy in the distant future, for practical purposes the league envisioned a mixed economy with a variety of industrial structures.

Recognizing that a mixed economy would exist, the authors saw the control of investment as necessary. They argued that under the National Planning Commission there should be an investment policy and that a national investment board should be set up to develop this policy under the aegis, as always, of the Cabinet. This policy would have two major aspects. First, the banking system would be centralized and would become publicly owned. The national planners and ultimately the government would thus be provided with a considerable source of investment funds which could be controlled for the purposes of the national economic plan. Indeed, the LSR authors saw this control as the major advantage of the socially owned banking system. Second, the authors recognized that capital funds were also available from other large financial institutions, particularly insurance companies, and they proposed that some of these funds be mobilized for purposes of the national plan. The LSR, therefore, proposed that considerable capital resources be made available to the national planners for their own purposes, which, of course, were public purposes according to the authors, since they would be ratified by the Cabinet and by Parliament.

In comparing these three documents one notes certain similarities. Clearly the League for Social Reconstruction foresaw a day when socialism would be triumphant in the sense that production would always be for use and not for profit and that it would essentially be controlled by the state. With less detail the CCF program held out a similar vision. Yet the LSR authors and the authors of the Ontario CCF first-term program acknowledged this to be a visionary prospect and instead devoted their attention to the foreseeable future and to the mechanics of producing a socialist economy in the period of a decade or so. In these terms the proposals made by both are almost exactly identical with the proposals made in 1971 by the New Democratic Party of Ontario. All three documents, and indeed all other CCF/NDP programmatic documents, emphasize the same fundamental points; they emphasize the democratic nature of the planning envisaged and the fact that it would take place within the constitutional framework, in a parliamentary democracy; the need to recognize the existence of a mixed economy; the need to mobilize capital resources and to use state agencies to allocate those resources; the need to recognize public opinion as the final arbiter of planning decisions; the need for a certain degree of social ownership, particularly in the resource industries and in the transportation field; and finally the need for a central planning organization – a planning commission – that would have sufficient expertise to develop workable co-ordinated plans. To put this more simply, the constant themes are constitutional conservatism coupled with the sovereignty of public opinion; socialism as a more effective and efficient economic system than capitalism is; and public ownership in the framework of an inevitable mixed economy. Certain details change but the principles first developed in *Social Planning for Canada* continue. Indeed, the only significant difference from 1932 to 1971, and it is a real difference, is the confidence in 1971, which one does not find even in 1948, that the province, if it must act alone, can develop a workable economic plan which will shift the balance of power away from the corporations to the state. In the 1930s this was heresy. It took the CCF/NDP thirty years for this reformation to be possible, though even in the midst of this reformation, its elder statesmen occasionally betray by their speeches a belief that the old centralization gods still occupy their thrones in the Socialist Valhalla.

The Canadian Constitution

In examining the CCF/NDP's attitude to the Canadian constitution there is no question that a significant shift took place from the 1940s to the late 1960s. It is clear that the CCF in its early days, indeed throughout its history, found comfort in the idea of a strong central government whose planning initiatives would solve most social problems. This orthodox position was laid down in the Regina Manifesto and in considerably more detail in *Social Planning for Canada*.

The League for Social Reconstruction proposed an amending formula for the Canadian constitution; it was a simple one consisting of three major proposals. First, the power of amendment should reside in Canada and all authority of the British Parliament should be ended. Second, ordinary amendments should be made by a majority vote of the Dominion Parliament assembled in joint session of the two Houses. Third, amendments affecting minority rights should require in addition to the approval of the Dominion Parliament the assent of all provincial legislatures and any province not dissenting within one year should be presumed to have given its assent.[33]

This proposal was certainly a centralist one. Although it called for the extraordinary procedure of a joint session of the two Houses in which the Senate would clearly be outvoted by the House of Commons, in fact since the LSR wished the abolition of the Senate, it foresaw that a simple majority in the House of Commons would be sufficient for ordinary amendments. And although the LSR would require the assent of all provincial legislatures to change those sections of the constitution affecting minority rights, it had a very restricted view of minority rights. The authors state:

The list of sections in the Act [the British North America Act] which requires special protection to quiet minority fears would be somewhat as follows: Sections 51 and 51A, dealing with representation in the Dominion Parliament; Section 92, subsection 1, dealing with provincial control over provincial constitutions; Section 92, subsection 12, dealing with the solemnization of matrimony in the provinces; Section 93 dealing with education; Section 135 dealing with the use of the French language; and the amending section itself. It will be quite impossible to concede "property and civil rights in the province" as a minority right unless provision is made for the extension of

Dominion Control over such portions of that subject as form part of every Dominion law controlling trade and commerce or labour conditions.[34]

The authors added the gratuitous comment that if property and civil rights were entrenched as minority rights and social planning became "dependent on provincial unanimity," then "the pace of progress would be the pace of Prince Edward Island." The league was not strongly represented in the Island province.

The authors argued strenuously for this centralist amending proposal. As they state:

Some people argue that in any federation the amending process must necessarily involve a vote by provinces or states, as is required by the American, Swiss and Australian constitutions. This is true of ordinary federations, but Canada is not an ordinary federation. Our constitution was carefully drawn so that we should not be ordinary. How else can we explain unfederal ideas as that the Dominion subsidizes the provinces, appoints and instructs and dismisses Lieutenant Governors, appoints provincial judges, appoints provincial representatives in the Senate, may veto provincial law, and may by declaration take over control of provincial works? These centralizing provisions are incompatible with ordinary conceptions of the federal state, and clearly indicate that we were intended to have a particularly unified form of federalism.[35]

Having decided the method of amendment, the LSR suggested in general terms what were the needed amendments.

The amendments which are immediately necessary lie chiefly in the field of social legislation. Without uniformity in some degree, laws dealing with wages, hours, insurance, benefits, health services, etc. must necessarily fail in their purpose, or at least work under enormous disadvantages and at greatly increased costs. The Dominion has done something to assist uniform standards, but its powers are cramped by the general understanding that social legislation belongs for the most part in the category of the provincial power over property and civil rights. Mr. Bennett's use of the treaty power, though probably sound, is somewhat uncertain; in any case there is no reason why Canada should be tied in these matters to the snail's pace of the other capitalist powers.[36]

An amendment is needed to transfer to the Dominion unquestionable power to establish a national labour code ... and to legislate regarding the subject of social legislation generally ...

... besides the matter of social legislation, amendments centralizing control over companies and insurance, and clarifying the whole subsidy and taxation basis of confederation, are highly desirable ... Further changes will be necessary when the planning commission and allied bodies are set up, to enable the national economic plan to be centrally adopted and carried out ... Control of this field should be added to the Dominion's more general power so as to make possible a unified national economic policy.[37]

The LSR, and its intellectual debtors in the CCF, were clearly of the view that the provinces were, or at least should be, creatures of the central government somewhat akin to county or municipal authorities in England.

An examination of the Ontario CCF's attitude to dominion-provincial relations is facilitated by a central document issued before the 1943 provincial election.[38] In it one finds this analysis: "The chief objective to be sought is to bring to an end the present situation in which the Dominion and Provinces deal with one another as though they were competing foreign powers, each manoeuvering to maintain or extend its separate sovereignty; and to substitute for this a process of cooperation in the good government of the Canadian nation." It welcomed the recommendations of the Rowell-Sirois Commission on Dominion-Provincial Relations and summarized them as:

1 The Dominion should assume provincial debts.

2 The Dominion should take over exclusive powers to collect personal income taxes, corporation taxes, succession duties.

3 The Dominion should take responsibility for relief of unemployed employables, unemployment insurance, contributory old age pensions (when established); leaving the provinces to run other social services, sharing the cost (to 75%) of non-contributory old age pensions, and administering health services concurrently with the provinces.

4 The Dominion should pay to the provinces an annual adjustment grant, reappraised every five years, based on what each province would need to maintain average social services; the amount of this grant to be determined by a finance commission.

5 The Dominion should also pay a special emergency grant to provinces such as Saskatchewan suffering from emergencies like that of the drought and depression of the 1930s.

The Ontario CCF agreed with these proposals, noting that "the CCF should accept these proposals for the readjustment of Dominion-

Provincial financial relations. It should agree with the Rowell-Sirois Commission that the proposals need to be accepted as a whole if they are to work properly." It suggested, however, that two modifications needed discussion.

1 Should health insurance or socialized medicine not be put entirely under Dominion control? Are there other social services which should be transferred to the Dominion? The Dominion should at least set up a social security administration for the integration of social services throughout the country.
2 Should some share in income tax (personal) be left to the provinces? The argument for this is that a province which wants to expand its services (say, in education) beyond the Dominion average, should not have to resort to indirect taxation, such as taxes on commodities – a socially undesirable form of taxation, to do so. The arguments against it are embodied in the Rowell-Sirois report. Income tax collected by the Dominion and distributed across the country in accordance with social need rather than with the wealth of different regions is the most powerful instrument for achieving a substantial equality of living standards and social services throughout the national community.

The Ontario CCF went on to make the following proposals. First, the Dominion should control minimum wages, maximum hours of work, age of employment, the status of trade unions, and the whole question of collective bargaining so that a national labour code similar to the American Wagner Act would be possible. Second, the Dominion should have full powers to implement international agreements such as the International Labor Organization conventions. Third, a federal bureau of education should be set up in Ottawa, though the provinces would continue to control education generally. Fourth, a bill of rights similar to that in the American constitution should be entrenched in the Canadian constitution, guaranteeing fundamental civil liberties. The entrenchment of a bill of rights was proposed on pragmatic political grounds – to take some of the sting out of the argument that the CCF was opposed to civil liberties – though the author of the proposal clearly approached it with a certain caution: "However, we should be made cautious by the fact that the protection which high minded Americans thought they were providing, in the Bill of Rights and in the 15th Amendment, for natural real persons, has turned out, in the hands of the Courts, to be a protection much more readily available for those fictitious legal persons, big business corporations." Fifth, the CCF proposed ending appeals to the Judicial Committee of the Privy Council.

The Ontario CCF further proposed a slightly different amending formula from that found in *Social Planning for Canada*. It was as follows:

1 Resolution by the House of Commons (the Senate having been abolished).
2 Ratification by a majority of the provinces (i.e., five provinces), such ratification to be the act of the provincial legislature (i.e., not of the provincial cabinet, nor of the people of the province voting in a plebiscite); the consent of a province to a proposed amendment to be assumed if its legislature has not within one year passed a resolution to the contrary. Certain provisions of the BNA Act which protects the French minority (representation of Quebec in the federal parliament, use of the French language, separate schools, and so on) should not be amended "except with the consent of all the provinces."

The author of this position paper, George Grube, continued: "The utmost care should be taken to avoid language which suggests the 'scrapping' of the BNA Act. Canadian unity is possible only in some kind of a federal setup and any possible federal constitution would consist mainly of clauses very much like those in the present Act." Moreover he strenuously opposed the proposal made by Frank Scott and David Lewis in *Make This Your Canada* to have a constituent assembly draw up a completely new Canadian constitution. As he stated: "This seems too romantic ... the constitutional convention would consist mainly of lawyers, and CCFers would be in a minority ... there will be much less energy expended if we concentrated on specific amendments as we need them and if we made use of techniques similar to those adopted by the New Deal to ensure that the Courts do not go too far in frustrating CCF legislation." Finally, Grube raised the possibility of transferring control of certain natural resources to the Dominion but admitted that this would "stir up a storm about provincial rights" and thus made his proposal tentative. This was not the official policy of the Ontario CCF on dominion-provincial relations, sanctified by convention resolution, but it served as a guide for candidates and officers of the party discussing the question and reflects accurately the position taken by the Ontario CCF leadership during the 1943 period.

The position of the Ontario CCF, which was certainly a centralist position, remained unchanged during the whole history of the party. Even by 1959 the CCF still was reluctant to consider any new constitutional arrangements except those which would put more power in the hands of the national government. By this period, however, Donald C. MacDonald, as leader of the party in Ontario, did demand that the Frost government be more aggressive in seeking more substantial funds from the federal government for social services. But he did not seek anything other than a better agreement and clearly favoured the tax rental scheme by which the federal government continued to collect personal income tax and corporation tax and returned but a small portion to the province as payment for the privilege of doing so. MacDonald would have liked a bigger portion, but he did not wish to see the province collecting its own income tax.[39]

With the formation of the New Democratic Party, there was a significant break with this strong centralist tradition. It was a break inspired by the beginnings of the Quiet Revolution in Quebec and by the concomitant demands by many Québécois for greater provincial autonomy. The founding convention of the party in 1961 passed a resolution stating that "true Canadian identity depends upon equal recognition and respect for both the main cultures of our Country."

That same convention saw an intense semantical debate take place over the substitution of the word "federal" for "national" in the party's constitution. The Quebec delegation was in favour of the substitution, and it was supported by the party leadership on the grounds that there were two nations in Canada and that Canada was best described as a federal state. Eugene Forsey, then director of research for the Canadian Labour Congress and a delegate to the convention, argued that the implications of this two nation position were incompatible with the traditional socialist belief in central planning. Forsey lost the argument (and subsequently quit the party); yet intellectually he correctly perceived that in what then came to be called federal-provincial relations the NDP was launched on a very different path from that followed by the CCF.

By 1965 the federal NDP was able to state more specifically just what were the consequences of this recognition of two nations. In a statement entitled "Federal-Provincial Planning," which was endorsed by the National Council on 10 July, the following points were made:

Since the end of the Second World War, there has been a shift in the economic relationship beween the Federal and Provincial Governments in Canada. In recent years, the provinces have taken on greater importance; there is no doubt that in future activities which lie within the provincial jurisdiction, such as schools, hospitals, roads and universities, will greatly expand. Recently, also, there has arisen in Canada a feeling of uncertainty about a national future, and tension between the two great cultures that make up Canada. This too has added to demands for revision of the economic relationships between Ottawa and the provinces.

In recognizing these facts, the federal NDP was not quite ready to abandon all central economic planning, but it was to propose such planning in a way rather different from that conceived by the LSR and expounded in countless CCF programs and speeches. The statement went on to say:

The New Democratic Party was the first to recognize the importance for economic policy of the recognition of our two cultures. Following on the guidelines laid down at our conventions in Ottawa and Regina, we have our program of planning on the following principles:
1 The federal government has a crucial role in assuring a full and sensible use of our productive resources and an equitable redistribution of income and services.
2 Planning in a varied economy like Canada should be kept as close to the people as possible. There is a strong case for many decisions and policies to be taken at the provincial level.
3 Quebec has a special place in a bi-cultural Canada and must be free to ensure the development of our unique heritage.

The statement proposed a number of changes in constitutional arrangements in Canada. Following from these principles, the first proposal was to give special status for the Province of Quebec.

At the same time Quebec must be allowed additional freedom of action in this field because of its special position at the centre of French culture on this continent. Many of the social policies followed in this field have a close or indirect bearing on the culture of the community. This is not only true of such obvious matters as education, but also of urban development and town planning. Quebec must be given the assurance that it can differ from the rest of Canada in these fields, and the real possibility to do so.

Finally, the rather curious suggestion was made that a federal initiating power in the social services field would be necessary "where backward provincial governments are in power." The authors of this proposal did not say who would decide on the backwardness of a particular provincial government or whether there would be two sets of rules, one for backward governments and one for progressive governments, in terms of this federal initiating power, but clearly the old CCF conscience was somewhat troubled by this full retreat from central economic planning. In addition the NDP endorsed increasing unconditional revenues to the provinces by a new tax-sharing arrangement. A more flexible conditional grant system was proposed whereby monies would be made available to the provinces, not just for specific programs, but for such broad fields as health and education. Thus programs suited to the needs of a particular province could be initiated.

By 1971 the Ontario NDP unashamedly proposed that in Ontario measures of economic planning be carried out by the Ontario government without federal intervention and indeed with little concern for the policies of the federal government, except where those policies prevented Ontario from raising sufficient revenue for its purposes. The NDP was still concerned with equalization among the provinces, but it no longer believed that equalization was simply the responsibility of federal politicians, just as it no longer believed that economic planning was the responsibility of the federal government. Moreover, this decentralist program was reinforced by a shift within the party itself. The centre of power in the party in the 1960s shifted from the national office to the provincial offices of the strongest provincial parties, those in British Columbia, Saskatchewan, and Ontario. The Ontario party finally came to have a sense of itself as a complete entity, and as noted previously, for many in the Ontario party federal politics became somewhat irrelevant.[40]

Symbolism and Ideology

The other shift in CCF/NDP attitudes is evident in those issues that are not central to fundamental party doctrine but that in fact symbolically come to represent, for members of the party, touchstones of its political condition. The myth of rightward drift has its basis, not in the debate over central economic questions, but in terms of changing cultural questions which agitate the party membership. Such issues as liquor control are fractious issues. The party was split on them. It was split between those who seek truth in holy writ and the doctrines of the past and those who seek it in the world, in the norms of the community – not the corporate community, but the community of industrial workers. The second group is other-directed and seeks the views of "average citizens." The first group is inner-directed, and as Ted Jolliffe notes in referring to the traditional left in the party, in many instances these members are conservatives. By this he means that they wish to conserve a revealed socialist tradition to be found in such documents as the Regina Manifesto or some previous party program or platform statement.[41] What they wish to preserve, however, is not the fundamental economic truths, on which agreement did exist, but rather the cultural attitudes of the past as manifested in such documents. And this division, in the context of more contemporary debates in the party, manifests itself differently throughout successive stages of development. The party's attitude towards consumption of liquor and liquor advertising in the 1940s and early 1950s is a case in point.

The CCF found itself with a large group of active prohibitionists who would be satisfied only if all alcoholic beverages were banned by law in the Province of Ontario. Canada has always had a strong prohibitionist element, arising in part from its position as a frontier society. As James Gray explained it for Western Canada, a frontier society has a strong two-fisted drinking tradition which manifests itself in a good deal of public drunkenness.[42] The churches in particular were appalled at the intellectual numbness and physical violence that accompanied drinking and reacted by calling for Prohibition. Groups such as the Women's Christian Temperance Union grew as part of this movement. That many CCFers were involved can be traced to three factors. First, as we have noted, since the CCF had many of its roots in the social gospel and was allied to many churchmen, if not the churches, many CCFers shared the temperance views of those clerics. Second, in Ontario the left had its one fling at power as a result of an alliance between MPPs representing the labour movement and those representing the farmers' movement who were associated with the Progressive party of Ontario in the United Farmers of Ontario. After the fall of that government most of those individuals drifted back to the Liberal party, which traditionally gained its strength from those parts of the province, particularly rural areas, which were dry and which were opposed to the "demon rum." The United Farmers of Ontario were very much a part of this prohibitionist sentiment, and there existed in the CCF, even though it had little strength in rural communities, a memory of the Farmer-Labour alliance, a certain knowledge that one of the key elements in that alliance was a recognition of the need for temperance and a remembrance of the hope for Prohibition. Third, the provision of alcoholic beverages to a large population is big business. The CCF was opposed to big business on moral as well as practical grounds. This feeling of righteousness was increased tenfold when the business was the liquor industry whose products clearly provided the immediate cause of a good deal of human misery.

At the same time it must be noted that by the 1940s a majority of the citizens of Ontario were undoubtedly opposed to Prohibition, and the same is true of the majority of the CCF. But for the CCF that fact meant that a good deal of disputation existed and that the leadership had to provide a policy which would take at least some cognizance of the very strong feelings of the minority in the party. One can find the official attitude of the party towards what was called the liquor question in *Information Bulletin Number 4* to CCF candidates in the 1943 provincial election. In part the party leaders argued:

We do not believe that the liquor question should be made into a first class issue in this election. Like some other issues, it is apt to arouse violent emotions, and to be thus considered in anything but a rational frame of mind ...

It is clear that measures of liquor control, sponsored and established by the present government, have failed in every respect. Profit seeking liquor interests have reached monopolistic proportions, and have a dangerous and corrupting influence on government. The CCF proposes:
1 To bring the manufacturer, as well as the wholesale distribution, of alcoholic beverages under public ownership – thus removing the vested private interests mentioned below.
2 To use part of the revenue from this source to provide a comprehensive programme of education as to the effect of the excessive use of alcohol.
3 Where beer is consumed, the consumer is entitled to proper surroundings. Better standards of cleanliness and accommodation should be enforced upon all licensed premises.
4 To devise and enforce a fairer system of rationing and hours of sale during the War, so that people will not be forced to stand in line or be denied the opportunity to purchase.
5 The wishes of the majority in any municipality as regards the number and locations of licensed premises will be respected.

There was naturally a certain tension in the party and very real divisions between those who were determined to control and even destroy the liquor industry and those who felt that it was necessary to recognize majority sentiment and to recognize also that Prohibition did not work and that it would not work in the 1940s and the 1950s. The great Prohibition experiment of the 1920s had failed in the United States as had lesser experiments in several places in Canada. For most people legal Prohibition, even if desirable, did not seem practicable after these events. Perhaps two letters which appeared in the *CCF News* in July 1956 express the tension best, as they reveal the position taken at conventions and elsewhere by the two sides. The letter is found under the heading "Liquor Resolutions":

Although myself a non-drinker, I am weary of prohibitionist attempts to use CCF conventions for ends on which CCFers, like members of other parties, are honestly divided. The excessive use of alcohol, and the appearance of alcoholism on a large scale, are symptoms of an insecurity and emptiness, which will not be cured by forbidding liquor advertising or even by forbidding liquor. The CCF program of service and brotherhood, social security and mental health, can give a meaning to life which makes drinking unnecessary, and we should not weaken our push for this great positive aim by constant bickering on side issues, whatever their emotional significance to individual members.

S.J. Dunkley, President, York East CCF

The second letter is under the title "First Drink Fatal":

You can't become a drunkard until you have had your first drink, so it is the first drink that is the danger, and the solution is to find means to stop the first drink, and that is the destruction of this "inhuman industry."

Professor Rogers, C.I.D., told that 40% of murders in Ontario are drunken brawls, and that up to 90% of highway accidents are the result of alcoholic liquors.

In convention, the CCF refused its efforts in this direction. Why be hypocritical about our CCF slogan "Humanity First"? Let's drop it, until we make up our minds that alcoholic liquors are our greatest detriments to human progress.

John N. Burnside, President, High Park CCF

The High Park CCF, led by William Temple, the man who defeated George Drew in the election of 1948, was the centre of the prohibitionist wing of the party. It should be noted that Temple, and many of the other prohibitionists, considered themselves to be on the left of the party, and they believed that their stand against the liquor companies was a more left-wing or progressive radical stance than that taken by the party as a whole. Thus at this stage in the party's development, because of the emotional content of questions concerning distribution of liquor and liquor advertising, the debate that raged within the party was seen to be one between the left and the right. In part it was this division and the consequent eroding of the position of the prohibitionists that led to the mistaken notion of a rightward drift. The question of Prohibition is not one that can be comfortably set on a left-right ideological scale; yet this was done in the Ontario CCF, and as a result the party and observers of the party mistakenly drew conclusions about its ideological position which were unwarranted. If one looks at more central issues such as economic planning and the revision of social security measures, another conclusion follows.

By the end of the 1950s the liquor controversy had lost all its symbolic potency except for a few individuals clustered around Bill Temple and the High Park CCF. The new issue which agitated the party was the question of Canada's membership in the North Atlantic Treaty Organization (NATO) alliance. Those with a watertight compartmental view of the Canadian constitution might feel that this was surely an issue for the federal party. In fact the provincial party debated it at a number of conventions.[43]

During this era great debates raged in the British Labour party between the unilaterialists, those on the left led by Aneurin Bevan, who wished Britain to renounce unilaterally nuclear weapons and to take an essentially neutral position in the cold war, and those led by party leader Hugh Gaitskill, who felt strongly that Britain was the chief ally of the United States and that under a Labour government it should remain so. They also felt that as an American ally it would be the height of folly for them to make a unilateral declaration abandoning their nuclear capability.

Canada was not at this time a nuclear power. Although the debate in the CCF was similar to that in the British Labour party and was clearly influenced by the cold war debate there, the issue was Canada's membership in NATO. The minority in the party argued that the cold war and the existence of nuclear weapons could lead only to a holocaust and that the only thing for decent people to do was to wash their hands of the East-West conflict and urge peace on both sides. The majority argued that they too were for peace but that peace could best be won by ensuring that the Soviet Union would not be tempted to intervene in the affairs of Western European states. To do so would provoke the NATO alliance, an alliance including the United States, against such intervention. The majority felt that the Communists in the Soviet Union, like the Communists in Canada, were not to be trusted. Canada was a natural ally of the United States and any attempt by a political party to end that alliance would be the equivalent of political suicide. The CCF, therefore, supported the United Nation's intervention in Korea (essentially an American intervention) and in almost all instances adopted the American view of the cold war.[44]

Again, this internal debate in the party was seen as a debate between the left and the right, the left for withdrawal from NATO, the right for supporting the United States. Yet in traditional socialist terms, there is no reason to make this kind of distinction. In fact the issue was as highly emotional as was the liquor question and as highly symbolic for both sides. The one side was most conscious of its socialism and therefore of its antipathy towards the United States as the world's greatest capitalist power. The other side was conscious of the sentiments of what it liked to call "ordinary Canadians," and certainly the sentiments of some of the leaders of ordinary Canadians in the industrial unions. As such, it felt that "no truck or trade with the Commies" was preferable to a similar sentiment about the "Yankees" because the latter sentiment would cut the party off from the vast bulk of its support.

Another more recent symbolic controversy concerned abortion on demand. In this instance one would be tempted to conclude that the left, which advocated abortion on demand, had taken control of the party, since the party endorsed a policy akin to that. Party leaders argued that such was not their position. The policy was put in these terms:

The NDP is associated – wrongly – as the party endorsing abortion on demand; accordingly, the issue is certain to arise despite the fact that it falls under federal, not provincial jurisdiction ... Our policy, as passed for the 1971 federal convention, states clearly that an NDP government would conduct research into safe methods of birth control and abortion, provide free information on conception control devices to anyone requesting them, and remove Section 251 from the Criminal Code (the latter constitutes the federal law on the matter) making abortion other than through therapeutic abortion committees and hospitals illegal ... Under no circumstances does the New Democratic Party support the notion that abortion is to be regarded as a form of birth control. The fact exists, although, that however undesirable it may be, it is sometimes necessary. There is nothing more unhappy and brutal than for a woman to be forced to bear an unwanted child or to resort in desperation, to a back street butcher. We all recognize that a woman desperate for an abortion will find one. Surely it is the best and human of alternatives that she have access to a free, legal and safe abortion.[45]

For a number of members of the party, certainly many Roman Catholic members, this last statement was unacceptable because it essentially called for abortion on demand without naming it that. The policy of the NDP had become one in which, for the reasons outlined, the party was prepared to say that if a woman insisted upon an abortion, she should have one. Attempts might be made to get her to change her mind, but if the woman "demanded" the abortion, it should be performed in safe surroundings rather than by "backroom butchers." Again, this is not a left-right issue. If it were, it would indicate that the party had moved to the left, since party policy was nearly the same as that of the left. In fact it was a symbolic issue for both sides in the dispute, the one side believing that the woman in the final analysis has the right to control her own body, the other side believing that the community has some rights in the matter as well.

These controversies, particularly the liquor and NATO questions, caused intense debate within the party. These were not, however, issues central to the party platform. The party consistently warned candidates to avoid them. By the late 1960s with the emergence of the Waffle movement some discussion and some very real disagreement arose over the central parts of the platform, particularly in terms of a resolution on the nationalization of resource industries in Ontario, but it is important to note also the party's subsequent repudiation of that resolution which was passed in convention. The party leadership remained steadfast in its traditional view that there should be a mixed economy and that while some resource industries might be nationalized, a resolution calling for a holus-bolus nationalization was dangerous, unnecessary, and unwanted.

As with many individuals, the Ontario CCF/NDP exhibited and lived with seeming contradiction. On the one hand, the party was remarkably constant in its fundamental beliefs through forty years of political life. On the other, the party was compelled to deal with issues which, though peripheral to its main ideological concerns, reflected its socio-cultural milieu. It might be said that its ability to live with this seeming contradiction essentially reflected its mature self-confident need to adjust to the world around it. The adjustment was made, but not at the price of abandoning fundamental beliefs. If this were not so, the party would either retreat into itself or become something very different from what it was. In either case it would not "survive" as a recognizable political institution.

PART THREE

The Mature Party: Adapting to Change

6

Caucus and Party

That the CCF/NDP in Ontario has remained fundamentally the same in its program and structure indicates, in terms of the human analogy, the existence of a consistent and integrated personality. This characterization does not, however, admit the conclusion that the Ontario CCF/NDP has failed to experience significant change and growth. The effluxion of time inevitably brings change, and the analysis of the stages of party development reflects the impact of such changes. The concept of secularization itself is fundamentally based on a description of significant changes in a party's response to external stimuli. Even a highly integrated personality must adjust to its environment, an environment in perpetual motion. The failure to adjust to such movement, or change, would inevitably inhibit the ability of the "person" to cope successfully and survive. If the CCF/NDP in Ontario has survived, it has necessarily undergone change.

The problem is to reconcile the observed changes with the regular patterns of party behaviour. How does the party respond to dramatic changes in its environment and yet continue as a recognizable entity? The personality analogy suggests a focus for solving this problem. In considering the stage by stage development of the party, distinctions were made in terms of the party's consciousness of itself as an actor in a particular environment. The focus, therefore, as for the study of the human individual, is on the processes of self-control in a constantly changing personal milieu. Change is ubiquitous, but so is a pattern of self-control, at least for the stable individual and so for the CCF/NDP of Ontario. More prosaically, the pattern of self-control in an institution is the same as the pattern of internal government – a central organizing principle for the traditional study of institutions.

Specifically the pattern of internal government of the Ontario CCF/NDP changes significantly in three ways: in the relationship between the legislative caucus and party leaders who do not hold public office; in the control exercised by certain party leaders over the selection of executive members; and in the ability of the party leadership to make effective use of the disciplinary machinery in the constitution.

In his classic study, *Political Parties*, Robert Michels turns our attention to these processes of internal government and argues that oligarchical control of any large-scale party organization is inevitable. He offers two explanations for his "iron law of oligarchy." First, the requirements of large organizations for representative leaders, which are by definition a step removed from the mass of individual members, place considerable formal and informal power in the hands of a minority of members chosen as those representatives. Second, the masses, according to Michels, have a psychological need to identify with the leaders they have chosen, and that identification gives those leaders a certain invulnerability from the assaults of putative rivals.[1] In addition, the very process of a party's adjustment to the world, analogous to a human individual's adjustment, requires a considerable degree of self-control and this control for the institutional personality is, again by definition, necessarily oligarchical, or more rarely monarchical. A great number of individuals in an organization cannot respond coherently to external stimuli; a few individuals or ipso facto one individual can. He who believes in responsiveness believes in oligarchy.

Evidence indicates that, among the various organs of the CCF/NDP in Ontario, the caucus of members elected to the Legislative Assembly has become increasingly important. In recent years it is hard to gainsay the view that it has become the most important party institution. Michels notes a similar development in a number of socialist parties in early twentieth-century Europe, and others, notably Maurice Duverger and Robert McKenzie, have made similar observations about the dominance of the elected deputy.[2] Two primary reasons are advanced to explain this phenomenon. First, the practice of paying an indemnity for the elected representatives' service in parliaments and legislatures grew, and he or she was able to spend more time in political activity than other members of the party leadership. Second, in a democratic polity election to public office is ideologically seen as a kind of sacrament, almost akin to priestly ordination, which inevitably gives the individual greater prestige in his own party than those party leaders who have not been so blessed by public opinion. These factors are relevant for the Ontario CCF/NDP, although the role of the caucus as an organ of the party is somewhat unique and the circumstances are so particular that it is imperative to seek other explanations for its increasing importance.

In any organization there are those who devote their attention and efforts to the internal concerns of the organization itself and those who are aware of, and to some extent respond to, the concerns and perceptions of the larger community. A sectarian organization has a preponderance of the former personalities; a secular organization, by definition, a preponderance of the latter. Certainly after 1942 many CCF leaders were aware of this organizational tension. Andrew Brewin recalls that during the early 1940s a struggle took place between those who wished to heed the wider community, a group led by Ted Jolliffe and himself, and those who were concerned primarily with the internal debate in the party, led by those Brewin referred to as "academics." The principal spokesman of this latter group was George Grube.[3] Grube himself was conscious of this tension, as shown in a letter to M.J. Coldwell: "I do not think it is being censorious to say that the Ontario member [Joe Noseworthy, MP from South York] does not have the 'feel' of the party in any full sense. I always feel that propaganda has to look both outward, toward those who might join us, and inward, toward the rank and file of the party. Joe is apt to look outward. I am probably apt to look exclusively inward. The two are necessary."[4] Inevitably, with one or two exceptions on the executive, those who "looked outward" were the elected members under Jolliffe's immediate leadership and those who tended to look inward were the members of the executive and council under the proximate leadership of George Grube, who in 1944 became president of the party in Ontario. A member of both groups as provincial leader, Jolliffe certainly recalls that his relationships were significantly easier with the caucus than with the executive.

I had no trouble with that caucus. I had far more difficulty and friction with the provincial executive and the Provincial Council over the years than I ever did with either the first caucus or the second ... There were too many people who were focused on a career within the party and a lot of them got elected to the Provincial Council and executive, although they had no interest whatever in getting elected to a municipal council or legislature of Parliament. They were having a little intramural career ... and such people can be troublesome.[5]

Others do not believe that the two official opposition caucuses of the 1940s were easy or manageable. Miller Stewart, sometime president of the Ontario CCF, states bluntly that the problem with the group elected in 1943 was that "there were at least six Commies in the caucus."[6] Jolliffe disputes this view, stating that only two members of the caucus, Nelson Alles and Leslie Hancock, were primarily influenced by A.A. McLeod, the leader of the Ontario Labour Progressive party, the name used by the Communist Party of Canada after it was outlawed by the War Measures Act in 1940. Other members of the party, however, were not so sanguine and were certain that both Robert Carlin of the Communist-dominated International Union of Mine, Mill, and Smelter Workers from Sudbury and Mae Luckock, the daughter of J.J. Morrison (for some years head of the United Farmers of Ontario), were also inclined to follow McLeod's lead and that two or three others were influenced by the two Labour Progressive members and by their own "Marxist" colleagues.

Aside from this distrust of several members of caucus held by key members of the executive,[7] others simply felt that both of the large caucuses in the 1940s were made up of relatively weak individuals. Jolliffe, when asked to name the key people in the 1943 caucus, names only four of the thirty-four, Agnes Macphail, Charles Millard, Les Wismer, and Bill Dennison, as having made an outstanding contribution. Andrew Brewin, who was a key officer in the Ontario party during this period, states: "I think it was a great weakness of both caucuses, particularly the first one, that they were inexperienced politically and weak on organization. I think that from Ted Jolliffe down they emphasized the legislative aspect of their work to the neglect of the organizational problems of local constituencies. I don't think they built firm organizations."[8]

With these misgivings about many individuals elected in 1943 and about the caucus generally, it is not surprising that the elected members did not immediately establish their pre-eminent authority in the party as the Michelsian corollary would have it. More important, the 1943 caucus suffered a fatal blow when most of its members lost their seats in the 1945 election. This blow was compounded by the fact that Jolliffe was defeated in his own constituency, and though he remained provincial leader, he was not in constant touch with the eight elected members. During the interregnum period from 1945 to 1948 it would have been very difficult for the leaderless caucus to assert itself fully in party councils. When the 1948 election produced a significantly larger caucus, many of the members had not been previously elected and it took some time for them to find their bearings in the assembly itself. By this point the habit of caucus subservience had been well established, and when the snap election called in 1951 reduced the caucus to an impotent two members with Jolliffe again out of the House, any possibility of the Michelsian prophecy becoming true in Ontario was shattered. Jolliffe himself was certainly a man devoted to the legislative process and to the assembly, and was seen by many in the party as a very eminent parliamentarian – Charles Millard states baldly that Jolliffe was the most brilliant man in the legislature[9] – but with his defeat, the caucus as a potentially dominant force in the Ontario CCF was also defeated.

From the election of 1951 to the middle 1960s, the caucus was certainly in a subordinate position within the Ontario CCF/NDP. It was a small caucus which expanded very slowly from two in 1951 to three in 1955, five in 1959, and seven in 1963. Moreover, although Don MacDonald as provincial leader was elected to a seat in the assembly in 1955 and retained it in each subsequent election, for many party activists MacDonald was seen as "basically ... an organizer. His idea of being leader was to organize the party and get it going."[10] Ken Bryden, a central figure in both the party and the caucus during much of this period, notes the good relationships that existed between the caucus and the party resulting from the fact that those in the caucus had all "come up through the party."[11] This was the case until Jim Renwick's election in the 1964 Riverdale by-election.

There were certainly some tensions. George Cadbury, provincial president from 1961 to 1966, recalls that he twice told MacDonald that he and the caucus had no business enunciating policy which had not been considered by the council, but generally relationships were very amicable and very different from those Cadbury observed in Saskatchewan. There, according to Cadbury, considerable tension existed between the party executive and the government caucus, even though a formal attempt to overcome such difficulties was made by the election of two members of the Provincial Council to liaise directly with the caucus and the Cabinet. Cadbury did not find similar problems in Ontario, although he complains that one or two individuals in the caucus were reluctant to co-operate with the executive and to recognize the pre-eminence of the executive and council in directing party affairs.[12] The executive pre-eminence was not challenged during this period by the caucus and was taken for granted by MacDonald and the other MPPs. The caucus was subordinate and accepted its subordination.

This state of affairs did not last. In part it did not last because the caucus was so much larger after 1967. The enhanced importance of the caucus, however, was noted by several observers before the 1967 election. Cadbury puts it this way:

I would say from 1966 on ... the authority in the party shifted almost completely from the executive. [John] Harney [then provincial secretary] spent more of his time, or a very great deal of his time, at Queen's Park ... he was always at Queen's Park when I asked for him and he seemed to have decided that that was where the focus of the provincial party was ... I think that there is no question that in the next two or three years, the whole control of the party – the focus and decision-making – was at Queen's Park.[13]

Aside from Harney's attendance on the caucus, other factors were at work. Fred Young, first elected to the assembly in 1963 after ten years as director of organization in Ontario, points to one:

The difficulty is that the party makes policy and theoretically the caucus has to carry out that policy, but there come times when the caucus is faced with a decision, not between the ideal policy which the party favours, but with the policy proposed by the Tories; between greys in other words. And sometimes on such issues which have never been discussed in party councils the caucus has to make a decision at that point for better or for worse. Caucus members have to vote in the legislature and they must vote as they see best. Sometimes the party may not entirely agree with what they do – there may be repercussions later on – but unless you have some method of calling together the party paraphernalia, the council and the executive, every time a vote is to be taken in the assembly on which there is no definitive party policy, then you're in trouble. And since it is impossible to call together the paraphernalia, the caucus has to have a great deal of freedom to act as it sees best.[14]

Also in 1966 the provincial caucus received additional funds, which enabled it to hire Terry Grier as MacDonald's assistant and Marion Bryden as research director. These resources gave the caucus more authority in party councils. Most important, of course, was the fact that after 1967 the caucus contained twenty members rather than eight, and this much larger group quite naturally included individuals with a multitude of talents. With a more important role to play in the legislature, the group as a whole had a great sense of esprit de corps and a concomitant sense of its own importance.

An equally important factor was the makeup of the caucus elected after 1967 which, as table 5 indicates, included a very representative group of Ontario – these were not marginal men. As table 6 shows, the 1943 caucus was also reasonably representative of the province. In comparing the caucuses of 1943 and 1967 with those of the Conservative and Liberals two statistics seem particularly significant. First, working-class people (blue collar workers and union representatives) are better represented in the CCF/NDP than in the other two parties where such individuals are almost nonexistent. Second, the CCF/NDP caucuses contain significantly more individuals who were born in the British Isles than do the other two. The first confirms that the party was in fact representative of the union class subculture with which it was most directly associated and from which it drew its immediate inspiration; the second suggests that the CCF/NDP more than the other parties was influenced by the colonial nature of the provincial political culture. Evidence shows that the party was greatly influenced by the debates and activities of the British Labour party, and given the composition of these caucuses, it is little wonder.

Moreover, as MacDonald acknowledges, the advent of the larger caucus took place in conjunction with a change in attitude of the government towards the legislature. MacDonald states that "John Robarts was the first person to bring the Ontario legislature into the twentieth century in terms of its basic operation." His "chairman of the board" attitude towards the legislature meant that the old feuds going back to the Hepburn era were set aside. Both the Liberals and the NDP received sufficient funds to enable them to employ an assistant for the leader, a public relations expert, and one or two research personnel, as well as half a secretary for each MPP. The resources were a far cry from those in earlier years when as MacDonald puts it: "I ran a one-man band."[15]

Stephen Lewis states of this period: "The caucus has always had a serious problem by viewing itself as the centrepiece of the party and viewing the party and its bureaucracy and constituency associations as a mere appendage, and only a reluctantly acceptable appendage of

TABLE 5
Portrait of Ontario MPPS, 1967

	Ontario Population 1971	Progressive Conservative	Liberal	NDP
Age (average):		51	43	44
Occupation:				
Teacher		4.7%	11.1%	23.8%
Blue collar worker		1.6	3.7	28.5
Lawyer		20.3	29.6	9.5
Farmer		14.1	11.1	0
Owner/manager/ white collar		53.1	37.0	4.7
Other professional		6.2	7.5	23.8
Union official		0	0	9.5
Religion:				
United Church	21.8	32.8	33.3	38.1
Anglican	15.8	39.1	7.4	14.3
Roman Catholic	33.3	10.9	22.2	14.3
Presbyterian	7.0	7.8	11.1	0
Other	22.1	9.4	26.0	33.3
Birthplace:				
Ontario, rural and small town (−30,000)		69.2	66.6	38.1
Ontario, urban (+30,000)		13.8	18.5	23.8
Other provinces		9.2	7.4	19.0
Canada, total	77.2	93.9	92.6	81.0
British Isles	7.6	4.6	0	14.3
Other	15.2	1.5	7.4	4.7

Sources: *Canadian Parliamentary Guide*, 1969; 1971 census.

TABLE 6
Portrait of Ontario MPPs, 1943

	Ontario Popula- tion 1941	Progressive Conservative	Liberal	CCF
Age (average):		52	54	46
Occupation:				
Teacher		0 %	0 %	12.9%
Worker		2.7	0	32.2
Lawyer		13.5	6.6	6.5
Farmer		29.7	46.6	3.2
Manager		40.5	46.6	25.8
Other professional		13.5	0	3.2
Union official		0	0	16.1
Religion:				
United Church	28.4	40.5	53.3	43.7
Anglican	21.6	40.5	0	15.6
Roman Catholic	22.5	2.7	33.3	6.2
Presbyterian	11.5	8.1	13.3	15.6
Other	16.0	8.1	0	18.7
Birthplace:				
Ontario, rural and small town		83.8	80.0	46.6
Ontario, urban		8.1	0	10.0
Other provinces		2.7	13.3	6.6
Canada, total	80.6	94.6	93.3	63.3
British Isles	11.9	5.4	6.6	36.6
Other	7.5	0	0	0

Sources: *Canadian Parliamentary Guide*, 1945; 1941 census.

the caucus, and that became extremely pronounced in the period 1967 to 1971."[16] John Harney, however, suggests that the caucus was not so overwhelmingly influential in this period that the party became a nullity. He asserts that both he and Gordon Vichert, the party president, frequently attended caucus meetings and were able to influence important decisions by reminding the caucus of the views of the executive and council.[17]

In the period after the election of Stephen Lewis as provincial leader, Lewis himself points out that Vichert and Gordon Brigden, the new provincial secretary, very infrequently attended meetings of the relatively unchanged caucus after the 1971 election.[18] As a result the caucus received little guidance from the officers of the party, the classic situation predicted by Michels. After 1970 the evidence indicates that the caucus came to dominate the party in Ontario not only because of Michels's predictions, but also because the caucus, as we have seen, was in large measure the most "secular" arm of the CCF/NDP in Ontario. Its members were more representative of the political culture of Ontario than were the members of other organs of the party, and as the party adjusted itself to that culture, it is hardly surprising that the most secularized section of the party should become dominant. By 1970 this most secularized institution in the party took control from the executive and the council because the party itself came to respect, more and more, the world about it.

7

Party Democracy

The striking idea of an "iron law of oligarchy" has been often alluded to in the case of the CCF/NDP.[1] Most students of the party have pointed to a small group of leaders who are seen to dominate continually at conventions and councils through a variety of manipulatory devices. Leadership in the CCF/NDP is usually examined in the context of the control exerted by party leaders in the various democratic forums of the party. For the national CCF, Walter Young provides a startling description of oligarchical control.

It is not surprising ... that the CCF was in many respects run by an oligarchy. "Who says organization, says oligarchy" wrote Michels. And the CCF, a party with a mass base in democratic institutions, was an organization and an oligarchy. If the personnel at the top in party executive positions is examined, this becomes fairly clear ...

... of a possible eighty different persons in office, on the basis of a complete change every convention, eleven persons occupied eighty posts over a twenty-eight year period ... From a survey of the length of time as either an executive member or one of the officers of the party, it emerges that the ruling elite in the CCF consisted of no more than twelve people.[2]

Of the twelve "oligarchs" named by Young three, David Lewis, Andrew Brewin, and George Grube, were also very influential in the Ontario party. Moreover, Young contends that this fairly small group of individuals was itself dominated in large part by one man, David Lewis, who, Young asserts, "was the party leader, although he was unable to win a seat in parliament."[3]

Lewis's authority did not simply derive from his offices in the party.

Peg Stewart, who served as both president and secretary of the Ontario CCF, states that Lewis's authority resulted from his extraordinary talents. She recalls a situation, one of many, which illustrates this:

There was a meeting in Hamilton and we went down from Toronto in the morning because a number of Commies and others were there. The whole thing was a shambles. I finally phoned for David to come over from Toronto and he arrived at noon. That was one of David's real accomplishments: he was able to go over there at noon, appear at noon, and then by the time he talked to enough people he knew exactly what the situation was and the thing just changed ... You know how he can exercise his authority or arrogance, whatever you want to call it, but it's a very useful commodity when you are in that kind of spot. He sure cleaned that thing up in about a half hour. He had the thing all on the rails and everything was fine. Oh, it was an intellectual achievement of great power.[4]

Zakuta also attests to the existence of an oligarchy in the Ontario CCF, although he suggests that this was not simply the formal oligarchy of party officers who through various devices perpetuated themselves in office. Rather, in Ontario, it was the rule of an informal group who, without necessarily holding party office, directed the organization.

The unofficial leadership was more homogeneous, more spontaneously chosen and, on the whole, more influential than the official set. The top officers played a major if indirect role in selecting both sets of leaders, but they chose the former simply as friends without having to consider either the public or the general membership. Several of these interlocked groups of friends formed the core of the CCF's leadership in Ontario from the mid 1930s and later in the national organization. They had many things in common, of which perhaps the most important for the party were a right-wing orientation and close connections with the trade unions.[5]

George Grube argues that Zakuta is wrong in asserting that an informal group were the effective leaders of the Ontario CCF. "He [Zakuta] says somewhere that a group of friends ran the party outside the executive. This is not true. The dissidents were a group of friends, but we beat them. We were elected every year."[6] Neither Grube nor other CCF/NDP leaders, however, dispute the essential point that the party was directed by a small group of individuals who knew each other well and who conformed to the Michelsian oligarchical pattern.

In considering the question of oligarchical control of the Ontario CCF/NDP, it is not necessary, therefore, to review Michels's sociology and apply it to the party in Ontario. That a few individuals were particularly influential in the CCF/NDP is unquestioned and their dominance has been adequately demonstrated. It remains to consider three subordinate questions: Who constituted the oligarchy in the Ontario party? How was the oligarchy renewed, that is, what were the patterns of recruitment to leadership positions in the party? What devices did the oligarchy adopt to maintain its control? Given the answers, we can analyse the processes of change in the internal government of the Ontario CCF/NDP.

Two methods may be used to identify the ruling group in an institution such as a political party. The first is to identify holders of key offices or positions in the party (in this instance executive members and caucus members) and to assume that this formal elite is essentially the same as the "ruling group." The difficulty with this method is that not all members of the formal elite have significant influence in formulating policies for the organization. This suggests the need for a second method, that of reputation. An attempt may be made, through interviews, to identify those individuals who have a reputation for possessing influence or power in the organization whether or not they hold formal positions of office. The difficulty with this approach is that it relies on subjective data which, unless carefully collected from a variety of sources, may contain a bias towards certain individuals either by ignoring them or by suggesting that they have an influence which in reality does not exist. The two methods are not mutually exclusive. With the expectation, not that the limitations will cease to exist, but that the additional evidence provided will make this identification of the Ontario CCF/NDP oligarchy more accurate, I have combined the two methods.

I consider, in the first instance, all those individuals who have held the most important offices in the party: leader, president, secretary, treasurer, deputy leader, and after 1967 all members of the working group of the Election Planning Committee. I have included this latter group because as Gordon Vichert, president of the Ontario party from 1968 to 1972, has stated of this period:

The Election Planning Committee is one of the most powerful bodies. There are a couple of caucus members on it; none of the rest are. The Election Planning Committee determines priorities for elections and has some influence on who actually gets elected; determines what kinds of things are said during election campaigns, what kinds of policies are emphasized and what ones are not emphasized; it determines what the leader is going to do, what his image should be, what the party is going to be insofar as that is within anyone's control; and it really makes a lot of important, long-range, and pragmatic decisions.[7]

For the years before 1967 I have chosen to look at the individuals who occupied the offices named because they were formally consulted about all major decisions of strategy and policy. Then relying on a series of interviews with key party activists, many of them members of the oligarchy as I am defining it, I have eliminated certain individuals who occupied these posts because, though formally consulted, their advice carried little weight. I have also added certain individuals when a consensus existed that no matter what position they might hold at a particular time they would always be consulted about critical and important decisions. Essentially I define the party oligarchy as that group of individuals who are invariably and inevitably consulted about all major party decisions and whose advice, if not followed, is always given a consideration that goes beyond a mere formality.

Two important characteristics of the Ontario oligarchy, identified by these techniques, emerge. First, the ruling group in Ontario does not have the same longevity that Young found for the ruling group in the national CCF. In fact in each stage of party development a different set of "oligarchs" emerges, although, as will be seen, the displacement from one set to another is never complete. Second, the oligarchy is remarkably small for the Ontario party, although it encompasses some ten individuals by 1970. By definition, of course, an oligarchy is small. A general pattern in both the Ontario party and the national party is to have critical decisions about the program and election planning taken by very few individuals. For example, both Terry Grier and Ken Bryden point out that the 1961 program for the new party was written by only four people, David Lewis, Frank Scott, Andrew Brewin, and Bryden himself. Grier recalls that the 1967 election campaign was essentially directed by MacDonald and himself with some advice from Stephen Lewis, Jim Renwick, and Marion Bryden. In 1970 when the Election Planning Committee grew to an unwieldy group of over twenty, a much smaller operations sub-committee which effectively assumed the functions of the main committee was formed.

I have not found it possible using the criteria mentioned to identify the oligarchy in the early sectarian stage of development. A few individuals, particularly Sam Lawrence, the lone CCF MPP during the 1930s; John Mitchell, the party president; Herbert Orloff, the party secretary; and Ted Jolliffe, then chairman of the Electoral Organization Committee, were certainly important. It is likely that others during the 1930s would meet the criteria of imperative consultation but there is insufficient evidence about this period.

By the second stage of development, from 1942 until 1951, it is easier to identify those individuals who fit the criteria. The party oligarchy consisted of six individuals: Ted Jolliffe, Andrew Brewin, George Grube, Charles Millard, Morden Lazarus, and David Lewis. Although they come from a variety of backgrounds, they are remarkably similar. Ted Jolliffe, born in China, is the son of missionary parents who were themselves the confident possessors of those middle-class Protestant virtues which characterized almost all leaders of Ontario society. Jolliffe, considered a brilliant young man, studied law in England as a prestigious Rhodes scholar and had few equals in debate either on the platform, in the legislature, or in the courtroom. He was only thirty-three when he became provincial leader in 1942.

Andrew Brewin was also the son of a churchman. His father was a Church of England clergyman whose parishioners included many prominent members of Canada's "aristocracy." Brewin's maternal grandfather, A.G. Blair, was premier of New Brunswick and later minister of railways and canals in Sir Wilfrid Laurier's first Cabinet. Brewin was educated at Radley Public School in England and read law at Osgoode Hall. He articled with J.C. McRuer, later chief justice of the High Court of Ontario. Brewin became a noted lawyer, ran unsuccessfully six times as a candidate for the CCF, and was finally elected to Parliament in 1962, serving until 1979.

George Grube, the Belgian-born professor of classics at Trinity College, University of Toronto, was never elected to public office but served continuously on both national and provincial party executives from the early 1940s until the mid-1960s, except for university sabbatical years. As president of the Ontario CCF and later as a member of the executive, Grube campaigned vigorously to ensure that both the national and provincial executives would be formally consulted before either the parliamentary or the legislative caucus made important decisions.

Charles Millard was undoubtedly the most powerful industrial union official in the country during the 1940s, and because of the rapid expansion of industrial unionism during the Second World War, probably Canada's most important union officer. He was also a devoted CCFer and was elected to the provincial assembly in 1943 and 1948. He served as a vice-president of the Ontario CCF throughout this period. Millard, a carpenter, joined the ranks of labour after his woodworking business venture had failed. Millard was employed at the General Motors factory in Oshawa in the early 1930s. As the workers in the factory began to organize, Millard was quickly chosen as their most important spokesman. When the bulk of the General Motors workers decided to affiliate with the United Auto Workers (UAW-CIO), Millard was chosen as the first president of Local 222 and later as the first Canadian director of the UAW. In 1939 Millard was defeated as UAW director by George Burt. Millard, however, had become so valuable to the burgeoning industrial labour movement that he was quickly appointed director in Canada for the CIO. After the formation in Canada of the United Steelworkers of America in 1941, he became the first national director. Until his retirement in 1953, when he left to take a post with the International Confederation of Free Trade Unions, he continued as the most dominant personality in the industrial union movement in the country. In addition to his labour and CCF activities, he was a prominent member of the United Church of Canada and associated his religious convictions with his political beliefs.[8]

Morden Lazarus was a skilful publicist who during the 1940s acted as the chief administrative officer of the party, although until 1948 the provincial secretary was Bert Leavens. Leavens, however, had little influence with the other officers of the party, while Lazarus offered much advice, often followed.[9] Lazarus comes from a middle-class background, but as a Jew he did not, like the others, have the same religious upbringing so characteristic of the Ontario middle class. Lazarus, a graduate pharmacist from the University of Toronto, did however marry Margaret Sedgewick, for some years treasurer of the Ontario CCF and the daughter of a former moderator of the Presbyterian Church of Canada, and so was certainly familiar with this fundamental aspect of Ontario culture. After his stint as provincial secretary, Lazarus became a political education director for the Ontario Federation of Labour, holding that post until his retirement in 1975.

David Lewis's background and career in the CCF have been described at length by Walter Young and by himself.[10] Lewis continued to be a most prominent member of the New Democratic Party after its formation, as an MP from 1962 to 1963 and from 1965 to 1974, as a vice-president from 1961 to 1971, and as federal leader from 1971 to 1975. After his retirement as leader, Lewis was made honorary president and as such was a member of the federal executive and council until his death in May 1981. Lewis first became a table officer in 1936 and remained an officer until his death.

Lewis's role in the Ontario party is somewhat more ambiguous than that in the national organization. He must be included as a member of the oligarchy, not because he held high office in the Ontario party (although he was briefly a member of the Provincial Council in 1947), but because all those interviewed about power relationships in the Ontario party agree that Lewis was always consulted about any major decision. During the early stage he was national secretary of the CCF and in that capacity was in constant touch with the provincial officers. Young argues vigorously not only that Lewis was primus inter pares in the national CCF but that in many instances he was a virtual dictator of party policy strategy.[11] It does not seem the case, however, that he directed the decisions of the provincial executive from his Ottawa office. Lewis was constantly consulted and he gave constant advice, but there is considerable evidence that he was treated as an equal colleague in the business of directing the Ontario movement and that in many instances his advice was not followed.[12] It is interesting to speculate that Lewis could dominate the national organization but not the Ontario CCF because in Ontario the other members of the party oligarchy were, like Lewis, men of very considerable talent, a talent which in most instances was recognized outside the CCF. People of such stature, with one or two exceptions in Saskatchewan and English-speaking Montreal, were not available to the party elsewhere in the country.

During the third stage of party development, from 1951 to 1964, the same methodology suggests an oligarchy of nine. Brewin, Grube, Lazarus, and Lewis continued to be consulted on all important questions, with Brewin and Grube serving on the Ontario executive throughout the period and Lazarus remaining an important figure in the party as director of the Ontario Federation of Labour's Political

Action Committee. After 1953 Millard resigned all his offices in the party. He returned to Canada in 1956 but was no longer a senior officer. He did, however, stand as a candidate for Parliament in the early 1960s and briefly served on the provincial executive at that time. He continued to be a respected figure but his opinion was not always sought on important questions. Jolliffe, who as leader was in many ways the most dominant member of the 1940s oligarchy became almost totally inactive after he gave up the leadership in the fall of 1953. He continued to be a part of the "movement" in Ontario as general counsel for the United Steelworkers and other unions, but all attempts to persuade him to take a place on the Provincial Council or executive failed and he essentially withdrew from active participation in the direction of party affairs.[13]

The new oligarchs were Donald C. MacDonald, Ken Bryden, Miller and Peg Stewart, and George Cadbury. Interestingly none of them were active trade unionists, and with Millard's retirement the CCF did not enjoy the advantages of having a prominent trade union leader (aside from Lazarus who was an employee but not an officer of the OFL) as part of the ruling group in the party. A number of key industrial unionists were often consulted, but the attitude of the trade unions was that the party was a separate organization and that they were too busy running their own organizations to spend much time directing the affairs of the CCF.[14] Leaders of the second and third rank in the labour movement were encouraged to sit on CCF executive bodies, but as in the British Labour party, the fact that they did not command their own organizations made their advice less valuable to the party and made it impossible for them to insist upon a particular course of action without going through the laborious process of bringing pressure from their union superiors on the party.

Of these new oligarchs undoubtedly Donald MacDonald was the most important. As provincial leader of the Ontario CCF/NDP from 1953 to 1970, he was certainly involved with every important question facing the party during this period. MacDonald spent his early years as a farm boy in that part of rural Quebec near the Ontario border. His background is not working class or "proletarian" nor is it wealthy or comfortable. He was forced to earn his BA by a combination of summer courses, correspondence courses, and one year of full-time university study in between teaching elementary school in the small towns of the Ottawa valley. Before the Second World War Queen's University, Kingston, harboured a number of such impoverished but "respectable" students and the best of them were encouraged to seek further education. MacDonald, therefore, was able to undertake an MA in history at Queen's at the end of which he won a travelling scholarship which enabled him to spend a year abroad, mostly in England, speaking to groups about Canada and her role in Anglo-American relations. He became a journalist, using the skills gained at the *Montreal Gazette* during his wartime service with the Royal Canadian Navy, and immediately after the war he was employed by David Lewis as education and information secretary for the national CCF. MacDonald's adult career has been spent primarily in the employ, in one capacity or another, of the party, and on his retirement as leader he continued to sit as the MPP for York South until his resignation in 1982, and for four years served as federal president of the NDP.

Ken Bryden is another son of the manse in the CCF/NDP. Bryden seemed originally destined for an academic career but his socialist commitment intervened, and with his doctorate in economics still uncompleted, he went to Saskatchewan to serve the new CCF government. He quickly rose to become deputy minister of labour, serving the Douglas government until 1949 when for personal reasons he decided to return to Ontario. He was seen as such a valuable person that Charles Millard arranged for funds to hire him as a research director of the party. He soon found himself out organizing and, after the resignation of Lazarus in 1952, became provincial secretary. Bryden held this post until 1959 when he was elected to the legislature from Toronto-Woodbine. He continued to be a member of the provincial executive, of the national executive, of both the National Committee for the New Party and the Ontario Committee for the New Party, as well as serving as deputy leader in the legislature. In 1967 Bryden decided not to seek re-election. Instead he took a teaching post at York University, completed his doctorate, this time in political science, and joined the Department of Political Economy at the University of Toronto.

Miller and Peg Stewart were again from middle-class professional backgrounds. Miller Stewart sold insurance and became a professional writer; Peg Stewart was also a professional writer and served as the full-time secretary of the CCF/NDP from 1959 through 1962. Both served as provincial president during the 1950s and are included among the oligarchy for this reason. In fact Peg Stewart became the more active of the two and as secretary fits the criteria as an oligarch more closely. It is useful, however, to include a husband and wife team in part to represent the facts that the wives of most oligarchs were themselves active in the CCF/NDP and that Peg Stewart carried this tradition to its conclusion by becoming for a period a more important figure in the party than her husband.

George Cadbury is also, inevitably it seems, from a background that is not working class. Indeed, as the eldest grandson of the Quaker founder of the Cadbury chocolate empire he would be considered in any country but Britain a member of the aristocracy. Cadbury is in a special position in this list inasmuch as he became central only after his election as president of the newly formed Ontario NDP in 1961. During his tenure as president, however, he was exceedingly influential and certainly fits the criteria as an oligarch. As might be expected, Cadbury's immediate election to the presidency shortly after arriving in Ontario caused a certain disquiet among many members of the NDP. Cadbury overcame this, not simply because the old oligarchy endorsed him (he was nominated for president at the Ontario founding convention by Andrew Brewin), but because his own background in the socialist movement was considerable. As the scion of a wealthy family he was financially able to give up a promising business career and devote himself to the international socialist movement. As a professional economist (he studied under John Maynard Keynes at Cambridge) Cadbury served the Saskatchewan government chiefly as director of economic planning. Later, as an international civil servant he served as a key adviser to Norman Manley's socialist government in Jamaica. After ceasing to be president of the Ontario NDP, Cadbury became treasurer of the federal party and later devoted most of his efforts to the International Planned Parenthood Federation, serving as its president.

After 1964, as the party moved into a different developmental stage, the composition of the oligarchy changed dramatically. MacDonald continued to be a central figure as provincial leader, but with the one exception of David Lewis all the other oligarchs of the 1940s and 1950s were no longer consulted, although many of them continued to be active in the party. The new elite that emerged, in addition to MacDonald, consisted of James Renwick, John Harney, Terry Grier, Ed Phillips, Gordon Vichert, Stephen Lewis, and Desmond Morton. By 1969 it is necessary to add John Brewin and Lynn Williams.

All have similar backgrounds, similar to each other and to the backgrounds of their oligarchical predecessors. Renwick, the son of a prosperous Toronto family, attended private school and then Trinity

College at the University of Toronto. During the war he served as an army officer and after returned to a corporation law practice and membership in the Conservative party. In 1963 he joined the New Democratic Party, ran in the general election of that year, but was defeated. Renwick was elected in Toronto-Riverdale in 1964 and has been re-elected since then.

John Harney has a somewhat different background as a Roman Catholic from Quebec City with a French-Canadian mother and an Irish-Canadian father, a prosperous contractor. Before being elected provincial secretary, Harney was an English professor at the University of Guelph. He served briefly in Parliament from 1972 to 1974 and has since returned to teaching English to university students.

Terry Grier is another scion of the "establishment." His father, Colonel Grier, was headmaster at the prestigious Bishop's College School in Lennoxville, Quebec. Grier took an MA in political science at the University of Toronto before going to work full time for the NDP. He was federal secretary of the party, special assistant to the leader of Ontario, and a member of the provincial and federal executives. He was also briefly an MP in the 1972–4 Parliament. Since his defeat Grier has returned to Ryerson Polytechnic as a senior administrator.

Ed Phillips, an Ontario Hydro engineer, is the son of C.E. Phillips, a well-known teacher and inspector of schools. Phillips served on the Ontario executive as vice-president and later treasurer. In 1968 he was effectively acting provincial secretary when John Harney was campaigning to become a Member of Parliament.

Gordon Vichert, like Ted Jolliffe, was born in China of missionary parents. He took a PH D in English literature at the University of London and returned to Canada to teach at McMaster University.

Stephen Lewis, the eldest son of David Lewis, was first elected an MPP in 1963 and served as provincial leader from 1970 to 1978.

Desmond Morton is the son of a brigadier general in the Canadian army and the grandson of another general, Sir William Otter, the founder of the Canadian Militia, whose life he has immortalized in a biography.[15] Morton himself served briefly in the Canadian army after training at the Royal Military College. He is a professor of history at Erindale College where he was academic vice-principal. He served the NDP as assistant provincial secretary from 1964 to 1966 and was a key member of the executive from 1968 to 1970.

John Brewin, the son of Andrew Brewin, trained as a lawyer at the University of Toronto. After two electoral defeats in Ontario, he moved to British Columbia where he was president of the British Columbia New Democratic Party in 1977–8.

Lynn Williams is another clergyman's son. He was educated at the University of Toronto where he took his MA in political science. Williams ran once for the CCF in 1954. He was director of District 6 of the United Steelworkers and is now the international president of the union.

One fundamental and important conclusion is evident from these brief sketches of party oligarchs. With but one exception, Charles Millard, every single person named is middle class, and in fact from that section of the middle class most comfortably assured of its important social role – the professional class. There are no oligarchs with an industrial working-class background, not even Millard and Williams, the two trade unionists. This phenomenon has been noted in other socialist parties. Michels points to the large number of middle-class leaders who play critical roles in the European social democratic parties about the turn of the century. Certainly every student of the British Labour party has noted, often with amazement, that many of its most important leaders have middle-class, not working-class, backgrounds. Yet in these European and British parties many socialist leaders are in fact from working-class backgrounds and are themselves "proletarians." The middle-class backgrounds of their colleagues are noted to show that even in political parties based on the trade union movement working-class individuals do not completely dominate leadership roles. For the Ontario CCF/NDP, however, there is no tension between middle- and working-class leaders simply because there have been no "oligarchical" leaders with working-class roots, save Millard, who as a skilled carpenter, and later the owner of a small business, had something akin to a middle-class background.

The commercial classes of society are also badly underrepresented in the CCF/NDP leadership. Almost all of these individuals are from backgrounds free from the taint of entrepreneurial activity. It is not surprising that middle-class individuals should become dominant in any organization, given the skills of articulation and expression they bring to social situations. It is certainly notable, however, that the Ontario party was led by individuals with such remarkably similar backgrounds and by individuals who, for the most part, were conscious that their political activity required significant financial and sometimes social sacrifices.

These individuals were not the only leaders of the CCF/NDP. Many others played critical roles. A number of trade union leaders, particularly, were consulted about decisions involving their organizations and they effectively exercised a veto over certain aspects of CCF/NDP policy and strategy.[16] Inevitably a few individuals, because they were consulted on one or two very critical and important decisions, had a longer-lasting impact on the fortunes of the CCF/NDP than some of those just named had. The definition employed for oligarchy is abstract and therefore an imperfect mirror of reality. But it is convenient to name individuals as an oligarchy and it is important to characterize that oligarchy in any analysis of the party.

G. Mosca, U. Pareta, R. Michels, and their contemporary disciples all focus on two fundamental problems of elites – recruitment and the maintenance of control. It matters not whether elites "circulate" or perpetuate themselves. There exists a logical and inevitable process of change in the individual actors who make up an elite. Moreover it matters not how closely knit or powerful an elite or oligarchy may be. The problem of maintaining its control, of exercising influence and power through a variety of devices, is ubiquitous.[17]

In the Ontario CCF/NDP members of the oligarchy have been recruited by a process of co-option. Although there have been very significant changes in the membership of the party oligarchy, there has also been a certain continuity. New members, even in periods of rapid change, have been recruited by those already conscious of their elite positions. For the first oligarchical generation of the 1940s, the process of co-option was essentially one of individuals choosing their political allies and consequently this oligarchy was based on equality. In subsequent periods some evidence suggests that certain individuals were co-opted not simply as allies but as disciples. However, the earlier habit remained, and for the most part those who came to be conscious of themselves as the party rulers had a collegial relationship with other oligarchs.[18]

Zakuta describes this process of co-option as one essentially involving the choosing of friends. He argues that the informal leadership of the party is in fact the most important leadership and that in the Ontario CCF group, "a dozen men and their wives most of whom lived in Toronto, [was a] nucleus [which] remained remarkably intact for over two decades [and that] similarities in age, education, occupation and interests made friendship easy."[19] The evidence, however, suggests that this is too much a conspiratorial interpretation. It is true that many of the oligarchy saw each other frequently on social occasions. It is also true, however, that the co-option tended to be on the basis not of previous friendships but of potential talent. Those chosen for admission to the "magic circle" were invariably individuals with formal talents such as law or journalism who, it was hoped, would prove helpful in directing party affairs in the future. Moreover, though undoubtedly individuals co-opted were expected to continue to work for the consensual principles held by other members of the party elite and thus help maintain elite control in the party, undoubtedly it was also hoped that they would help the whole party, including individual elite members, achieve its wider electoral ambitions.

In terms of the actual process of recruitment, it is useful to analyse some examples. George Cadbury recalls being approached to run for president by Ken Bryden. Cadbury speculates that he was approached because at the time of the founding of the new party in Ontario the oligarchy wanted an independent person who was not identified with either the trade union movement or the old CCF or indeed the New Party clubs and yet was clearly a party regular.[20] Gordon Vichert, who was asked to run for president in 1968, was approached by Stewart Cooke, the area supervisor for the Steelworkers in Hamilton. Cooke is not named as an oligarch here because he does not fit the criterion of someone consulted on all major issues, since his residence in Hamilton rather than Toronto made it difficult for him to attend all the necessary meetings. But Cooke, another university-educated union leader, certainly had very close links to the oligarchy and served as a key officer of the party from the early 1950s to the 1970s. Since Vichert was also from Hamilton, Cooke's approach to him was quite natural, but as Vichert suggests, it was one inspired not simply by Cooke himself but by others in the party hierarchy anxious to prevent Val Scott, a man seen as a maverick, from becoming president.[21] In the case of persuading John Harney to become provincial secretary, Don MacDonald, Stephen Lewis, and Jim Renwick visited Harney in Guelph and urged him to take the post.[22] In all these instances the individuals recruited were approached by key persons who were themselves central to the party leadership or who had the confidence of the party leadership. In all instances those recruited were individuals with considerable talent who could be elected at a convention to party office. Cadbury had been a successful businessman and international civil servant as well as a policy adviser in Saskatchewan. Harney and Vichert were both university professors of English and were seen as literate, articulate, and persuasive individuals.

The maintenance of the leadership's control over the party organization has been consistent throughout the history of the Ontario CCF/NDP. On no occasion have the elected officers, executive and council, been prevented from directing party affairs between conventions, and although significant challenges have been made to the hegemony of the oligarchical leadership at convention, these challenges have always failed. Between conventions control over the direction of the party has been maintained by the leadership because there has been an overwhelming acceptance by members of the party of the hierarchical structure contained in the constitution; control has been maintained at conventions because the leadership has skilfully employed three political devices to that end.

The first device adopted by the members of the oligarchy was the simple expedient of maintaining close personal relations among themselves and with as many other key active party workers as possible. There should be no question at this point that a great many individuals other than those identified as oligarchs played critical and important roles in the CCF/NDP of Ontario. As discussed previously, a number of key trade unionists were always consulted on issues involving the labour movement itself and, less often, on other important programmatic concerns. Local leaders, presidents of riding associations, provincial council delegates, backbench MPPs, and others holding some formal post found themselves in fairly continual contact with the central leadership core. Samuel Eldersveld, in his study of Michigan political parties in which he develops the idea of a hierarchy of elites – a "stratarchy" – finds that no matter how competent or efficient local precinct leaders are, the frequency of contact with the "top elite" in the party is very similar between precincts.[23] It is the top elite which initiates contacts with local party leaders, a pattern evident in the Ontario CCF/NDP. Friendships and political alliances would be formed between conventions and at conventions local leaders of importance would be consulted about resolutions, constitutional amendments, and the election of council and executive members. Since the oligarchs often worked full time at political activity, or at least devoted most of their spare time to such activity, they had the "leisure" to maintain these contacts and consequently were able to persuade personally the key trade union and local constituency leaders much more readily than were any opponents who surfaced at a particular convention.

Second, the very highly developed oratorical skills of the leadership were heavily employed at party conventions to maintain control of decisions by the ability to persuade. These skills were particularly important at the provincial convention after the formation of the New Democratic Party, which attracted over one thousand delegates. It has become fashionable in recent years to suggest that in the McLuhanesque age of television "hot" personalities such as the political orators of old are a dying breed and that the new way to political success is to exude a cool image of technocratic competency. It is argued, in other words, that in the modern age people distrust those who seem too glib or too facile with words. Such may be the case for politicians campaigning on television for the allegiance of the mass electorate, but in conventions where leaders can be seen in the flesh, and in a party where debate is believed to be important, the ability to speak well should not be undervalued. Without exception, members of the oligarchy of the party in Ontario were skilful orators and many of them, like David Lewis, were exceptionally powerful in debate. These oratorical skills, combined with effective control of convention agendas, made it possible for party leaders to persuade rank and file delegates that they were right.

Finally, the leadership maintained its control by its use of the official slate. Much was expected of the official slate and sometimes everything, or at least everything to do with the loss of democracy and the rule of oligarchy was blamed on this mighty artifact. At conventions the official slate was always the subject of intense conversation, quiet rumour, and noisy denunciation by those hostile to the leadership. The slate was a simple device constructed for a more complicated purpose. As the number of posts elected by convention increased and as conventions themselves became large gatherings, the problem of ensuring that the "right" people were elected to these posts became increasingly difficult. During the 1960s it was not unusual for forty or fifty individuals to seek election to the fifteen positions for member at large on the provincial executive. Most of these individuals if elected would be acceptable to the party oligarchy; most of them were not fundamentally opposed to the incumbent leadership but simply had an ambition to work in the party in a broader capacity. The difficulty was that certain combinations that might result from a free-for-all election would be embarrassing. For example, it would be very awkward if all of the members at large happened to come from the Toronto-Hamilton area, or embarrassing if it turned out that no women were elected to the executive or that a farm union official who agreed to allow his name to stand was defeated. Consequently the delegates needed some assistance in filling out ballots which would result in a balanced executive. The official slate was the form that this assistance took. The slate was a piece of paper listing all the posts to be filled at the convention from leader to member at large and, beside the positions, the names chosen by the slate makers to fill them. The choice of names was complicated and those few who drew up the slate spent considerable effort consulting with various groups in the party to ensure that an appropriate balance had been struck, so that all significant groups would have some form of representation and that at the same time key individuals, oligarchs, or putative oligarchs would also be elected.[24]

The slate was invariably denounced on the floor of each convention undoubtedly because it was a most successful device. To have one's name included on the official slate did not make election a complete certainty. However, it guaranteed a considerable vote and usually only two or three individuals named on the slate would find themselves defeated. Often those defeated were trade union officials of the second rank whose names were not well known to the constituency delegates and often those who replaced them were MPs or MPPs whose names were very well known. The slate was rarely broken and as a result those actively opposed to the party leadership would attempt to combat the slate by issuing their own slate of preferred candidates. This attempt inevitably failed, and despite the ideological appeals which usually attended such dissident slates, the official slate, shorn of any decoration save positions and names, was always recognized as authentic. This was so in large part because of its puritan format and also because it was handed around by individuals known to be agents of the party establishment.[25]

It is tempting to conclude that the employment of these devices indicates that the Ontario CCF/NDP "enjoyed" an oligarchical government so strict that any effective participation by ordinary members of the party, or even by constituency activists, was rendered useless and ultimately frustrating. This Michelsian "paradise lost" however is based on only partial evidence and the epic conclusion is therefore suspect. The membership of the oligarchy changed throughout the stages of the development of the party in Ontario, and these changing leaders pursued somewhat different strategies which in large mea-sure characterize the different stages of party development. The party leadership, both oligarchs and those associated with them just below the summit of power, were certainly not of one mind, and as Michels predicted, when they fell out among themselves there was an opportunity for "paradise regained" or, at least, for democracy to function. Choices had to be made between the alternatives put by different oligarchical factions. This falling-out was not common but it has always occurred in the Ontario CCF/NDP over the question of who should be elected provincial leader.

The provincial leader is certainly the key figure in the Ontario party. He provides the most immediate link between the caucus and the party executive, by right of office he sits on every important caucus and party committee, and as a full-time officer and the senior figure in the hierarchy he, like the provincial secretary, is able to command the staff resources available to the caucus and the party itself. Moreover, his unique position as the key spokesman of the party gives him a prestige among the rank and file not available to the other officers.

Because of the critical nature of the leader's position, the choice of leader provides a focus for any ongoing debate among members of the oligarchy. The election of a leader is a symbolic act for the party in the sense that the person chosen is ordained as the only legitimate spokesman of party feeling. Others may, of course, announce specific policies but they are expected to do so with the leader's permission. The leader himself is expected to follow the policies of the party as laid down by convention, but it is he who makes these policies a reality in the external world and is therefore seen as the symbol of the party's inner character. The choice of provincial leader is akin to that of a chief by primitive tribes, or indeed to that of a president of the United States by the citizens of that republic, who endow the elected president with the mythical qualities they desire for the people as a whole. On a more mundane level individuals seeking the party leadership naturally have friends who hope for preferment should their man be chosen and consequently they are prepared to work to that end.

Thus when the oligarchy is divided, leadership conventions in the CCF/NDP provide the secondary leaders from the labour movement and from the constituencies with an opportunity to participate genuinely in a critical decision. Indeed, without their participation the possibility exists that the leader would not be seen to have any special characteristics, would not be able to become a symbol of the party's fundamental beliefs, and would thereby find his position considerably weakened. The post of provincial leader is important, the struggle for that post equally important, and the consequences of that struggle in terms of the oligarchy momentous.

Formally all CCF/NDP conventions are leadership conventions in the sense that the leader must submit himself for election along with all the other officers. To 1972 the post had been won by acclamation on all but five occasions, three of which have been significant. The two not-so-important contests are little known even to amateur historians of the party in Ontario. They occurred in 1942 and in 1946. Ted Jolliffe emerged as the victor in both contests, and as this was universally expected, they did not arouse the passions that surrounded the three later contests. In 1942 the CCF for the first time decided to elect a provincial leader and Jolliffe was the nearly unanimous choice for the post.[26] Since it was the first leadership convention, Murray Cotterill, later public relations director for the United Steelworkers, felt that it would be useful to have a contest and so he allowed his name to be placed in nomination and took the occasion to deliver a spirited address.[27] Jolliffe was not challenged again until 1946 when Lewis Duncan, a recent convert to the party and for a time acting mayor of Toronto, decided to seek the post. Again the party leadership was almost unanimously united behind Jolliffe, and it was no surprise when Jolliffe was handily elected.[28]

When Jolliffe resigned as provincial leader in 1953, a special leadership convention was called to choose his successor. Three men sought the post: Andrew Brewin, Don MacDonald, and Fred Young. Each was supported by different groups in the party. Brewin drew his support from a number of Toronto constituencies and from individuals like Charles Millard who had worked with him during the 1940s.[29] Millard, however, did not campaign actively, and MacDonald was able to draw much of his support from the trade union movement and from constituencies outside Toronto which he had visited fairly frequently as national organizer. Young jumped into the race almost at the last moment, and though a Steelworkers' staff representative, he was supported primarily by the anti-establishment forces who saw both Brewin and MacDonald as too right wing.

Interestingly all three candidates perceived it to be a very low key campaign. As MacDonald put it: "The campaign, to the degree that you would find unbelievable, was an unorganized campaign ... In fact, I have often commented that I think it was one of the most civilized leadership campaigns that was ever fought because Andy and Fred and I all knew each other well. We were all close friends."[30] Young recalls: "It was a pretty free and open convention. There wasn't the pre-election organization as we know it today, not the same hulla-baloo, and we didn't have the signs and banners and all the rest of it and I don't think we even had pins, lapel pins or other gimmicks."[31] Bryden, who was not a candidate and was officially neutral as provincial secretary, though he in fact supported MacDonald,[32] suggests that hard campaigning did take place despite the veneer of civilization at the convention.

In relation to the size of the party membership and the resources of the party, I would say there was as much campaigning as there was in subsequent leadership contests – in fact, a very, very active campaign was put on by two real campaigners on behalf of Fred Young, namely, Marj Pinney and Joan McIntosh. Everything was on a smaller scale, and very little money was involved, but people were certainly campaigning. They were trying to rig the representation from the boondocks, they were trying to get their people in, and when they got them down there, they were still working them over.[33]

The results of this campaigning, gentlemanly or otherwise, were fairly close. On the first ballot Young received 154 votes, MacDonald 127, and Brewin 75. Brewin was eliminated and his vote went predominately to MacDonald. The final ballot gave MacDonald 181 votes and Young 175.[34] Jolliffe explains MacDonald's victory in this way:

I think there was a feeling that Fred Young just wasn't strong enough and there was also a feeling, which was expressed to me by some people, that Don MacDonald had been, for a long time, a party functionary and, well, one word that was used to me, was that he was expendable, which wasn't a very nice thing to say. I think in addition that a lot of people probably felt that if they chose Andrew it would be more of the same. Too much my approach because I was a lawyer too, and so Don represented a sort of compromise between those who would have liked to see a rugged trade unionist and those who wanted a leader with a more broadly based appeal. Don was confident looking, he was popular in the party, and as far as I knew, he had at that point never gotten into any very serious wrangles. In fact, being in the federal picture he hadn't been terribly active in the provincial, and he was in a similar position to Mackenzie King, coming back from the United States to the 1919 Liberal convention – there was nobody organized to cut his throat.[35]

In making this assessment Jolliffe suggests that MacDonald represented a different approach to strategy from his. Certainly the change in leadership heralded a significant change in the oligarchy and consequently in the character of the party.

MacDonald was acclaimed as provincial leader in each succeeding convention until 1968. A few individuals approached Bryden at the time of the formation of the new party in 1961 to see if he was interested in contesting the leadership. Bryden stated that he was not.[36] In 1968, however, Jim Renwick concluded that MacDonald could never lead the party to power and felt that his own chances of doing so were considerably better. Consequently he announced to a somewhat surprised MacDonald that he would seek the leadership in that year. Renwick made his announcement in the early summer, and from that time until the November convention both candidates put forward a considerable campaign effort.

The campaign began with speculation in the party that MacDonald was indeed vulnerable and that Renwick, who had replaced Bryden as deputy leader in the caucus and had been elected federal president in 1967, was an attractive personality who might well have a wide public appeal.[37] Having caught MacDonald completely by surprise, Renwick failed to press his advantage in the early days of his campaign. Instead MacDonald was given time to mobilize his own forces quickly, which he did with considerable skill by personally calling three hundred or so key party and trade union activists to enlist their support. Most of them bowed to this persuasion and MacDonald entered the public phase of the campaign secure in the knowledge that the majority of the secondary leadership in the party was formally committed to his cause.[38]

The second phase of the campaign proved even more disastrous for Renwick. George Cadbury notes: "Poor old Renwick didn't know what was happening to him, and his campaign was horrible – I mean, you do not go around saying that if this other man wins, we're done for, and then the other man wins."[39] Stephen Lewis, who nominated Renwick and acted as one of his key advisers, similarly analysed the Renwick campaign.

I think that in fact the party, while it had an immense loyalty to Don, was in a mood to listen to the argument that he had led the party long enough and that a change in leadership would be valuable, but Renwick's personal mishandling of the whole thing was so disastrous that it was never serious at any time. Had he been a more serious campaigner, had he presented the arguments as some of us thought they should be presented, rather than losing control almost from day one, then I think, although there is no doubt in my mind that Donald would have remained as leader, it would have been seen as a serious challenge. As it was, it wasn't a serious challenge at all. It did, however, serve ironically to engage the trade union movement in the life of the party in a way no other single event had served, including the election of 1967.[40]

Undoubtedly the major incident during the campaign was Renwick's attack on two Steelworkers' officials. In a public speech Renwick blamed them and the Steelworkers for the difficulties in his campaign and the unions were quick to respond angrily.[41] Consequently a real bitterness arose at the 1968 convention, and although Renwick was handily defeated by a vote of 859 to 370, the campaign itself was surrounded with considerable emotion.

The passions aroused in the party by the 1968 leadership convention did not immediately dissipate. Tension between MacDonald and those members of the caucus who had supported Renwick continued to fester. This very unstable political situation within the NDP set the stage for another challenge to MacDonald's leadership, this time by Stephen Lewis. Lewis affirms that the decision was his own and that it was taken for reasons very similar to those advanced by Renwick.

I decided to run because I felt that Donald couldn't take us further. In the final analysis I guess it's as simple as that. Now, it may have been completely wrong. I can't judge that now, although like a great many other people in the party I've thought about it. I was influenced by the situation in the caucus [many caucus members wanted a change in leadership] but not overly influenced. It was clearly important in the crude calculation of political strength whether you had x caucus members but in terms of influencing my decision it wasn't that important. I was much more influenced by my own feelings and by some of those around me. I guess a pretty good example of the group that urged me very strongly to run was people like the Bigelows, who are an example of the riding association types who were beginning to emerge in the party.[42]

Gordon Vichert, then party president and a very quiet supporter of Lewis's challenge, makes this observation:

There was an overwhelming feeling of large numbers of people in the party that everybody was just weary of Donald. They'd heard the same speeches and the same phrases and the same rhetoric from Donald for too many years and the people were turning off. In retrospect I think it's clear that a lot of people in the party were turned off by Donald and were therefore projecting their reaction onto the Ontario public who hadn't heard Donald nearly as much and who were not necessarily tired of Donald. There was a very strong sense of just plain weariness, however, that Donald was just somehow no longer relevant, that he'd had his day, and that if the party was to go anywhere it had to have a new, brighter, younger image than Donald could provide. There is no possible way now of judging whether that was correct; it did involve a certain amount of wishful thinking I suspect. Certainly subsequent events [the 1971 election] have demonstrated that Stephen couldn't do appreciably more than Donald could have done under the same circumstances.[43]

Lewis decided that he should very actively explore the possibility of a challenge late in 1969. He made his opening move when both MacDonald and Renwick were away from the Ontario legislature attending the federal convention of the NDP held in Winnipeg. During that week Lewis provided the inspirational leadership for the caucus and devoted himself to helping his colleagues with their speeches and generally lending a sympathetic ear to their frustrations and their grievances. By the time MacDonald returned to Queen's Park the overwhelming majority of the caucus were prepared to support Lewis's bid for the leadership if it should come at the next convention.

MacDonald did not become immediately aware of this changed feeling among his colleagues in the caucus.[44] It was not until February 1970 that rumours of Lewis's challenge became so persistent that MacDonald decided to check them out. He approached Lewis, who denied that he had decided to run for leader at the 1970 convention, although he did indicate that he had listened to a number of individuals who suggested that he should make that challenge and that a change in leadership might be necessary.[45] Lewis subsequently intensified his efforts to survey groups and individuals in the party about his chances by asking them whether he should stand for nomination. During this period MacDonald found himself in a very awkward position, since Lewis was not officially a leadership candidate and yet at the same time was conducting a campaign, not simply to seek opinion about the appropriateness of his challenge, but to persuade certain people that he in fact should make that challenge. It was not, however, a leadership campaign and Mac-Donald was not able, therefore, to launch his own campaign. He was in the hands of events.

The most important crisis in this sounding-board campaign occurred at the convention of the Canadian Labour Congress held in Edmonton in May 1970. Lewis asked key Ontario trade unionists there whether he should challenge MacDonald. After some deliberation the trade union leaders pronounced that such a challenge would be "inappropriate" and urged Lewis to postpone his ambition. Two consequences followed. Lewis was fortunate that the Ontario party learned the labour leaders' views in a story written by Mark Zwelling, then labour reporter for the *Toronto Telegram*. Zwelling, an active New Democrat and a strong supporter of Lewis, cast his story in such a way that it appeared that the labour leaders had vetoed the democratic possibility of a contest for the post of provincial leader. The reaction in the constituencies was instantaneous; even individuals who generally favoured MacDonald were outraged at the idea that a few trade union officials could seemingly dictate to Lewis and to the party that a leadership contest would not take place. Lewis gained a great many constituency adherents as a result. The second related to the fact the trade union leaders were not unanimous in their decision, and led by Dennis McDermott, Canadian director of the powerful United Auto Workers, the resolve of the other union leaders to prevent a leadership contest quickly collapsed. Lewis suddenly found himself with very considerable support for the idea of a challenge in the constituency parties and with the promise of significant trade union backing from the UAW.

MacDonald quickly reacted to this changed circumstance by having two of his closest associates in the party telephone both key trade unionists and constituency leaders to see if he could still count on their support if a challenge did come. He discovered that opinion in the party was extremely divided and that Lewis's challenge, if not successful, would certainly be a powerful one, and even if he retained his post, he would do so only by a very narrow margin. After a weekend of considerable thought, MacDonald decided to resign. As he explains:

It was really the result of a mix of things. One, I had always promised myself that when the time came to get out, I was going to get out. I wasn't going to pull a Diefenbaker and hang on to the accompaniment of tensions and bloodletting and all that. Combined with this was the feeling, which while it had probably reached its peak by 1970, was very prevalent throughout the 1960s, that it was time for younger men to take over the leadership of the party – the whole Kennedy kick from the States and that sort of pattern that Kennedy established in public thinking. A willingness to entertain the idea of young leaders, indeed to welcome it, was influential … I think the clincher quite frankly was the conviction that knowing Stephen's organizational capacity and knowing both the length of time and the care with which he had built up an organization, he had not only enlisted all those who were disaffected in any way – all those who, as inevitably would be the case with any leader, were opposed to me, or, I suppose, for reasons that had been accumulating since 1953 – but in addition he had fired up the trade union movement because of his working relationship with them. A lot of people who were normally apathetic towards the leadership, who had gone along fairly enthusiastically in fact with my leadership, suddenly said "By gad, here's a fresh new opportunity" … I still feel that if I'd decided to slug it out I could have won. I have no illusions it would have been a tough and nasty fight … and I didn't want that.[46]

Lewis was left with a clear field for the moment but he did not expect that that situation would long continue. "My view was, first, that we would win, and, second, that there would have to be an opponent because the animus towards me, the resentment, the feeling within the party, was so strong in a number of quarters that it had to have an expression and I assumed then it would be Walter [Pitman] because he seemed to be the most logical choice."[47] In fact, after considerable persuasion, Walter Pitman decided to run and make it a contest. He did not begin to campaign instantly. MacDonald resigned at the end of June 1970. Pitman had promised his family that they would spend July driving to and from the West Coast of Canada and the United States and he was unwilling to abandon his plans. As a result the Pitman campaign did not get fully under way until early August, although Pitman's key supporters had spent much of July preparing the groundwork.[48]

In the end Lewis's victory was clear-cut. He received 1,188 votes and Pitman received 642.[49] The actual campaign was not so clear-cut. Lewis's early start had given him an advantage and in addition to the trade union backing he had enjoyed considerable support from the constituencies. However, the majority of the party oligarchy had supported Pitman, and in the contest to list prestigious and well-known names Pitman had upstaged Lewis. John Brewin, one of Pitman's campaign managers, states: "We knew it was an uphill battle. But on the other hand we knew we had a majority of the executive and that the key people in most constituencies, the ones who really ran the constituency whether or not they were president or some other officer, were for the most part nervous about Stephen's somewhat hawkish image and inclined to favour Pitman as the individual most likely to lead the party to victory. We gave them a real scare."[50] Gordon Vichert, who as party president was ostensibly neutral, analyses the support received as follows:

As far as the union support is concerned, Stephen had most of it, but this was not the result of a carefully organized union plot. Only one union had what might be called enthusiasm for Stephen – a very powerful union – but a union which has been less central to the party's affairs than the Steelworkers ... Union support for Stephen was by and large a reluctant lesser of two evils type of support. In addition ... Stephen had almost the whole left of the party at that stage, whoever they were, and they contained a large number of middle-class individuals ... He was more radical, more willing to use socialist rhetoric, than either Donald or Walter ... He looked more radical, more of a firebrand, and there was a tremendous desire in the party for some kind of excitement at that stage ... I had the impression that Stephen's support was pretty general in the riding. One could find support for Stephen in almost every riding association and in almost every constituency, and it had more to do with personality than with class or anything else. As for Pitman's support, if it can be characterized at all, it was people – it's hard to find the right phrase because I am tempted to say conservative but that isn't true – it was the people who had worked longest and hardest for the party in a sense and that of course is an insidious statement because it reflects some of the people who supported Stephen. I don't mean it that way, but it was the party loyalists, people who had been presidents of riding associations for years, people who had worked on the provincial executive for a long time, and so on – those who were not drawn to the flashy or what they perceived as the flashy youthful image making of Stephen but who were more concerned with the qualities that might be called solid, moderate, and so on and saw the party in those images.[51]

Despite the final voting tally, the campaign was perceived as a close one, as both camps had experienced a good deal of nervous anticipation.[52] In the final analysis Lewis's union support had proved telling and by careful organization he had managed to encourage some eight hundred union delegates out of a convention total of over eighteen hundred to register. There seems every reason to believe that they provided the margin of his victory. Certainly the Pitman forces believed that they had won a majority of the votes from the constituency delegates,[53] and Lewis himself, when he met the caucus for the first time the day following his victory, stated very clearly that in his opinion Pitman had carried the constituency vote.[54]

An analysis of these leadership contests yields three important conclusions. First, it seems evident that after 1967 the caucus came to play an increasingly important role in the direction of party affairs and in the making of critical and fundamental decisions. Renwick's campaign faltered as his caucus colleagues rallied to support Mac-Donald, and MacDonald's position two years later became untenable when the overwhelming majority of MPPs decided that a change in leadership would be desirable. Indeed, before his resignation Mac-Donald clearly had a majority of trade unionists prepared to support him and constituency association activists were perceived to be divided so that MacDonald could realistically have won a majority, albeit a narrow one, among them. The executive had a majority which favoured MacDonald continuing as leader. Only the caucus was overwhelmingly opposed to MacDonald but in the final analysis the caucus had its wish.

Second, the hoopla associated with presidential conventions in the United States – balloons, signs, buttons, and all the other paraphernalia of mobilized enthusiasm – became much more apparent in the Ontario CCF/NDP in each succeeding leadership convention. The worldliness of the electioneering in other parties intruded upon the consciousness of the New Democrats and they imitated the American and Canadian examples before them. This is not to say that the campaigns of 1968 and 1970 were entirely different from that of 1953. The choice of leader was important at all three conventions and the campaigning was as fierce.What changed was not the intensity but the style of the campaign. In the early years CCFers had prided themselves on conducting their business in a fashion very different from that of other parties, both Canadian and American. In later years this pride was replaced by a new pride of being able to campaign as colourfully and as effectively as other parties.

Finally, these leadership contests were important because they heralded a fundamental change in the internal government of the party. The leader as the central figure, a kind of chieftain, is the symbol of the party leadership, and his replacement portends a change not only in the one office but in the oligarchy itself. After Lewis was elected, the oligarchy described previously ceased to be an oligarchy in the sense that it is defined here, and a new set of individuals were consulted on the important issues facing the party. In particular Gerry Caplan, Lewis's long-time friend, then a professor at the Ontario Institute for Studies in Education, became Lewis's executive assistant, a member at large on the provincial executive, and a key strategist for the 1971 election. Unlike the national party the Ontario party once again changed the guard.

8

Party Discipline

An examination of the party's disciplinary practice reveals one more important aspect of the party's domestic life in which significant changes arise from the socio-cultural milieu of Ontario. The Ontario CCF/NDP experienced five major crises in which the disciplinary provisions of the constitution were employed. The first need not be considered in any detail, since in fact the constitution was not invoked and it occurred in 1934 during the sectarian phase of party development.

Woodsworth, more than any other leader in the fledgling CCF, had a horror of any proposed common front of alliance with the Communists,[1] and when such a proposition was endorsed by the Ontario CCF, he reacted swiftly and vigorously. Without consulting his own national executive or council, he appeared at a meeting of the Ontario Provincial Council and announced that the organization in Ontario was dissolved and that a new one loyal to the national organization would be formed. Woodsworth's stature in the party was such that a decision of this sort by him could not be questioned and it was swiftly endorsed by the National Council.

The lessons of this intense drama of dissolution remained with the Ontario CCF and re-emerged after the party had become a significant electoral force and had elected thirty-four MPPs, some of whom were suspected of having Communist sympathies. The initial concern arose, not from the election of these members, but rather from a motion passed by the Provincial Council of the British Columbia CCF, favouring co-operation with the Communist party.[2] This resolution caused concern in all sections of the CCF and George Grube, then vice-president of the Ontario party, wrote to the secretary of the BC party, expressing the concerns of the Ontario executive about a common front. He said, in part:

In considering our attitude to the Communist party, the following should be the premise on which our argument must be based. A good deal of unnecessary confusion is caused by some who believe that the CCF and the Communists have the same ends in view, but differ as to methods. Actually the kind of world the Communists seek to establish is widely different ... because they are convinced of their own infallibility ... they seem incapable of loyal co-operation. Essentially they try to control every organization they use or else break it up. This attitude is only too frequent in unions they control ... There is still a struggle in this country as to who – CCF or Communists – is going to control the radical forces. Their renewed desire for co-operation is due to the fact that we are, at the moment, stronger ... they will take every chance, therefore, to weaken us, from without or from within ... It is unpleasant because in most cases where a "united front" has been tried the Communists have not lived up to their undertakings. This was especially clear in France. The Communists cheerfully made an alliance with Hepburn [then premier of Ontario] only eighteen months ago. Only our own more radical and consistently socialist position caused them to abandon those tactics. Their claim to be the extreme left-wing is a fake, in my opinion.[3]

Not surprisingly Grube concluded by urging the British Columbia party to give up any idea of co-operation with the Communists and instead to build its own organization.

Grube's analysis of the "common or united front" and the dangers of any alliance with the Communist party was generally accepted by the Ontario leadership. The British Columbia CCF initiative provided the opportunity for a position to be established in full, but it was political events in Ontario and in the Ontario party which not only crystallized that position but turned it into political reality.

In late September 1944 a number of known trade union supporters of the Labour Progressive party and other union members launched a campaign to encourage the CCF to enter a coalition with the Liberals and the LPP to replace the Conservative minority government under George Drew. The spearhead of this movement was found in Windsor, Ontario, where sixty-six individuals published a large advertisement calling for such a coalition. The advertisement was in the form of an open letter to the three CCF MPPs from the Windsor area, and it appeared at the same time as several labour councils and local unions throughout the province sent similar messages in the form of resolutions to Ted Jolliffe and other CCF members. Because one of the Windsor MPPS, Nelson Alles, was extremely sympathetic to this appeal for a "coalition,"[4] Jolliffe set down before the caucus a detailed argument against such a move.

The LPP argument proceeds along these lines. 1. That Drew and the Tory party represent the spearhead of reaction in this country and that every effort must be made to get rid of them. This premise is only half true. Actually the Tory party has no strength outside Ontario and Mr. Bracken [then national leader of the Progressive Conservative party] as anybody can see, is losing ground everywhere. As for Drew, he is extremely unpopular outside Ontario ... the real spearhead of reaction is the Liberal party and it will get the backing of the big business interests because they know that the Liberal party alone has a national organization with some chance of success. 2. The LPP argument goes on that the Drew government is a minority government, having thirty-eight seats while other groups have fifty-two, and that all the opposition groups are on record against the Drew government. Mr. Hepburn is not on record against Drew; he is on record against King. The only issue on which the Liberals have gone on record against Drew is the family allowance issue. On every other important question they have supported the Drew government. 3. The LPP then use the term "coalition" incorrectly to suggest that Drew can be voted out only by a "coalition" ... No coalition is necessary to out-vote Drew ... 4. ... they [the LPP] imply that the defeat of Drew would be followed by the formation of a "coalition government." Of course this is nonsense. What Drew would undoubtedly try to do would be to bring on an election ... If the CCF were foolish to fall for the "coalition" cry, the LPP would demand in the next Ontario election we divide up constituencies – i.e., that the Liberals get so many constituencies and the LPP so many constituencies, unopposed. This would be a considerable advantage to weak parties like the Ontario Liberal Party and the LPP and the best possible way of weakening the CCF.[5]

Jolliffe's analysis was shared by all members of the party leadership,[6] and undoubtedly accepted by most CCFers, but there were those who could not agree with his conclusions. This fact caused considerable tension and inevitably led to the threat of disciplinary sanctions on those who dissented.

From 1943 to 1945 the Communists in Canada, through the Labour Progressive party and labour organizations, continued to push vigorously for a coalition among the CCF, themselves, and the Liberals. For example, considerable pressure was brought to bear on the CCF to withdraw its candidate in the Grey North by-election to ensure the seat for General McNaughton, the new minister of defence and Liberal party candidate.[7] Two CCF MPPs agreed with the coalition strategy and finally decided to resign from the CCF in opposition to Jolliffe's views. They were Nelson Alles (Essex North) and Leslie Hancock (Wellington North), the first resigning late in 1944, the second early in 1945. Although these resignations caused a certain concern in the party, they were both seen as essentially personal decisions and no significant ruction was caused.[8]

A similar calmness did not prevail in the case of Robert Carlin, MPP from Sudbury. Carlin was elected to the legislature in 1943 but unlike many he was re-elected in 1945. It was during this second term while Jolliffe was out of the assembly that the difficulty with Carlin emerged. While serving as MPP Carlin was also an executive board member for the International Union of Mine, Mill, and Smelter Workers of America from Canada. As such he was an important figure in the industrial union movement and his importance was enhanced by his obvious popularity in Sudbury which had translated into his legislative seat. Carlin's union "Mine-Mill," was believed to be in the hands of members of the Communist party of the United States and certainly it consistently opposed the political program of the CIO. As a result Carlin, as a CCF MPP, was particularly vulnerable to political initiatives made by the LPP and by Communist sympathizers in trade unions.[9] Millard wrote to him about this.

More than three years ago ... we discussed at length the whole question of Communist influence and control in the Canadian labour movement, especially in your union. You maintained then – and you appear to hold the same opinion still – that you could succeed in building your union by using appeasement policies between union-CCF forces on the one hand and Communist agents on the other ... I left Sudbury very discouraged. I was quite sure that you were adopting an attitude toward Communist party people which would result in their control of the Mine-Mill union in Canada and your personal subservience, or if they failed in their purpose, the wrecking of all you and your friends in that union and the Congress it struggled to build. You will remember that I urged you to rid your union of well known Communist party people in Canada and to use your influence to change your international leadership. In a very personal sense I very deeply regret that you did not feel free to accept my advice.[10]

The view that Carlin and the whole of the Mine-Mill leadership in Canada were coming more and more under Communist influence gradually became more widespread. By 1948 the Ontario CCF leadership was persuaded that Carlin was considering the interests of the Communist party both in his own union and in a wider political sense. Moreover, by 1948 a deep and bitter split had developed in Mine-Mill between those who supported Carlin's leadership and those who were determined to defeat the individuals they believed to be Communists or Communist sympathizers. In working towards this goal within Mine-Mill the anti-Communist forces received support from both the Canadian Congress of Labour and the Steelworkers. In addition this anti-Communist movement was supported by large numbers of rank and file of members of Mine-Mill and included a number of important subsidiary leaders of the union, such as Ralph Carlin, Robert Carlin's brother.

By 1948 these two forces, the CCF leadership and the anti-Communist group in Mine-Mill, had come together. In the same year both the Trades and Labour Congress and the Canadian Congress of Labour moved to discipline those unions they felt had become dominated by Communist leaders. Mine-Mill was formally expelled from the congress in 1949.[11] Given all these forces, the situation as it existed could not long continue.

Following a suggestion made by Carlin's opponents in northern Ontario,[12] members of the provincial executive decided to interview Carlin to determine whether they should again endorse him as the official CCF candidate in Sudbury for the 1948 election. This meeting, held 13 April 1948, resulted, after some very close questioning of Carlin, particularly by Millard, Jolliffe, and Brewin, in a decision to deny Carlin endorsation.[13] Carlin's supporters reacted swiftly, declaring that if the decision was put into effect they would run independent candidates in Sudbury, Timiskaming, and South Cochrane with the intention of splitting the labour vote and defeating the CCF in those seats.[14] The executive temporized for a week in the face of these threats but then proceeded to make it clear that Carlin would not be accepted as an official CCF candidate and that if he persisted in his stated intention of running in any event he would be automatically expelled from the party. Carlin insisted that he had been nominated by the Sudbury CCF association as a candidate and he would continue to seek re-election as a CCFer. On 29 May 1948 the Sudbury Riding Association was officially notified by Morden Lazarus, provincial secretary, that as a consequence of this stated intention Carlin was no longer to be considered a member of the CCF.[15] Carlin contested the general election as an independent CCF candidate; he lost the seat but placed a close second. The official CCF candidate garnered few votes and placed a dismal fourth.

Carlin's expulsion was symbolically very important for the party. The process of the party's alienation from Carlin was lengthy and aroused strong emotions in both those who supported Carlin and those who felt that his renomination as an official candidate was a political impossibility. The former generally sympathized with the view that all progressive forces should unite against the "reactionaries," particularly Conservative party reactionaries, while the latter group came more and more to believe that such a strategy would ultimately deliver the CCF and the labour movement into the hands of the Communist party. Carlin symbolized this fundamental division and his expulsion symbolized the victory of those who believed that it was important to have, in Doc Ames's words, "no truck nor trade with the Communists." It is of some importance to note that Carlin himself was well liked both by those who supported him and by those who disagreed with his political strategy. Despite his personal popularity, the Ontario CCF decided that Carlin was in the long term a political liability and the executive set aside personal considerations to rid itself of that perceived liability.

The consequence of Carlin's expulsion was to align the Ontario CCF firmly with those forces in the Canadian labour movement and in the democratic left generally who were determined to rout out Communists from all positions of political influence. By 1950 the Provincial Council was able to pass a resolution stating: "This provincial council asks all CCF members to respect the national policy of this party by taking the utmost care to refrain from giving or appearing to give, directly or indirectly, any kind of encouragement or assistance to representatives of the Communist party in the trade unions or in any other organization wherever they may be found."[16] Woodsworth's anti-united front policy had completely triumphed and the measure of its triumph was the logical desire found in the CCF to destroy all Communist party influence in Canada.

Jolliffe notes that the struggle with the Communists had its costs. "A large part of the valuable time of our most useful and valuable people was spent in battling the LPP influence in the unions. An enormous amount of time and energy was wasted in these struggles."[17] Yet he concludes that for the CCF the struggle, though wasteful, was inevitable. It had its own internal dynamics. Jolliffe argues:

The cold war mentality had little or nothing to do with [the purge of Communists in the trade union movement] in this country. It did in the United States where the Communists, incidentally, were not nearly as strong in the unions as in Canada. Canada attracted very able people and they collared some pretty influential spots in the labour movement union including the office of secretary-treasurer of the Trades and Labour Congress ... there were these [able men] scattered all over the country in key positions. Now if they had behaved in a legitimate way and if they had consistently served the interests of their people and their unions as some academics seem to believe, they'd be there yet. They were thrown out because it became increasingly apparent that they'd be satisfied with nothing less than control, and one of their principal objectives was to exclude the CCF and destroy the CCF influence in the labour movement. In short, they were thrown out, reluctantly, only because they had become such a disruptive influence that the Canadian trade union movement just couldn't live with them any longer. It had nothing to do with the cold war except in this sense: they had shown their hand repeatedly by taking a pro-Russian line where it was indefensible, as in their opposition to the Marshall Plan and in their attempt to sabotage the delivery of Marshall Plan supplies. This was a give-away, and it was not lost on active trade unionists in the labour movement.[18]

Although the victory of those who opposed Communist influence in the CCF and the trade union movement was complete in the Ontario party, nonetheless in the 1950s and early 1960s the party found itself in the toils of expulsions and other forms of disciplinary action on several occasions. By this point the party was no longer concerned about Communist infiltration. Instead, it was bothered by a small sectarian group whose leaders had formed the Revolutionary Workers Party (RWP) after the Second World War. After the dissolution of that party, the members were simply identified as Trotskyists or Trotskyites. The leader of this group, Ross Dowson, had his application for CCF membership accepted by the High Park Riding Association, but it was turned down by the provincial executive on 23 September 1953.[19] This decision was later upheld by the Provincial Council and the provincial convention. The decision to reject Dowson's membership caused little distress in the party. As Ken Bryden, then provincial secretary, is reported to have said at the council meeting which considered the executive's recommendation for rejection,

A person who is dedicated to the struggles which the RWP when it existed was dedicated could not conscientiously subscribe to the principles and policies of the CCF. He said that he would be prepared (even though with considerable misgiving) to accept the application of a person such as Dowson if that person was prepared to make an unequivocal statement to the effect that he had repudiated his former Trotskyist philosophy and now accepted the democratic socialist philosophy of the CCF. Dowson, however, had made it abundantly clear, both orally and in writing, that he was not prepared to do any such thing.[20]

All but one member of the council agreed with these sentiments, and since Dowson was clearly the leader of this Trotskyist group and since he had not been a member of the CCF, the decision to refuse his membership was accepted with equanimity.

The decision taken a year later to expel from the party certain members who were said to have associated with Dowson and his Trotskyist group raised considerably more controversy. The sequence of events was as follows. A member of the Trotskyists, Leslie Dawson, approached Bryden with an offer to provide information on members of the Trotskyist organization who were also members of the CCF. Bryden informed the executive that this information existed and that Dawson was prepared to be questioned. The executive appointed a committee, consisting of Bryden, George Grube, and William Newcombe, to question Dawson and to examine the information he provided. The committee reported that fifteen individuals, thirteen in Toronto ridings, held dual membership in the CCF and the Trotskyist group. The executive then decided that written charges of dual membership should be sent to each by registered mail and that the charges would be placed on the agenda of the next Provincial Council meeting at which those accused of dual membership were invited to appear. In addition a copy of each charge was made available to the secretaries of those ridings affected and the ridings were notified that they could send an observer to the council meeting when the charges were considered. Before the Provincial Council meeting, the Toronto and District CCF Council appointed a committee of three to interview the provincial executive about the charges. At the Provincial Council meeting on 30 and 31 October 1954 charges against eight persons who had appeared were heard with most of the evidence against them being supplied by Dawson. Of the eight members charged, one was "acquitted." The Provincial Council appointed another committee, consisting of George Grube as chairman, Andrew Brewin, Pat Lawlor, and Harry Hatfield, to hear evidence in the cases of the seven individuals who had failed to attend the council meeting. This committee met on 25 and 26 November and found that all seven were guilty of being members of another political party which, it stated, was "contrary to Article III, Section (iv) of the Constitution and that under Article III, Section (iv) of the Constitution their membership in another political party cancels their membership in the CCF and they are therefore not members of the CCF." The executive approved all sections of the committee's report unanimously and this report was sustained by the Provincial Council and ultimately by the convention.[21]

This elaborate procedure had the effect of persuading the majority of members of the party that it was a fair one and that the Trotskyists deserved expulsion.[22] Ross Dowson's group continued to plague the Ontario party for some years after and although the executive was always required to justify any action it took against individuals, it continued to have little trouble in either refusing memberships or expelling those who it believed were also active members of Dowson's new group, the League for Socialist Action (LSA).

Despite this outcome, the executive was consistently reluctant to expel one or two individuals who it believed were Trotskyists and preferred instead that local riding associations handle these "difficult people" by themselves. After the formation of the New Democratic Party, however, a number of individuals associated themselves with Dowson and at the same time were members of the Young New Democrats. On two occasions in the 1960s the Ontario party acted to rid itself of those it considered were key trouble-makers.

The first occasion was in 1963 and here the executive followed a complex procedure very similar to that used in 1954. A subcommittee of the executive first met to consider charges against the individuals; the subcommittee reported to the executive, who decided that expulsions were necessary; the Provincial Council met to consider the decision and authorized the executive to take further action. The executive formally "tried" the individuals involved and ten of the eleven individuals named in the original subcommittee report were in fact expelled. The expulsions were upheld by an overwhelming majority at the Provincial Council.[23]

The second wave of expulsions occurred in 1967. Over a period of two years all the officers of the Ontario Young New Democrats (OYND) had come to believe that a very significant number of OYND members had also become members of the League for Socialist Action and that they took instruction from the LSA leadership. At an OYND executive meeting held 15 February 1967 the youth executive discussed the political activities of sixty-eight individuals and decided that forty-seven of them should be expelled from the party.[24] The provincial executive of the party decided not to proceed with such a decimation of the OYND, but it agreed with the executive that Trotskyist influence was growing in the youth organization and substituted a more modest decision to refuse the memberships of twelve individuals who were believed to be the key Trotskyists active in the OYND. A resolution condemning the action of the executive in "expelling" these twelve people was brought to the 11 and 12 May Provincial Council meeting. However, a substitute resolution endorsing the executive's decision was overwhelmingly carried, and Trotskyist activities soon ceased to be a significant factor in the Ontario NDP.

The next disciplinary issue was not decided with such few tears. During the late spring and early summer of 1969, Jim Laxer, a doctoral student in the Department of History at Queen's University, organized several meetings to draft a statement of socialist and nationalist principles to be presented to the convention of the federal party scheduled for Winnipeg later that year. Since the early 1960s, certainly before it was fashionable, Laxer had been one of those Canadian intellectuals who strongly believed that Canada had become dominated by the United States and that this relationship was ultimately detrimental to the best interests of the Canadian people. Unlike many Canadian nationalists, however, Laxer, who was the product of an intellectual Marxist family, came to the view that only through the development of a socialist economy and society would Canadians be able to assert themselves vis-à-vis the United States. Laxer very effectively promoted this view at a number of seminars and other symposia, as well as in private conversation.

By 1969 a number of Canadians connected with the universities had become persuaded that socialism, indeed, was Canada's only hope of escaping the horrors of continentalism. Among the converts to this view was Professor Mel Watkins of the Department of Political Economy at the University of Toronto, who had served as chairman of a federal government task force to investigate the impact of the United States on the Canadian economy. Until 1969 Watkins had firmly advocated a strategy of strengthening Canadian capitalism as the means of lessening American influence.[25] However, Watkins experienced a sudden conversion to the view that socialism was a prerequisite for Canadian economic independence, and he happily joined the meetings which considered this statement of principles.

Others who helped prepare the statement included Gerry Caplan; Don Taylor, the assistant research director of the United Steelworkers; and Ed Broadbent, later federal leader of the NDP. They, and several other individuals who, like them, had been long-time members of the party, were particularly keen about the Laxer-Watkins initiative because of what they sensed was a growing feeling that the NDP, primarily the federal NDP, had become stodgy and unimaginative and that a bolder program, what some would describe as a more thoroughgoing left-wing socialist program, was needed. The statement, which was entitled "For an Independent Socialist Canada" and which came to be known as the "Watkins Manifesto,"[26] called for the ending of American economic domination in Canada by a strategy of massive industrial nationalization.

The manifesto attracted considerable initial support. Ninety-four individuals signed it. These included almost the whole leadership of the British Columbia party and a number of key individuals in the federal party.[27] Yet, without exception, all the party notables in the Ontario NDP, including Ed Broadbent, who had written much of the document, and Stephen Lewis, who was then perceived as the spokesman of the "left" in the province, declined to add their signatures. Moreover, when it became clear that Laxer and Watkins did not intend to permit the manifesto to be dealt with simply as a discussion paper, a number of signatories repudiated it and supported an alternative resolution which had been drafted by David Lewis and Charles Taylor (who, in fact had signed the manifesto) and was presented by the National Council. An intense and lively debate took place at the 1969 convention on the issues raised in the manifesto, and although it attracted considerable support, it was finally defeated by a vote of over two to one.

Unlike other left-wing coalitions which emerged at the time of party conventions, the Waffle group, as it came to be known,[28] did not disappear. Instead Laxer and Watkins organized within the party to create a group which would continue to press for the position developed in the manifesto and which would at the same time continue to oppose the views of the party leadership. The stage was set for an inevitable confrontation in the Ontario NDP.

The confrontation was inevitable, however, only because the Waffle stayed in existence as an organized group. Initially there was considerable sympathy for the manifesto. As Stephen Lewis recalls: "I know that I came fairly close to signing that original document myself because I felt I had a similar view of the left. I think I was scared off by David [Lewis]. I think it was a severe parental admonition – he scared me off – and it was ironic that I didn't rebel by signing ... it was only after that that I became persuaded in my own mind that it really was going to be bad for the party."[29] Others, without that parental guidance, although often with David Lewis's help, similarly concluded that the Waffle, although it had been a good thing in the beginning, now threatened the very existence of the party, or at least the party as the leadership and their allies in the riding associations and trade unions understood it.[30]

The crisis did not come until 1972. From 1969 to 1972 the Waffle continued to grow and to focus all party debates on its own concerns. It won a number of symbolic victories, the most notable of which was Laxer's second-place finish in the federal leadership race with David Lewis in 1971. This, combined with victories on many resolutions presented at the 1970 Ontario convention and at the 1971 federal convention, gave Laxer, Watkins, and all those associated with the Waffle the encouragement to continue to oppose the party establishment.

Finally, after considerable pressure from key trade unionists and from certain riding associations, particularly Hamilton Mountain, Stephen Lewis decided that it was necessary for him as leader to deal frankly and publicly with the whole question of the Waffle group and its impact on the Ontario party. In a powerful and emotional speech Lewis insisted that the situation between the Waffle and the party could not continue. In part he stated:

There has crept into the party evidence of acrimony and bitterness without precedent. I have attended meetings in the last few months which I find hard to believe – meetings where hurtful and wounding things have seethed to the surface from all sides. There is a strong polarization under way; there is evidence of distrust and intolerance. People quick to anger, groups meeting separately, secretly. Nominations fought on a pro or anti-Waffle basis; the energies of a powerful political movement drained in a fruitless series of skirmishes. It's just not characteristic of our party and it leaves our people bewildered and lost. When the solidarity goes, confusion takes over ...

... As a matter of fact, I think it's fair to say that for most people who are apprehensive about the Waffle, the focus tends to be on the structure. That seems to me a legitimate focus – if truth be known, some Wafflers are also concerned. It's not really a very difficult set of propositions to state: To what extent can the New Democratic Party accommodate a highly organized internal group whose structures and activities are often competitive with those of the party?[31]

Following Lewis's speech a stunned Provincial Council voted to direct the executive to prepare a statement outlining the responsibilities and obligations of members of the party. The vote was 157 to 62. The executive quickly established a commission to draft the statement. It consisted of the president, Gordon Vichert; the treasurer, John Brewin; and Gerry Caplan. The commission held regional meetings in Thunder Bay, Sudbury, Timmins, Ottawa, London, and Toronto, and its report states, "approximately 500 persons attended these meetings. One hundred and three written briefs were received and more than one hundred persons made oral presentations."[32] Never before had a question of the internal government of the party received such intense consideration from so many members of the party.

After finishing its investigation, the commission concluded:

We undertook our commission from the executive with the hope that a formula could be found for peace and tolerance within the party. While recognizing the depth of feelings surrounding the Waffle, we hoped that the basic loyalty of members to the party would enable us to find an amicable compromise. Regretfully we have concluded that such a compromise is impossible because the Waffle, in demanding their right to continue as an organized opposition within the party, is making an unacceptable demand of the party.[33]

The commission went on to make several recommendations, only one of which was seen as important by both Waffle and anti-Waffle forces and which began an even more intense and acrimonious debate in the party. That recommendation was:

It is contrary to the spirit and meaning of the constitution of the New Democratic Party for members to participate actively in a group organized on a continuing basis for the express purpose of securing fundamental changes in the strategies, structure, leadership, policies, and principles of the party.

The Waffle has become such a group and must therefore be dissolved as soon as possible.

Any member of the party who thereafter actively participates in the group described in the first paragraph of this resolution will be subject to the disciplinary provisions of the constitution.[34]

Vichert explains its impact:

Certainly I became convinced of two things. First of all ... my background in the Baptist church where my father fought his whole life against the fundamentalists, the literal interpreters of the Bible, served me well because I recognized the same kind of stridency, the same kind of intolerance on the part of the Waffle, that I knew from childhood and I knew there was no compromising with fundamentalists. They had the divine word and that was it. Over and over again, wherever we went, we were subjected to that kind of blood test on the part of the Waffle who set up its own strict interpretation of what the policy of the party ought to be, and then called everyone a heathen who didn't adhere to those policies ...

... The second thing that became increasingly evident was that the Waffle was really being used for power; that really we were faced with an attempt to take over the party in the interests of a group within the party – and that was articulated again in different forms. It was very clear that we were not only dealing here with an ideological movement but with a movement for the leadership of Jim Laxer and Mel Watkins, for their own prestige and power within the party, and that seemed to us intolerable.[35]

The executive adopted the commission's report, Waffle members of the executive walked out of the meeting, and war was declared. The party was in a complete turmoil – charges, countercharges, demands for expulsion, demands for the resignation of the executive, were flying in all directions. As Vichert explains:

The party, by and large, took fright because it's not natural for a party like this to engage in what was bound to be interpreted as an ideological purge. The party consists basically of pretty decent people, who don't like to tell other decent people that they must stop doing what they are doing, that they must stop thinking the thoughts they are thinking, and that sort of thing. So all those people who hadn't had the experience of going around the province and listening to the Waffle abuse assumed that there must be some compromise available between the hard-line commissioners and the Waffle. It's part of the standard liberal mythology of North America in which we are all steeped that there always has to be a middle road. In this case it just didn't happen to be.[36]

The crisis continued and deepened. There was no consensus, either pro-Waffle or anti-Waffle. Some members of the Waffle took fright themselves and sought a compromise with the rest of the party which would allow them to maintain their organization but which would see that organization become less publicly active between conventions.[37] The majority of the Waffle refused to consider any compromise and decided that the commission's report could be defeated at the Provincial Council. They concluded:

In the view of Waffle supporters, the edict of the Vichert-Brewin-Caplan commission that the Waffle must disband is a rejection of an important part of our party's history for the past three years. It is an untenable attempt on the part of some to turn the clock back to the days of non-debate in the party ... The Waffle group will not disband and give up its efforts to contribute to the party and the Canadian Socialist movement. Party members who wish to avoid a purge should urge their ridings and affiliated locals to oppose the executive recommendation.[38]

More important than the divisions within the Waffle were the divisions among New Democrats who did not support the Waffle. Some, particularly trade unionists, felt that the report was long overdue and that it was imperative that it be passed. Others, including a number of key party leaders, were concerned that the report had gone too far, that its solution was too draconian, and that some middle ground had to be found. An explanation of this position is found in a letter from Walter Pitman and John Harney to those on the party mailing list.

The provincial executive proposal recommending the dissolution of the Waffle, a recommendation which, we believe, was made in good faith but under the intense pressure which has existed in the party over the last several months now, has met with rejection or distaste from a large section of the party and will be understood by the public as a purge at worst or a suppression of dissent at best.

Not only Ontario, but all of Canada, is watching to see how a socialist party can resolve its differences, for many citizens will not put the government of their country in the hands of a party which cannot deal with its own affairs in a decent, humane and effective fashion.

It is essential that a common ground be found ...

There have been a number of proposals. They can generally be categorized either in the "rules of behaviour" approach or an "affiliation-association" approach. So far, all have failed to obtain a broad and general support by themselves. One of the writers of this letter, Walter Pitman, has suggested proposals of both kinds, the other, John Harney, has urged the adoption of the latter kind, but both now come together to appeal to all delegates to seek compromise and be prepared to consider supporting either "rules" or "association" in the effort to find a common ground for all.[39]

Confusion reigned in the debate and no one was certain what the outcome at the Provincial Council would be. Stephen Lewis and the Ontario party leadership were under intense pressure from key party figures throughout the country, including Davis Lewis, now federal leader, to abandon the central demand that the Waffle disband or face expulsion. A compromise resolution was prepared by Gordon Vichert and Gerry Caplan and presented to a meeting held in Peterborough. Though it condemned certain activities of Waffle members, the proposal fell short of demanding the complete dissolution of the group. Stephen Lewis supported this Peterborough compromise and an emergency meeting of the Administrative Committee of the executive was called to consider this new proposal so that it might be presented to the executive and ultimately to the council. The Administrative Committee, however, deeply influenced by Lynn Williams of the Steelworkers, decided it preferred the original recommendation and refused to permit the executive to be called together to consider any new proposal.[40]

Stephen Lewis has described in some detail the intense pressures of those weeks of indecision in the party.

We decided the Waffle had to be disbanded for two reasons. Primarily we [the leadership] were persuaded that the Waffle was destroying the party, both in its internal operation morale and also in the external perceptions of the party. Partly also, and there is no use denying it, there was an unstated ultimatum from the trade union movement which weighed very heavily on the party leadership ... for some people ... it was terrifying that the trade union movement should be threatening to tell the party to shove it, that they weren't going to continue to be a part as long as people like Watkins and Laxer called the shots ...

... there were two meetings at the Ontario Federation of Labour building which I would sooner forget at which father and son were at bitter loggerheads … There was one meeting attended by David, by Mahoney, by Dowling, by Larry Sefton, by Lynn, by Don Taylor, by Montgomery, by Bud Clark, Sam Fox, David Archer, Dennis, Vichert, and myself at which David made a strong appeal that we shouldn't do it, that we should lay off. I was taking an absolutely intransigent line; so was Sefton; so was Williams. McDermott was touch and go. McDermott wasn't sure – he wanted to move the Waffle out but he didn't want to offend the old man – none of them did. It was the first time in my life with David that I had ever seen him at odds with the leadership of the trade union movement that way.[41]

… After the report came out, party reaction was so violent and so strong that we were headed for a close outcome on the vote and that for us was a defeat. Defeat didn't have to be measured by winning or losing absolutely. It could be measured by the size of the opposition strength, and it was clear that the report was just engendering so much antagonism that the party was cohering against it and its recommendation and that the trade union movement was cohering for it, and that we were heading for one of the most unspeakable confrontations in the party's history … I was in the position of desperately trying to persuade the trade unionists that alternative wording had to be found – there had to be a way of making this acceptable to the decent, so-called middle of the party. Lynn Williams, who was the bargainer for the trade union movement, was treating me like INCO and he just wasn't moving an inch. There were midnight meetings at the Royal York Hotel, the Westbury Hotel. I can remember an absolutely impossible meeting with Larry [Sefton] and Lynn [Williams] one afternoon, with Larry, who I knew was dying of cancer, saying, "You have no right to come to me as leader of the party and ask me to jettison everything that is important about the party and my life." That was the clear message; those weren't the exact words but that was the clear message. Larry said to me that he and others had fought for this party, built it, fought the Communists in the trade union movement, had brought it to this point today, and you're asking me to give in to these pathological guys, I won't …

I nearly disintegrated. Really, it was just awful. I went back to Michelle [Lewis], and said, "It's all over. We're going to Orillia. The party is going to absolutely disintegrate and there is nothing that can be done about it because there's just no way. I can't do that with Larry; I can't tell him he's wrong because I think he's probably right. He recapitulated in five poignant, savage minutes his whole history in the party – what he and a million others had done for it and why they were being kicked in the teeth and they would not allow it." The only thing that kept me sort of in the mediating role, if that's what it was called, was a phone call from Dennis [McDermott], who said, "They'll [the Steelworkers' leadership] take you right up to the brink, but if you come up with anything, they'll back off, so don't despair."

... So then of course there was this extraordinary assemblage of the middle. I mean really, they were the most remarkable group, Broadbent and Harney and Pitman, the Pattersons, and we went to the Sunday meeting [after the Administrative Committee decision] and told them, "It's just no go. We cannot move the trade union movement. You have to know that and either you are going to come down with them for the future of the party or you're going to come down against them" ... Well, Broadbent came up with the alternative wording which was of course identical with the original wording in meaning. Vichert was speechless. Caplan left the room because he couldn't believe what was happening, and I actually said to them, "Do you not realize that what you are advocating here is identical with the effects of the report from John [Brewin], Gord [Vichert], and Gerry [Caplan]." No, they saw it as different and I said that no one in the world could interpret it differently. But they said, no, it was different, so I said that I'd take it up with the trade unions. I took it back to Lynn and Lynn threw me out of his office. He said he was not prepared to accept a comma amended, so I phoned and begged and I pleaded – he would have nothing to do with me. On Friday I finally got through to him, and he made a one-adjective amendment, which was then acceptable to the Pattersons and Broadbent and Morton and others. Then Lynn said to me that he didn't know whether it could be sold to the trade union movement and I told him that was nonsense. I didn't realize then, what I realized subsequently, that he had in fact taken it so far down the road that to alter any of it would run into great resistance ... The night before the council meeting, at the beer-drinking hall where the dance was after the executive meeting, the trade union delegates were brought into the backroom in groups of between fifteen and twenty. Pilkey was there, Lynn was there, Bob McKenzie was there. They would talk to the delegates to explain the change in the report and why it was acceptable to them ... I was at the hall from 9:00 PM until 3:00 in the morning ... I went in to reinforce the decision that had been made and in a couple of those groups ... all hell broke loose.[42]

The climax came on 23 June 1972 at the Provincial Council meeting held in the small Ontario town of Orillia. The so called Riverdale compromise, which replaced the Peterborough compromise and which insisted that the Waffle disband, was passed by a vote of 217 to 88.[43] After the meeting Waffle leaders took two months to decide what to do. Finally the majority of them, under the leadership of Laxer and Watkins, decided to leave the party and form their own organization called the Movement for an Independent Socialist Canada, while a minority, though completely opposed to the Ontario leadership, decided to stay as individual party members. The Waffle era in the Ontario NDP was over.[44]

Changes in the party in terms of the exercise of discipline are evident. In dealing with the Communists and the Trotskyists the party leadership was able to act reasonably, swiftly, and effectively. It was united in its action and most of the secondary leadership was prepared to follow its lead. There was dissent, but that dissent was kept inside the party for the most part, with little public attention being focused on the internal debate. The party leadership knew its own mind and its actions reflected that consensus. By the 1970s it was no longer possible for severe political conflicts within the party to escape the attention of the media – the Waffle controversy engendered considerable publicity and party leaders were concerned about the nature of the attention the dispute received. Partly as a result, the leadership was greatly divided about the appropriate course of action. Schemes of all sorts were advanced, and as they attracted media attention, they were seriously considered by various groupings within the party. The new left doctrines of participatory democracy had made many party members suspicious of the control of formally elected bodies, such as the executive and the council, and consequently they were not prepared simply to "follow the leader." Undoubtedly this dissension in the party reflected similar tensions in Ontario society as a whole. Ontario had come to heed a multitude of metropolitical cultural masters, American, British, European, and others, and Ontario society reflected the diversity of socio-cultural opinion and tradition to which its citizens subscribed. In handling the Waffle, the Ontario NDP reflected a growing anarchistic impulse that derives from the combination of a logical liberalism and a colonialism of many masters.[45]

In the final analysis the Ontario party still acted as it had acted in the past – its actions were predictable, as would be expected from a stable personality. At the same time it acted in a very different context and the character of its disciplinary action reflected that changed context. Like many human individuals, the party, as it came to maturity, to a knowledge of a wider world, was still recognizable as the same person it always had been. But the greater complexity of its wider environment made the party less certain about the right course to follow, and it becomes more difficult for an observer to predict its behaviour.

PART FOUR

A Conclusion

9

The Significance of
Party Personality

From the late 1930s to the 1950s a number of scholars – social philosophers and social scientists – all deeply influenced by Max Weber's social interactionist writings, began to question and combat the popularity of Marxist economic determinism with an alternative theory of social behaviour. Two social mechanisms held considerable attraction for such a purpose. The first was the free market tending to equilibrium; the second, the maintenance in a community of a prevailing ethical religion.

It is easy to understand why the doctrines of the marketplace, as developed by neo-classical economists, had a considerable fascination for these scholars. A market which is seen to regulate itself automatically by the operation of the impersonal forces of supply and demand suggests a wider vision of societal self-regulation in which impersonal rules and institutions automatically control the competing social desires of individual citizens. As in the market, however, participants in society are not merely subject to these impersonal forces but can, by their own actions, influence outcomes. The free market in its broad context implies individual choice; its tendency to equilibrium implies that the outcome of a multitude of individual choices will be an observable order.

The maintenance of a prevailing ethical religion is also fundamentally concerned with social order. This is so because a widely accepted public religion implies, in its ethical life, that its adherents and all those it influences will share sufficient norms and values to predicate orderly behaviour. A public religion, whether or not of a transcendental character, assumes the existence of wilful individuals (individuals who "choose" one course of action over some other course of action), who, in a social circumstance, must inevitably "will" conflicting ends and therefore must inevitably seek to eliminate other wills, and thereby society, unless they accept instruction implicit in the ethical rules of public religion. The maintenance of religion, then, is the sine qua non of social order.

The Marxists also focus on social order. For them, the laws of history inexorably change a prevailing order and create a new order. For the anti-Marxist scholars, whose leader was Talcott Parsons,[1] order is not determined by history or by factors of production. It is created, and re-created, in society by individuals exercising choices.

David Easton has developed these Parsonian themes in political science. Easton's political system provides order by automatic regulatory processes, which, if they break down, herald the destruction of the system.[2] Easton's later interest in childhood socialization was undertaken, in part, to show that the successful intergenerational transmission of certain fundamental social norms serves to maintain the regulatory processes of the political system by providing external support for key political institutions.[3]

Ironically, at the same time as these "grand theories" of social order were being expounded and became fashionable, the free market tending to equilibrium was seen to fail. John Maynard Keynes was the progenitor of this perception of failure with his argument that state intervention in a capitalist economy was necessary and desirable.[4] Kenneth Galbraith, in *The Affluent Society* and in subsequent books, completed the shattering of the free market illusion by demonstrating that both governments and corporations possessed and used monopolistic powers.[5] Advocates of the market, such as Milton Friedman, agreed that even in the United States the free market economy had disappeared.[6]

Simultaneously, the public religion of North America was perceived to have collapsed. David Riesman and his colleagues argued that the traditional norms internalized by individuals had so little impact on most people that the majority were directed to behave in a particular way, not by their own beliefs, but rather by observation and by imitation of the behaviour of others.[7] More recently Samuel Beer has noted the decline of public religion or of shared moral values and suggested that this inevitably is a cause of what he terms "the disorders of modernity," disorders which he sees as limiting, indeed prohibiting, genuine individual choice.[8]

Yet while the free market and public religion are perceived to have failed, so Marxism is also perceived as a failure. The laws of historical development are violated throughout the world in Communist as well as non-Communist countries. Ennui remains. But ennui, the feeling of helplessness and hopelessness is, by definition, a subjective state; an objective external reality also continues, and a part of that reality is social institutions.

Institutions, social, cultural, economic, and political, are shaped and changed by forces about them, but except by some solipsistic sleight of hand, they have a fundamental reality and provide the external world with a basic order. Institutions, because they are made up of human individuals, by definition reflect their socio-cultural milieu; because of their objective reality, because they are perceived to exist and do exist, they also affect that socio-cultural milieu. As Ostrogorski noted of party organizations in nineteenth-century England: "They have a fundamental effect on human individuals because they are a 'device' for keeping in check the free impulses of the members of society after the State has been reduced."[9] As the link, therefore, between individuals and social order, institutions must be explained and understood by social science.

More specifically it is necessary to understand political parties because in their institutional existence they symbolize a particular order, but at the same time, unlike the state, they are not universal agents of order and so permit individuals to accept or reject them in terms of their fundamental conceptions of an ordered society. As institutions, parties link individuals who make choices with an objective ordered reality.

In this context, parties are not to be understood as empty vessels filled by the impersonal forces of the external environment. At the same time parties cannot be understood apart from their socio-cultural milieu. It is helpful, therefore, to consider parties, and all institutions, as individuals in order to understand and explain their characteristics apart from some determinist framework. It is necessary because no determinist framework, including a Marxist one, is satisfactory, and necessary because interactionist frameworks based on the free market tending to equilibrium or the internalization of prevailing religious norms have also become unsatisfying as a consequence of their antecedent assumptions. The consideration of parties as individuals, with the attendant consideration of the principles of individual psychology, provides a means of examining the fundamental problem of the link between social order and individual choice.

In this study I have examined the interaction between the Ontario CCF/NDP and the political culture of Ontario. In a sense, therefore, this study has been a biographical examination of the party. Since the CCF/NDP has interacted with its external environment in a particular way, it has been possible, by examining those particularities, to define and, hence, understand the CCF/NDP in Ontario. In terms of that definition of the party, several conclusions have become manifest. Interestingly, these conclusions about the Ontario CCF/NDP, derived from the interactionist framework of the "party individual," generally contradict the conventional wisdoms. The most important conclusions to emerge from this study have been:

1 The description of the party's stages of development provides a convenient framework for the analysis of party character. The comparison between the party's stages of development and those of the human individual indicates a pattern of development which ends, but need not have ended, with a consciousness in the Ontario CCF/NDP of wholeness and integrity – a concept attached to human personal growth by Erikson. This provides considerable support for the secularization hypothesis of party growth, a hypothesis which predicts party survival based on a successful internal adjustment to the constraints of the external milieu.

Even if we set aside any relationship between these descriptive stages of party development and the concept of the institutional personality, the straightforward description of these stages is, in itself, helpful in providing a plausible, empirically based, interpretation for the CCF/NDP of Ontario. In the first place, the stages propounded in chapter 3 are different than those suggested by Caplan and Zakuta and, as suggested previously, imply a different interpretation of party crises and their consequences. Most notably, the evidence suggests that the party continued to expect an early victory after the 1945 electoral setbacks and did not abandon such hope until 1951 and, in addition, that the party's electoral self-confidence was not immediately restored in Ontario after the formation of the NDP in 1961.

2 The analysis of the party's program, that is, of successive expressions of that program, contradicts the usual view that the Ontario CCF/NDP became ideologically more conservative, or "right wing," with each succeeding year. Considerable evidence has been offered which indicates that on matters of substantial ideological concern for democratic socialists the party program, in its various

guises, showed a remarkable continuity from the 1930s to the 1970s. There were, however, two areas of important change. First, the party, in recognizing the growing importance from 1960 onwards of provincial governments, was less inclined to advocate centralist solutions to social and economic problems. More important, the issues which in fact divided the party were those which were not central to socialist ideology, but rather had a symbolic potency in the context of the party's interaction with a wider community. That wider community was divided on such questions as liquor distribution, sixty-cycle hydroelectric power, Canadian support for NATO and for the Korean War, unilateral disarmament, and abortion on demand. The community had also divided on socialist planning but in this instance the party had always been united. In these other instances the party itself was divided, and the divisions symbolized for party members the debate between those who believed principles were more important than public support and those who believed that principles were derived from the felt needs and real necessities of ordinary men and women. This underlying debate is not susceptible to a "right-left" model but the symbolic issues can be associated with either a conservative or liberal view of human nature. Thus, the fashionableness of the issue notwithstanding, its resolution at any given time tended to suggest that the party was becoming conservative or was drifting to the right. In fact, the party generally, but not always, was responding to the conservatism of its immediate milieu – the union class subculture. Yet this response, in terms of fundamental socialist concerns, could be profoundly radical in dealing with the immediate realities and deprivations of an Ontario working-class existence. In short, the issues which divided the party divided it emotionally, not intellectually or ideologically, and the outcome of these divisions must therefore be evaluated in terms of culture, not ideology.

3 Party structures and decision-making processes changed little from those of the early 1940s either in substance or style. This structure was not set at the founding of the party in 1932. It emerged only after the principle of restricted membership implicit in the concept of autonomous clubs had been abandoned and the principle of one annointed spokesman, the provincial leader, had been accepted with Jolliffe's selection in 1942. Once these changes had been made, the conduct of party business had a continuity and sameness which were scarcely altered even by the formation of the

New Democratic Party as a formal alliance between the old CCF, the labour movement, and "liberally minded" individuals. This structural orthodoxy[10] promoted an essential stability for the CCF/NDP of Ontario.

4 This stable personality, that is, the Ontario CCF/NDP, interacts with a particular external environment, suggesting a particular, and different, interpretation of the party's internal political culture, or, to use words associated with the analogy, the party's personality. The party's personality is stable, but not rigid; it is always coherent and recognizable but it responds to external circumstance. Instead of an iron law of oligarchy, or a reciprocal deference structure, there is the law of successful adjustment to the changing external reality of actual success and actual failure. This successful adjustment implies secularization, or, to use Erikson's categories, psycho-social integrity rather than despair. The evidence for this integrated personality is substantial. It includes the fact that more authority in the party came to be exercised by the legislative caucus rather than by the provincial executive. The caucus, as the most secularized or worldly official group within the Ontario CCF/NDP, was never a group born of despair but instead consisted solely of individuals who had enjoyed electoral success. Even the smallest caucus did not experience the fullness of political defeat and despair. Caucus members perceived themselves, as party standard-bearers, to have adjusted successfully to an external reality.

Second, the genuine nature of contests for the post of provincial leader, and the importance of that office, are twin phenomena which suggest that genuine change is possible for the party. If a party's internal life is utterly rigid, if changes can never occur no matter what the external provocation, then the idea of choice is negated. If an individual, human or institutional, cannot choose a course of action, it cannot hope for a more desirable set of circumstances. Even in Eden the Fall is inevitable; in other climes despair ensues. In the Ontario CCF/NDP a genuine choice has been possible; as a result changes, at least in emphasis, have occurred and as a consequence of change, despair is banished or, at least, mitigated.

In this context perhaps the most startling change occurred in the homogeneity of the party leadership and its concomitant ability to impose a particular set of values on the party membership. Until the middle 1960s the socialist generation of leaders which had emerged in the early 1940s had little difficulty in maintaining cohesion among the leadership and control within the party. The essential unanimity of the party about such emotional matters as individual discipline for members who were seen to be linked with either the Communists or the Trotskyists is evidence of this. By the late 1960s, however, this cohesion and control had significantly weakened and the party's confused and disjointed response to the Waffle crisis indicates this. This change was not entirely unpredictable. No single individual ever came to dominate the Ontario CCF/NDP, either intellectually or politically, as David Lewis was seen to have dominated the national CCF.[11] Even David Lewis did not. Moreover, by 1968 a new generation of leaders had come to the fore, which did not, of course, represent a complete break with the past. Many leaders of the socialist generation still played important roles, particularly as activist trade unionists and as members of the party caucus in the House of Commons. More important, many of the new generation had been introduced to the party through the University of Toronto CCF Club in the late 1950s, and their political socialization in a group dominated by the children of key party leaders provided a certain continuity of perspective. At the same time the old cohesion could not be maintained between generations and consequently neither could the old control. Yet the party did not fall apart as a result. It adjusted to the inevitable change in generational leadership and it adjusted to the inevitable differences which must occur between generations raised in a different cultural environment. That adjustment to a new world, though it brought a dissonance in party affairs, reflected a similar dissonance and confusion in the wider community. The difficulties the Ontario NDP had in dealing with the Waffle, so different from the ease with which the party had dealt with Communists and Trotskyists, reflected nonetheless a successful adjustment to a more difficult and less certain society.

Two other conclusions emerge from this study. The first concerns the characterization of Ontario political culture as colonial-liberal with the identification of the party's immediate environment as the union class subculture. The party's ability to avoid despair in the face of an ideologically hostile environment and with the experience of significant electoral defeats is largely explained by the existence of this union class culture – a culture legitimated in large part because the colonial aspect of the larger Ontario community makes easy the acceptance of a British trade union ideology – providing the party with material and psychological succor.

The second is associated with the explanation for the survival of the CCF/NDP of Ontario, which derives from the interactionist theory of party arising from the concept of institutional personality. It is evident that survival was not inevitable. Choices were made and different choices would have yielded a different consequence. A different environment, perhaps one even more hostile, would have made the party's adjustment to external circumstances more difficult, producing, therefore, a very different survival outcome.

In this instance, the development of the concept of an "integrated personality" adjusting to external reality, that is, becoming "secular-ized," has permitted an understanding of the interactive process between the Ontario CCF/NDP and Ontario society, in particular the union class in that society. The party survived because it maintained a "personal" integrity; it remained recognizable as an entity, and yet, at the same time, it adjusted to the particularities of its immediate environment.

It must be noted that party survival does not equal party success. Survival by maintaining integrity and adjusting to the real world may bring success. But, as with human individuals, the process of adjustment may be one which brings a recognition of ultimate limitations and, in an objective sense, of inevitable worldly failure. The question of success or failure for the Ontario CCF/NDP is yet unanswered and unanswerable.

Afterword: 1972 Onwards

Biographers of men and women in public life, if they are wise, will wait until their great personage has passed form the scene either through death or genuine retirement. They will do so because living men and women cannot be counted upon to show a proper obedience to the behaviourial dictates of a biographer's scholarly conclusions touching their own characters. Subsequent events may not only embarrass public figures, but as well they may embarrass those who pretend to understand those public figures and through a biography have committed themselves in print to a particular understanding. Unfortunately the chronicler of an institutional persona does not usually have the same options as other biographers, since human mortality is generally shorter than is institutional mortality. It is because of this that I feel compelled to say something about the nature of my conclusions in the light of events that surrounded the Ontario NDP from 1972 to 1982.

I do not intend a recantation. Indeed I would argue, perhaps a little boldly, that the events to 1982 have confirmed my conclusions, although the structure of my analysis of the CCF/NDP is not so powerful as to have actually predicted these events. Certainly the party remained secular in the sense that it avoided sectarianism by remaining committed to the political process and to winning support in the community at large. Some, of course, might prefer a formulation that the party continued to be opportunistic. But no matter; there is no need here for a moral judgment, only a need to show that in the conduct of both federal and provincial election campaigns, in the conduct of leadership conventions, and in the development of new programs there remained a real consistency between present and past behaviour and present and past attitude.

Specifically, for the Ontario NDP in the decade from 1972 to 1982 the conclusions advanced in the last chapter may be extended in these ways. There were no major changes in the fundamental program, either as passed at conventions or as publicized on the hustings. The platform of the party, however, did not remain constant between elections and its policy did change in interesting ways. The party clearly responded to changed external circumstances and advocated a number of strategies for maintaining employment in Ontario and for redistributing income. Nonetheless, the belief in a mixed economy was certainly not repudiated. Several spokesmen for the party gave different emphases to the importance of the various sectors of the economy and to the desirability of some form of public ownership. Yet fundamentally, the party remained committed to the maintenance of a significant private sector as it also remained committed to some form of central economic planning, now referred to as an industrial strategy. Although fierce debates took place over the economic program, a consensus on these broad principles also existed.

As it was before 1972 the lack of consensus within the party was most manifest around social and cultural issues, issues which symbolized a particular kind of life-style. After 1972 the NDP in Ontario found itself divided on issues such as abortion on demand, the rights of homosexual teachers, the control and direction of municipal police forces, and the reliance in Ontario on nuclear power plants. These specific issues were associated with the emergence of broader social movements advocating feminism, gay liberation, and an environmentally pure society. As with the introduction of margarine and the control of liquor, they were divisive because they related to fundamental beliefs about the nature of the world. It was around these issues, therefore, that the different sections of the party, which self-consciously saw themselves as either left or moderate, rallied. The symbolic issues changed over time but the condition of divisions on social and cultural matters, as opposed to economic matters, remained.

In the 1970s the party remained remarkably consistent in structure and organization as it had for over forty years. Since 1972 there have, of course, been amendments to the constitution of the party. The status of the youth section changed and slightly different representational rules came to apply for conventions, but the forms of membership combined with the representational and nonexclusivity principles have all survived since 1972. The party has not suffered any mid-life crisis that has caused it to change its way of governing itself and governing the behaviour of its members.

Moreover, remarkably few changes occurred in the organizational structure. The party's enhanced ability to raise funds as a result of both the federal Election Expenses Act and a similar provincial act has been reflected in an increased staff. A federal tax credit providing a direct rebate of 75 per cent of the first one hundred dollars contributed to a political party and a lesser percentage for amounts over that dramatically increased the number of people who found it possible to contribute that amount or more to the Ontario NDP. The party responded by employing a full-time fund raiser, with the title of development director, who was responsible for ensuring that opportunities for donating existed in each year, such as at special functions, fund-raising drives, conventions, and membership renewal campaigns. Some of these funds were used to employ organizers who were to ensure that a significant electoral effort would be made in a majority of provincial constituencies. This goal provided a somewhat different focus for organizers. Through the 1960s and early 1970s, the party had attempted to concentrate on those seats it had a chance of winning. But with an expanded organizational staff and more importantly new provincial legislation which provided public money to party campaigns in those constituencies in which the party achieved more than 15 per cent of the vote, there was a concomitant desire to do well in all but the most hopeless constituencies. This approach seemed not only financially desirable but considerably more feasible after an upset victory by George Samis in the eastern Ontario riding of Stormont in October 1974. This victory, combined with Samis's re-election in the general election of 1975 and a parallel upsurge of support for other NDP candidates in traditionally conservative eastern Ontario, encouraged the party to believe, once the Ontario Election Expenses Act was in place after 1975, that it could achieve the 15 per cent minimum in most provincial constituencies.

These changes in organizational strategy, though important, could not be said to change the organizational character of the party. Party organizers and other officials continued to be responsible to an elected provincial secretary and continued to perform the time-honoured tasks of co-ordinating membership drives and other fund-raising campaigns. The party continued to concentrate on key ridings in election campaigns, and although the number of key ridings was expanded as a result of increased resources, the strategy of concentration was not abandoned. The pattern of "peacetime" organization between elections at the provincial office also continued as did the pattern of constituency and regional organization. The party experienced growth, but it no more experienced a change in organizational priorities, with the modest exceptions noted, than it did in programmatic priorities.

One characteristic of the maturing secular party before 1972 was the growing dominance of the full-time politician, in particular, the member of caucus. The importance of the caucus itself has remained; the importance of members of the caucus has been somewhat diluted by the fact that other full-time party activists (including members of the federal caucus from Ontario) have come to exercise a considerable influence since 1972. Perhaps the symbol of this diminution of caucus dominance was the election of Michael Cassidy in 1978 as Ontario leader to replace Stephen Lewis. Cassidy went into the convention with almost no support in the caucus. His chief rival, Ian Deans, had the overwhelming endorsation of most members of caucus, and Mike Breaugh, who finished third, also was more popular than Cassidy among fellow MPPs. Despite his lack of caucus support, Cassidy defeated Deans by a vote of 980 to 809. His election was fairly dramatic evidence that the caucus could not dominate the party; it did not, however, mean a return to the caucus subservience of the 1950s. The caucus never became reconciled to Cassidy, and even before the 1981 provincial election call, several members of caucus actively voiced their displeasure with his leadership. After the party's poor showing in 1981, Cassidy was quickly forced to announce his resignation.

The fact that caucus was no longer as dominant as it had been with Stephen Lewis as leader did not mean that the "iron law of oligarchy" was now inoperative in the Ontario NDP. In some sense the 1970s saw a broadening of the full-time professional cadre of party leaders. It included the caucus, it included members of the federal caucus, and it included an enlarged organizational staff. There was, for example, no widespread change in staff following the election of a new provincial secretary. Indeed, the pattern in the party was for individuals such as Penny Dickens to serve as an organizer or director of organization, then to be elected provincial secretary, and after relinquising that post to return to the full-time organizing staff. Provincial secretaries after 1972, Gordon Brigden, Gordon Vichert, Penny Dickens, Jack Murray, and Michael Lewis, came to the post after having served either as president of the Ontario NDP (Vichert and Murray) or as full-time organizers who had made the party a career. The executive during the 1970s did not regain its former prestige and ability to direct party affairs but the caucus had to surrender some of its new-found authority to the other full-time party functionaries.

From 1972 to 1982 the Ontario NDP had three leaders: Stephen Lewis, Michael Cassidy, and Robert Rae. Following the NDP's reversion to third-party status in the legislature after the 1977 election, Stephen Lewis decided to resign the leadership in order to spend more time with his young family. In addition, Lewis had found the 1977 campaign particularly frustrating and he was not anxious to repeat the gruelling experience of a campaign that, despite planning and good intentions, fails to run smoothly. Lewis subsequently resigned his seat in the legislature and withdrew from active participation in politics.

Three MPPs sought the vacant post. The front-runner, seen by many as the obvious successor, was Ian Deans, first elected as MPP for Wentworth in 1967. Deans, a fireman before his election to the legislature, had been an effective critic of several government departments during his eleven years in the House. Party oligarchs and members of caucus were not wildly enthusiastic about Deans, and many lived in hope that Walter Pitman or some other prominent New Democrat outside the caucus would respond to the call of duty. Nonetheless they generally felt that Deans was the safest bet, certainly safer than the other candidates, Michael Cassidy and Mike Breaugh. The NDP, after all, like the labour movement, believed in seniority, and Cassidy, MPP for Ottawa Centre, and Breaugh, MPP for Oshawa, were not elected to the legislature until 1971 and 1975 respectively. Moreover Cassidy, as a leadership contestant, was burdened with the reputation of being an abrasive individual. Before his election to the legislature he had been a journalist with the prestigious *Financial Times*. His parents, Harry and Bea Cassidy, had both been active in the League for Social Reconstruction. His father had, like many Canadians on the left before and after him, briefly succumbed to the blandishments of the Liberals and had actually contested the Ontario leadership of the Liberals in the early 1950s. This last fact was not well known within the NDP, but other aspects of Cassidy's background, in particular his academic manner, provided him with a considerable handicap. The third candidate, Mike Breaugh, proved to be an attractive personality but he was a relative newcomer in the party and was almost unknown.

At the convention, held in February 1978, the party surprised itself.

Cassidy's intellectual grasp of economic problems enabled him to perform incisively and decisively at the convention. He persuaded delegates that he could turn the economic programs of the party to the same good political advantage as Lewis had turned the social programs. He impressed the delegates with his ability to speak fluent French. In the end he swept past Deans and Breaugh and seized the prize.

Unhappily for Cassidy and the party, the new leader was fairly quickly put on the defensive both in the legislature and in the province as a whole. Some MPPs continued an underground opposition to him, as did some members of the executive who had been chagrined by the spontaneous nature of his support at the convention. Moreover, he was quite naturally unable to establish immediately the same presence in the province as Stephen Lewis had enjoyed because in part he needed time to establish an image and in part he was unable to articulate his concerns in the same fashion as Lewis had. Cassidy, therefore, was never able to put his own stamp on the party and on its hierarchy as had Ted Jolliffe, Don MacDonald, and Stephen Lewis. He was somewhat reluctantly permitted one election, and he quickly acceded to party sentiment after the 1981 results by resigning.

Cassidy announced that he would not seek re-election as leader in April 1981. In that same month the provincial executive decided to hold its regular bi-annual convention in February 1982. Until that convention Cassidy would remain as leader. Again, a number of key members of the party, feeling that there was no one in the caucus, and now a much-reduced caucus, who could be the kind of inspirational leader that Jolliffe, MacDonald and Lewis had been, attempted to persuade Walter Pitman, president of Ryerson Institute, to return to politics and throw his hat in the ring. Pitman proved to be steadfastly unpersuadable, but one other "outsider" was not so reluctant. Bob Rae had already had a meteoric rise within the party. Rae, son of a prominent Canadian diplomat, did not become active in the party until the 1970s when he was still in his late twenties. In a startling upset he defeated John Harney for the party's nomination in a federal by-election in Broadview-Greenwood. This was as safe a seat as any the party had in Ontario and had been held for some years by John Gilbert, who had resigned in order to become a county court judge.

Not only did Rae win the nomination, but he won the by-election and quickly established himself as a formidable presence in the House of Commons where he served as a high-profile finance critic. Many observers were persuaded that Rae would eventually succeed Ed Broadbent as federal leader. Broadbent, however, had no intention of stepping down and a number of senior Ontario activists, led by Don MacDonald and Terry Grier, were persuaded that Rae could best serve the party as provincial leader. They argued, as party activists had always argued, that Ontario was the key to any real national success. After some courting, Rae became persuaded and, with very substantial backing, announced his candidacy. His opponents were Richard Johnston, who had succeeded Stephen Lewis as the MPP for Scarborough West, and Jim Foulds, MPP for Port Arthur. Neither had a chance. The campaign was a triumphal procession for Rae and the convention, a coronation. Moreover, the three candidates proved to be personally compatible and most New Democrats, though they preferred Rae, were not unhappy with the idea of a contest which would provide publicity for the party and which would permit the airing of certain issues. Unlike Cassidy, Rae, with this kind of mandate and support, was in a position to encourage some changes on the executive, including the election of Michael Lewis as provincial secretary and the promotion of an important policy change in lifting the ban on receiving party contributions from small business.

The breakdown of the consensus which had been built by the socialist generation of leaders, in part reflecting the dissonance in the wider Ontario community, continued through the 1970s into the 1980s. The Dowsons and some of their followers from the old Trotskyists were finally admitted to party membership: no principle could be summoned to exclude them. The leadership of the party came to reflect a more plural society and therefore had a less sharp and vivid definition of the role of the party in the world; the socialist generation was retired and many of its sons and daughters who had seemed destined to carry the torch in the early 1970s drifted away to other concerns and other causes. The party, however, had not lost touch with its roots. Of the 136 hosts of the 1982 leaders' levee, no less than 36 had been prominent in the party around the time of its founding in the early 1960s. Many of them in fact had been active in the CCF in the 1940s and 1950s. At the sàme time it is clear that in the 1970s the party developed a much broader leadership, which reflected the party's continuing adjustment to the wider society.

After 1972, as before, the critical events that impinged on the Ontario NDP – leadership conventions, federal and provincial elections, by-elections, internal organization and reorganization – shaped and changed the party's character. New people came to the fore; new policies were developed; the party lived with new external circumstances and responded to those circumstances. But it was still the same party with, if I can be forgiven one last reference to my analogy, the same personality. Despite some tension the Ontario NDP maintained its close relationship with the labour movement, particularly with those unions that came out of the old CCL. Although it broadened its base of support throughout the province, it still campaigned most effectively, with the best electoral results, in those areas of the province with a high trade union concentration, the areas with a union class base.

Provincial election results after 1971 suggest that the party had the same strength and weaknesses as it had before. A small turnout, as in 1981 when only 58 per cent of the electorate voted, brought with it a dramatic fall in NDP support. It fell to levels similar to those in the 1950s and suggests that the party machine, when it is weak or demoralized, fails to get out its vote. Potential NDP voters, no doubt because they are more likely to be cross-pressured about their "deviant" political behaviour and because they are more likely to have fewer resources, both financial and intellectual, to follow provincial politics closely, are harder to turn out to the polls than are supporters of other parties. More than the other parties the NDP needs a vibrant political machine. Yet at the same time a true heavy turnout as in 1971, when 73.5 per cent of the electorate voted, is also difficult for the NDP. A turnout of this magnitude seems to come about, as it did in 1945, when there is a general fear, at least among some elements of the population who do not ordinarily vote, that socialism will be triumphant: triumph they perceive to be bad for them. This pattern obviously creates a problem for the NDP. It has to maintain an effective election machine without exciting the dormant antisocialist forces in the province. But it is an old dilemma that forms a part, perhaps the major part, of the CCF/NDP struggle to cope with the external world. Consequently it helps the party to maintain its particular persona. Stability and change – bound together they define a mature person.

Appendix

Extensive interviews were conducted for this study with these people.

Andrew and Peggy Brewin	April 1974
John Brewin	September 1976
Ken Bryden	June 1973
George Cadbury	June 1972
Terry Grier	April 1974
George and Gwynneth Grube	May 1972
John Harney	April 1974
E.B. Jolliffe	April 1974
Stephen Lewis	June 1973
Donald C. MacDonald	June 1973
Charles Millard	June 1972
Larry Sefton	June 1972
Miller and Peg Stewart	May 1972
Gordon Vichert	June 1973
Fred Young	June 1973

Notes

Chapter 1
An Analogy: The Party Personality

1 Desmond Morton, "Effectiveness of Political Campaigning: The NDP in the 1967 Ontario Election," *Journal of Canadian Studies* 4 (August 1969): 21–33.

2 Frederick C. Englemann, "Membership Participation in Policy-making in the CCF," *Canadian Journal of Economics and Political Science* 22 (May 1956): 161–73, based on his PH D dissertation, "The Co-operative Commonwealth Federation of Canada: A Study of Membership Participation in Policy-Making" (Yale University 1954). Stanley Knowles, *The New Party* (Toronto: McClelland and Stewart 1969).

3 (Toronto: University of Toronto Press 1968).

4 See John M. Wilson, "Politics and Social Class in Canada: The Case of Waterloo South," *Canadian Journal of Political Science* 1 (September 1968): 288–309.

5 See Fred I. Greenstein, "Personality and Politics," in Fred I. Greenstein and Nelson W. Polsby, eds., *Micropolitical Theory: Handbook of Political Science*, vol. 2 (Reading, Mass.: Addison-Wesley Publishing 1975), for a comprehensive discussion of the analytical questions surrounding the role of personality in political life.

6 Amitai Etzioni, *The Active Society: A Theory of Societal and Political Processes* (London: Collier-Macmillan 1968).

7 Ernest Troeltsch, *The Social Teachings of the Christian Churches* (London: Allen and Unwin 1956).

8 Samuel H. Beer, *Modern Political Development* (New York: Random House 1973), 59.

9 Ibid., 94 ff.

Chapter 2
The Setting: Political Culture and Ontario

1 *International Encyclopedia of Social Sciences* (New York: Macmillan and Free Press 1969), 12: 218.

2 Lucien Pye, "Culture and Political Science," in Louis Schneider and Charles Bonjean, eds., *The Idea of Culture in the Social Sciences* (Cambridge: Cambridge University Press 1973), 68.

3 The inspiration for these studies is Garbiel Almond and Sidney Verba, *The Civic Culture* (Boston: Little, Brown 1963), which characterizes and compares the political cultures of five nations with data collected from five major surveys.

4 See Pye, "Culture and Political Science," 67.

5 Daniel H. Levine, "Issues in the Study of Culture and Politics: A View from Latin America," *Publius* 4, no. 2 (1974): 78.

6 Leslie White, *The Evolution of Culture: The Development of Civilization to the Fall of Rome* (New York: McGraw-Hill 1959).

7 Ibid.

8 See T.S. Eliot, *Notes towards the Definition of Culture* (London: Faber and Faber 1948).

9 Eliot's religious reductionism is not unknown to social science. Talcott Parsons, for example, arrives at his complex conception of the social system, in part from an earlier interest in the religious basis of cultural mores. See "The Theoretical Development of the Sociology of Religion," in Talcott Parsons, *Essays in Sociological Theory* (Glencoe, Ill.: Free Press 1959), 197–211.

10 Daniel Levine, "Issues in the Study of Culture and Politics in Latin America," typescript 1972, 6.

11 For example, both C.B. Macpherson, *Democracy in Alberta* (Toronto: University of Toronto Press 1953), and S.M. Lipset, *Agrarian Socialism* (1950; reprint, New York: Doubleday 1968), adumbrate various social and economic factors and attempt to use some combination of these factors as an explanation for the peculiar pattern of political life they observe in Alberta and Saskatchewan.

12 Wilson, "The Ontario Political Culture," in D.C. MacDonald, ed., *Government and Politics of Ontario* (Toronto: Macmillan 1975), 211–33, and Gingras, "Ontario," in Bellamy et al., eds., *The Provincial Political Systems* (Toronto: Methuen 1976), 31–45. Gingras makes use of both demographic data and survey data, primarily data first reported by Richard Simeon and David Elkins in "Regional Political Cultures in

Canada," *Canadian Journal of Political Science* 7, no. 3 (September 1974): 397–437. Wilson also makes use of aggregate and survey information.

13 See Daniel Bell, *The Coming of Post-Industrial Society* (New York: Basic Books 1973), for a discussion of the cultural effects of the economic shift from secondary manufacturing to an expansion of the tertiary sector, which relies heavily on "knowledge" industries.

14 See Bruce Hodgins's study of John Sandfield Macdonald, Ontario's first premier, who, though he supported John A. Macdonald's vision of Confederation, began his political life as a Baldwin reformer, in *John Sandfield Macdonald* (Toronto: University of Toronto Press 1971). See also Donald Swainson, ed., *Oliver Mowat's Ontario* (Toronto: Macmillan 1972), which contains several useful descriptions of Ontario political life and Ontario society in the last years of the last century.

15 Dennis Wrong, "Ontario Provincial Elections, 1934–1955: A Preliminary Survey of Voting," *Canadian Journal of Economics and Political Science* 23 (August 1975): 395–403.

16 John Wilson and David Hoffman, "The Liberal Party in Ontario," *Canadian Journal of Political Science* 3, no. 2 (June 1970), and "Ontario: A Three Party System in Transition," in Martin Robin, ed., *Canadian Provincial Politics* (Scarborough: Prentice-Hall 1972). The election results of 1975, 1977, and 1981 make their latter argument of minority status for the Liberal party somewhat suspect.

17 Wrong, "Ontario Provincial Elections, 1934–1955," 395–403.

18 Jack Granatstein, "York South By-election of February 9, 1942: A Turning Point in Canadian Politics," *The Canadian Historical Review* 48 (June 1967): 142–58.

19 A copy of this pamphlet may be found in the Ontario CCF/NDP Papers, deposited in the Queen's University Archives, Douglas Library, Queen's University, Kingston, Ontario. The Ontario CCF/NDP Papers include material from the 1930s to the 1970s and have been donated by George Grube, Donald C. MacDonald, and the New Democratic Party of Ontario. I have not used box or carton numbers, since at the time the research was conducted the papers were not catalogued. Further reference to these papers will be styled QA (CCF/NDP).

20 Desmond Morton, "The Politics of Polarization," 18 April 1970, QA (CCF/NDP).

21 John Wilson, memorandum to the Pitman committee on the nature of Ontario politics and the question of the provincial leadership, August 1970, QA (CCF/NDP).

22 John Wilson, "The Ontario Political Culture," in D.C. MacDonald, ed., *Government and Politics in Ontario* (Toronto: Macmillan 1975).

23 A.G. Bailey, *Culture and Nationality* (Toronto: McClelland and Stewart 1972), 178–99.

24 Millard interview.

25 Donald C. MacDonald interview.

26 Douglas Hamilton, *Trade Unions in Canada* (Toronto: Ontario Federation of Labour 1967), 2.

27 Ibid., 3.

28 Ibid.

29 Larry Sefton interview.

30 E.R. Black and A.C. Cairns, "A Different Perspective on Canadian Federalism," in J.P. Meekison, ed., *Canadian Federalism: Myth or Reality*, 3d ed. (Toronto: Methuen 1977), 31–49.

31 Sefton interview.

32 See, generally, Richard Perlman, *Labour Theory* (New York: Wiley 1969), and John R. Commons et al., *History of Labour in the United States* (New York: Macmillan 1921).

33 Frank Parkin, *Class Inequality and Political Order: Social Stratification in Capitalist and Communist Societies* (London: MacGibbon and Kee 1971).

Chapter 3
The Party in the World

1 See Erik H. Erikson, *Identity Youth and Crisis* (New York: W.W. Norton 1968), especially chap. 3.

2 Ibid., 105.

3 Ibid., 92.

4 Ibid., 92, 93.

5 Ibid., 138.

6 Gerald L. Caplan, *The Dilemma of Canadian Socialism: The CCF in Ontario* (Toronto: McClelland and Stewart 1973).

7 Leo Zakuta, *A Protest Movement Becalmed: A Study of Change in the CCF* (Toronto: University of Toronto Press 1964).

8 See Kenneth McNaught, *J.S. Woodsworth: A Prophet in Politics* (Toronto: University of Toronto Press 1959), and Grace MacInnis, *J.S. Woodsworth: A Man to Remember* (Toronto: Macmillan 1953). Both biographies, the first by a University of Toronto historian, the second by Woodsworth's daughter, suggest that Woodsworth was a saintly man, almost too good for the mundane world of political life in Canada.

9 Walter D. Young, *The Anatomy of a Party: The National CCF, 1932 – 1961* (Toronto: University of Toronto Press 1969), 41–2.

10 See Caplan, *The Dilemma of Canadian Socialism*, for a useful picture of the early days.

11 Ibid., 22, 23.

12 More details of this conference may be found in a paper by John Buckley entitled "Ontario's First Labour Party," QA (CCF/NDP). Buckley was president of the Independent Labour Party from 1917 to 1923, and later was president of the Toronto and District Trades and Labour Council and secretary-treasurer of the Trades and Labour Congress.

13 See W.C. Good, *Farmer Citizen* (Toronto: Ryerson 1959), and David Hoffman, "Farmer-Labour Government in Ontario, 1919–1923" (MA thesis, University of Toronto 1959), for a full discussion of the events which led to the defeat of the Drury government.

14 Caplan, *The Dilemma of Canadian Socialism*, chap. 3.

15 Ibid., 47.

16 Ibid., 56. Chapter 4 contains a much fuller discussion of these events.

17 Annual report of the executive committee of the CCF (Ontario section) from 20 April 1935 to 31 March 1936, QA (CCF/NDP).

18 Andrew Brewin interview.

19 Annual report of the executive committee of the CCF (Ontario section) from 20 April 1935 to 31 March 1936, QA (CCF/NDP).

20 For a full account of the attempt to dismiss Underhill and Grube, see Michiel Horn, *The League for Social Reconstruction: Intellectual Origins of the Democratic Left in Canada, 1930–1942* (Toronto: University of Toronto Press 1980), chap. 10.

21 Jolliffe interview.

22 Andrew Brewin interview.

23 Executive minutes, 2 January 1942, QA (CCF/NDP).

24 Andrew Brewin interview.

25 Jolliffe interview.

26 Ibid.

27 Young interview.

28 Executive minutes, 17 January 1941, QA (CCF/NDP).

29 For a description of the 1964 Riverdale campaign, seen as a model campaign, see Desmond Morton, *The Riverdale Story* (Ontario New Democratic Party 1964).

30 See Gregory Clark, "Dollar Bills and Stamps Paid Noseworthy Election," *Toronto Daily Star*, 23 February 1942, 16.

31 Andrew Brewin interview.

32 Atkinson himself later contributed five hundred dollars to the CCF. Andrew Brewin interview and South York campaign account books in the possession of the author.

33 The CCF also opposed Humphrey Mitchell, King's minister of labour and a long-time trade unionist, who was running on the same day in a by-election for the Welland riding. Mitchell was elected.

34 In 1936, for example, the membership of the party in Ontario totalled some thirty-seven hundred. Executive minutes, 1 September 1937, QA (CCF/NDP).

35 See Neil McKenty, *Mitch Hepburn* (Toronto: McClelland and Stewart 1967), esp. chaps. 15 and 16, for a fascinating account of this period.

36 Jolliffe interview.

37 A copy of this report may be found in QA (CCF/NDP). No doubt other copies exist.

38 A copy of this speech is found in QA (CCF/NDP).

39 Caplan, *The Dilemma of Canadian Socialism*, 171, and David Lewis, *The Good Fight: Political Memoirs, 1909 – 1958* (Toronto: Macmillan 1981), chap. 12. Lewis, relying on material from the Public Archives of Canada, suggests that Drew may have known more than he revealed to the LeBel Commission.

40 Caplan, *The Dilemma of Canadian Socialism*, 171.

41 Pemberton to Grube, 30 June 1945, QA (CCF/NDP).

42 Interview with Miller and Peg Stewart.

43 Ibid.

44 Millard interview. Millard refused to say who had approached him, but the Stewarts and others indicated that it was this group, the intellectual left of the party, grouped around the *Canadian Forum* and Frank Underhill.

45 Zakuta, *A Protest Movement Becalmed*, chap. 6.

46 Andrew Brewin interview.

47 The text of this speech is found in QA (CCF/NDP).

48 Samuel Beer, *British Politics in the Collectivist Age* (New York: Knopf 1965), 154, 155.

49 Guenther Roth, *The Social Democrats of Imperial Germany* (Totowa, NJ: Bedminster Press 1963).

50 Memo from Morden Lazarus to candidates, November 1951, QA (CCF/NDP).

51 Stewarts and Andrew Brewin interviews.

52 Jolliffe interview.

53 QA (CCF/NDP).

54 Executive minutes, 14 April 1951, QA (CCF/NDP).

55 Sefton interview.

56 Bryden interview.

57 Executive minutes, 10 February 1953, QA (CCF/NDP).

58 David Lewis, *The Good Fight*, chap. 19 et 6 seq.

59 Zakuta, *A Protest Movement Becalmed*, 132.

60 Council minutes, 21, 22 September 1955, QA (CCF/NDP).

61 See Horowitz, *Canadian Labour in Politics*, 178, for the text of this resolution.

62 Ibid., 194–5.

63 John Brewin interview.

64 It is interesting to note that as a token of appreciation for his assistance with a television program featuring Donald MacDonald, Alan Anderson was sent a copy of Galbraith's book. Executive minutes, 1959, QA (CCF/NDP).

65 See Desmond Sparham, report on New Party clubs, July 1961, QA (CCF/NDP). Sparham was national director of New Party clubs employed by the National Committee for the New Party.

66 CCF National Council minutes, 25 August 1959, QA (CCF/NDP).

67 Donald C. MacDonald to Grace MacInnis, 2 September 1959, QA (CCF/NDP).

68 Ellen Camnitzer to George Grube, 30 October 1959, QA (CCF/NDP).

69 Press release, 17 October 1959, QA (CCF/NDP).

70 Members of the National Committee for the New Party, 1958–61, were CLC representatives Claude Jodoin, Donald MacDonald, William Dodge, Stanley Knowles, George Burt, Frank Hall, William Mahoney, Joe Morris, Roger Provost, and William Smith, and CCF representatives David Lewis, Hazen Argue, Thérèse Casgrain, Andrew Brewin, Carl Hamilton, T.C. Douglas, Gérard Picard, Harold Winch, Ken Bryden, and Frank Scott. Additional members appointed from New Party clubs in January 1961 were Walter Pitman, Walter Kontak, Walter Young, Sam Bowman, W. Edgar Mullen, Louis Lloyd, Leo McIsaac, and Leonard Laventure. Alternates appointed were Woodrow Lloyd, Donald C. MacDonald, and Michael Oliver. The chairman was Stanley Knowles, the executive secretary was Carl Hamilton, and an honorary member was M.J. Coldwell.

71 QA (CCF/NDP).

72 MacDonald to Peg Stewart, 7 July 1960, QA (CCF/NDP).

73 MacDonald to Peg Stewart, 22 July 1960, QA (CCF/NDP).

74 Walter Young, "The Peterborough By-Election," *Dalhousie Review* (Winter 1960–1): 505–19.

75 I have chosen not to reveal the author or the recipient of this letter. It is dated 17 May 1961, QA (CCF/NDP).

76 Stewart to Francis Eady, 19 May 1961, QA (CCF/NDP).

77 "A Lift for Democracy," *Ottawa Journal*, 8 August 1961.

78 *Saturday Night*, September 1961.
79 The Credentials Committee reported the following breakdowns: Ontario Committee for the New Party 26, CCF Provincial Council 48, Ontario Federation of Labour executive council 16, MPPS 1, Farm Committee and New Party clubs 155, CLC Labour Council 23, local union delegates 519, and CCF constituency association delegates 256. In addition there were 38 alternate delegates and 92 registered visitors, for a total of 1,174 registrants.
80 Terry Grier interview.
81 Executive minutes, 21 July 1962, QA (CCF/NDP).
82 See, generally, Robin F. Badgley and Samuel Wolfe, *Doctors' Strike: Medical Care and Conflict in Saskatchewan* (Toronto: Macmillan 1967).
83 Grier interview.
84 Cadbury interview.
85 Pierre Trudeau, "The Practice and Theory of Federalism," in Michael Oliver, ed., *Social Purpose for Canada* (Toronto: University of Toronto Press 1961), 371–93.
86 See, generally, Peter Stursberg, *Diefenbaker: Leadership Lost, 1962–1967* (Toronto: University of Toronto Press 1976); J.G. Diefenbaker, *One Canada: Memoirs of the Right Honourable John G. Diefenbaker* (Toronto: Macmillan 1975); James Johnston, *The Party's Over* (Don Mills, Ont.: Longman 1971).
87 Knowles to MacDonald, 14 April 1963, QA (CCF/NDP).
88 Trotskyists were left-wing Communists, who had adopted a conscious strategy of infiltrating social democratic parties to prevent those parties from gaining social office. The Trotskyists feared that social democratic policies would ameliorate the living conditions of the working class and the poor and would thereby hinder the inevitable revolution. See chapter 8 for a fuller discussion of the party's disciplinary problems.
89 Executive minutes, 15 November 1963, QA (CCF/NDP).
90 QA (CCF/NDP).
91 For a very full description of this campaign, see Morton, *The Riverdale Story*.
92 See Young, *Anatomy of a Party*, chap. 9, and Horowitz, *Canadian Labour in Politics*, esp. chap. 3.
93 Council minutes, 12 and 13 January 1953, QA (CCF/NDP).
94 Executive minutes, 5 January 1952, QA (CCF/NDP).
95 Executive minutes, 8 March 1952, QA (CCF/NDP).
96 Stewarts interview.
97 Frank Underhill, "Power Politics in the Ontario CCF," *Canadian Forum* 32 (April 1952): 7, 8.

98 Executive minutes, 6 December 1952, QA (CCF/NDP).

99 Executive minutes, 31 July 1951, QA (CCF/NDP).

100 See letter to MacDonald from E. Park, 14 October 1960, QA (CCF/NDP) in which Park castigates MacDonald for his "obsession with scandal."

101 Beer, *Modern Political Development*, 97.

102 For an exhaustive description of this period, see Desmond Morton, "Report of the Assistant Provincial Secretary," 1964 and 1965, QA (CCF/NDP). The question is from the 1965 report.

103 Morton to Jack Granatstein, 13 November 1965, QA (CCF/NDP).

104 Grier interview.

105 MacDonald and Harney interviews.

106 A number of key individuals including Cadbury tried to persuade Wally Ross, a Steelworkers' staff representative, to stand against Harney, Ross toyed with the idea for a time but decided instead to accept the post of director of organization with a promise that he would be in charge of the organizational side of the provincial office. MacDonald interview.

107 Harney and Grier interviews.

108 Harney to Scotton, 25 April 1968, QA (CCF/NDP).

109 Stephen Lewis interview.

110 Erikson, *Identity Youth and Crisis*, 95.

Chapter 4
Party Structure

1 Report to the Provincial Council entitled "CCF Organization," January 1942, QA (CCF/NDP).

2 Ibid. Throughout the internal documents of the Ontario CCF/NDP the terms "constituency" and "riding" are used interchangeably to refer to an electoral district returning a representative to either Parliament or the Legislative Assembly. I have chosen to follow that rule of interchangeability.

3 Ibid.

4 See John Austin, *Lectures on Jurisprudence*, 4th ed. 2 vols. (London 1873).

5 CCF Provincial Constitution, 1955, QA (CCF/NDP).

6 Ibid.

7 Bryden interview.

8 Minutes of the CLC/CCF subcommittee on structure, 8 August 1958, QA (CCF/NDP).

9 It is interesting to note that the Canadian Labour Congress is a loose federation, not of provincial federations of labour, but of affiliated unions. The provincial federations of labour are, in fact, creatures of the CLC.

10 Minutes of the CLC/CCF subcommittee on structure, 8 August 1958, QA (CCF/NDP).
11 Ibid.
12 MacDonald to Archer, 16 July 1961, QA (CCF/NDP).
13 QA (CCF/NDP).
14 Sefton interview.
15 Young, *Anatomy of a Party*, esp. chap. 6, and Lewis, *The Good Fight*, chaps. 5 to 18.
16 Dean McHenry, *The Third Force in Canada* (Berkeley: University of California Press 1950), 78.
17 Bryden interview.
18 Jolliffe interview.
19 Ibid.
20 MacDonald interview.
21 Lewis interview.
22 John Brewin interview.
23 Cadbury interview.
24 MacDonald interview.

Chapter 5
Party Ideas

1 See James Bryce, *The American Commonwealth*, 3d ed. (New York, Macmillan 1895), and Woodrow Wilson, *Congressional Government: A Study in American Politics* (Boston: Houghton Mifflin 1900).
2 See Michael Cross, *The Decline and Fall of a Good Idea: CCF-NDP Manifestoes, 1932 to 1969* (Toronto: New Hogtown Press 1974), for the most comprehensive retailing of this view.
3 John Brewin interview.
4 For different analyses of left- and right-wing socialism, see Anthony Crosland, *The Future of Socialism* (London: Cape 1956); Richard Crossman, *The Politics of Socialism* (New York: Atheneum 1965); Michael Harrington, *Socialism* (New York: Saturday Review Press 1972); and Ralph Milibind, *Parliamentary Socialism* (New York: Monthly Review Press 1964).
5 See Michiel Horn, *The League for Social Reconstruction*, for a thorough analysis of the league.
6 Andrew Brewin interview.
7 George Bernard Shaw, *The Intelligent Woman's Guide to Socialism and Capitalism* (London: Constable 1928), 4.

8 R.H. Tawney, *Equality* (London: G. Allen and Unwin 1931). John Wilson has further developed this area in explaining democratic socialism in "Toward a Society of Friends," *Canadian Journal of Political Science* 3, no. 4 (December 1970): 628–54.

9 See Herbert Morrison et al., *Can Planning be Democratic?* 1944; W.A. Robson, ed., *Social Security*, 1943; Abel Smith et al., *Socialism and Affluence*, 1967; A.C. Jones, ed., *New Fabian Colonial Essays*, 1950; Harold J. Laski et al., *Where Stands Democracy?* 1970; and Peter Townsend et al., *Social Services for All*, 1968, for examples of the range of Fabian proposals as presented in a multitude of pamphlets published by the society. See also Margaret Cole, *The Story of Fabian Socialism* (London: Heinemann 1961), for a more analytical consideration of Fabian proposals.

10 See E.P. Thompson, *The Making of the English Working Class*, rev. ed. (London: Penguin 1968).

11 Richard Allen, *The Social Passion: Religion and Social Reform in Canada, 1914–1928* (Toronto: University of Toronto Press 1973).

12 Andrew Brewin interview.

13 See Ross Johnson, "No Compromise–No Political Trading: The Marxian Socialist Tradition in British Columbia," (PH D diss., University of British Columbia 1975), and Walter Young, "Ideology, Personality and the Origin of the CCF in British Columbia," *B.C. Studies* 32 (Winter 1976–7): 139–62.

14 Jolliffe interview.

15 See George Bernard Shaw, *An Intelligent Woman's Guide to Capitalism, Socialism, Sovietism and Fascism* (Middlesex: Penguin 1937), esp. section 84, for a 1930s glowing account of Soviet prospects.

16 See John R. Commons et al., *History of Labour in the United States*, and Richard Perlman, *Labour Theory*.

17 Grier interview.

18 Zakuta, *A Protest Movement Becalmed*, 103.

19 Desmond Morton, *Social Democracy in Canada* (Toronto: Samuel Stevens, Hakkert and Company 1977), esp. chap. 7.

20 See Resolutions Book, Ontario New Democratic Party convention, 1970.

21 Grier interview.

22 Bryden interview. Jolliffe, when interviewed, also referred to the dissidents in the party as "conservative."

23 Clifford Geertz, "Ideology as a Cultural System," in David Apter, ed., *Ideology and Discontent* (New York: Free Press 1964), 48.

24 See Michael Cross, *CCF-NDP Manifestoes*.

25 Program of the New Democratic Party of Ontario, 1971.

26 The term "prime minister" was in use in Ontario during John Robarts's premiership and was imitated by the NDP.

27 See League for Social Reconstruction, *Social Planning for Canada* (reprint, Toronto: University of Toronto Press 1975).

28 Ibid., 229, 230.

29 Ibid., 235.

30 Ibid., 242, 243.

31 Ibid., 245.

32 Ibid., 266, 267.

33 Ibid., 509.

34 Ibid., 508.

35 Ibid., 509.

36 This statement was written before the Labour Conventions case was decided in 1937, ending all speculation on the use of section 132 of the British North America Act. Afterwards the treaty-making power was a dead letter.

37 *Social Planning for Canada*, 505, 506.

38 George Grube, "Constitutional Proposals, A Position Paper," 1943, QA (CCF/NDP).

39 Press release, April 1959, QA (CCF/NDP).

40 John Brewin interview.

41 Jolliffe interview.

42 James Gray, *Booze: The Impact of Whisky on the Prairie West* (Toronto: Macmillan 1972).

43 See, for example, the report of the Resolutions Committee of the 1959 Ontario CCF convention, QA (CCF/NDP).

44 See Andrew Brewin, *Stand on Guard* (Toronto: McClelland and Stewart 1965), for a comprehensive statement of the majority view.

45 NDP position papers, 1975, in author's possession.

Chapter 6
Caucus and Party

1 Robert Michels, *Political Parties: A Sociological Study of the Oligarchical Tendencies of Modern Democracy* (New York: Free Press 1962, first published in 1911), esp. pt. 1.

2 Michels, *Political Parties*, pt. 3; Maurice Duverger, *Political Parties* (London: Methuen 1954), esp. chap. 3; and Robert McKenzie, *British Political Parties* (London: Heinemann 1955), esp. chap. 7.

3 Andrew Brewin interview.
4 Grube to Coldwell, 10 July 1942, QA (CCF/NDP).
5 Jolliffe interview.
6 Stewarts interview.
7 Grube and Stewarts interviews.
8 Andrew Brewin interview.
9 Millard interview.
10 Stewarts interview.
11 Bryden interview.
12 Cadbury interview.
13 Ibid. Queen's Park is the location of the Legislative Assembly in Ontario.
14 Young interview.
15 MacDonald interview.
16 Lewis interview.
17 Harney interview.
18 Lewis interview.

Chapter 7
Party Democracy

1 See, in particular, Walter Young, *Anatomy of a Party*, esp. chap. 6; Zakuta, *A Protest Movement Becalmed*, chap. 4; and Lipset, *Agrarian Socialism*, chap. 9.
2 Young, *Anatomy of a Party*, 167, 168.
3 Ibid., 163.
4 Stewarts interview.
5 Zakuta, *A Protest Movement Becalmed*, 25.
6 Grube interview.
7 Vichert interview.
8 Sefton and Jolliffe interviews.
9 Andrew Brewin interview.
10 Young, *Anatomy of a Party*, and David Lewis, *The Good Fight*.
11 Young, *Anatomy of a Party*, esp. chap. 6.
12 Jolliffe, Andrew Brewin, and Millard interviews.
13 Stewarts interview.
14 Sefton interview.
15 Desmond Morton, *The Canadian General: Sir William Otter* (Toronto: Hakkert 1974).
16 Bryden interview.

17 See U. Pareto, *The Rise and Fall of the Elites* (reprint, Totowa, NJ: Bedminster Press 1968); G. Mosca, *The Ruling Class* (New York and London: McGraw-Hill 1939); and R. Michels, *Political Parties.*

18 John Brewin interview.

19 Zakuta, *A Protest Movement Becalmed,* 25.

20 Cadbury interview.

21 Vichert interview. Harney felt he could not continue as provincial secretary if Scott were elected president. Harney interview.

22 MacDonald interview.

23 See Samuel J. Eldersveld, *Political Parties: A Behavioral Analysis* (Chicago: Rand McNally 1964), 100 ff.

24 Grier interview.

25 John Brewin interview.

26 Andrew Brewin interview.

27 Jolliffe interview.

28 This unanimity did not mean that everyone in the party leadership was content with Jolliffe as leader, but because they were very suspicious of Duncan, they had no difficulty in uniting behind Jolliffe. If Millard had yielded to entreaties that he stand for the post, there is little doubt that a genuine contest would have ensued in which the oligarchy would have been divided. Stewarts interview.

29 Millard interview.

30 MacDonald interview.

31 Young interview.

32 Bryden interview.

33 Ibid.

34 These voter totals are not extant. Party records of them were no doubt destroyed. MacDonald, however, recalls these figures and believes his recollection to be quite exact. MacDonald interview.

35 Jolliffe interview.

36 Bryden interview.

37 Harney interview.

38 Grier interview.

39 Cadbury interview.

40 Lewis interview.

41 Sefton interview.

42 Lewis interview.

43 Vichert interview.

44 Grier interview.

45 MacDonald interview.

46 Ibid.
47 Max Saltsman, the MP from Waterloo South, briefly toyed with the idea
of opposing Lewis and telephoned Lewis to announce this intention.
He soon abandoned the idea. Lewis interview.
48 John Brewin interview.
49 A fringe candidate, Douglas Campbell, received twenty-one votes.
50 John Brewin interview.
51 Vichert interview.
52 Lewis and John Brewin interviews.
53 John Brewin interview.
54 The author was present at that meeting.

Chapter 8
Party Discipline

1 Bryden interview.
2 See letter from Frank Scott, national chairman of the CCF, to Frank
McKenzie, secretary of the British Columbia CCF, 27 July 1943, QA
(CCF/NDP), in which Scott firmly asserts that the National Council must
be responsible for such a major decision.
3 Grube to McKenzie, 11 August 1943, QA (CCF/NDP).
4 Jolliffe interview.
5 Memorandum from Jolliffe to Nelson Alles, MPP for Essex North;
William Riggs, MPP for Windsor Walkerville; and George Bennett, MPP
for Windsor Sandwich, 26 September 1944, QA (CCF/NDP).
6 Andrew Brewin interview.
7 See, for example, a letter to Jolliffe from Helen Duckworth, secretary of
the Niagara Falls Labour Progressive party, 4 January 1945, QA (CCF/NDP),
in which she states: "There is a definite possibility that a CCF candidate
may secure enough support from progressive people of that riding to
ensure the defeat of McNaughton and the election of a Tory candidate.
Such an outcome would not be in the best interests of the majority of
Canadians in that it would strengthen the position of reactionary
elements in Canada."
8 See Jolliffe to Alles, 13 December 1944, QA (CCF/NDP).
9 Millard interview.
10 Millard to Carlin, 12 April 1948, QA (CCF/NDP).
11 For a full discussion of the battles in Mine-Mill, see Irving Martin Abella,
Nationalism, Communism and Canadian Labour (Toronto: University of
Toronto Press 1973), chap. 6.

12 Ames to Lazarus, 7 April 1948, QA (CCF/NDP).

13 Executive minutes, 13 April 1948, QA (CCF/NDP).

14 See letter from Ames to Lazarus, 27 April 1948, QA (CCF/NDP).

15 Lazarus to president, Sudbury CCF Riding Association, 29 May 1948, QA (CCF/NDP).

16 Council minutes, 12 February 1950, QA (CCF/NDP).

17 Jolliffe interview.

18 Ibid.

19 Executive minutes, 23 September 1953, QA (CCF/NDP).

20 Council minutes, October 1953, QA (CCF/NDP).

21 An outline of these procedures and events is found in a paper attached to the minutes of the Provincial Council meeting of 30 and 31 October 1954 with the title "Procedure etc. re Expulsion of Trotskyites," QA (CCF/NDP).

22 Stewarts interview.

23 For an outline of this procedure, see letter from Jim Bury, provincial secretary of the Ontario NDP, to Jessie Mendels, provincial secretary of the British Columbia NDP, 25 April 1963, QA (CCF/NDP).

24 Because of a constitutional change at the 1966 provincial convention, it was not necessary to "expel" these individuals in the technical sense the term is used in the Ontario NDP constitution. The 1966 convention voted to require that youth membership be "integrated" with regular party membership. As a consequence the provincial executive ruled that in 1967 all applications for membership from individuals who had been members of the OYND would be treated as new applications. This meant that the executive could turn down any application it desired without the individual having an automatic right of appeal to the Provincial Council. In fact, the council considered these membership referrals on the grounds that it could always review any decision of the executive.

25 See Mel Watkins, "A New National Policy," in Trevor Lloyd and J.T. McLeod, eds., Agenda 1970 (Toronto: University of Toronto Press 1969), esp. 175.

26 Although as Desmond Morton reveals in Social Democracy in Canada, 92, "The chief authors, so far as a collective enterprise could have them, were Laxer, Broadbent and Caplan."

27 Document entitled "List of Signatories of the Statement, For an Independent Socialist Canada," 2 September 1969, QA (CCF/NDP).

28 Morton points out that the name Waffle developed as a kind of joke by Broadbent, who stated that if the document like all documents

"waffled," it would "waffle" to the left rather than to the right. Morton, *Social Democracy in Canada*, 92.

29 Lewis interview.

30 Grier interview.

31 Stephen Lewis, *A Report to the Provincial Council* (New Democratic Party of Ontario 1972), QA (CCF/NDP).

32 Gordon Vichert, John Brewin, and Gerald Caplan, "Report to Provincial Executive" 6 May 1972, QA (CCF/NDP).

33 Ibid.

34 Ibid.

35 Vichert interview.

36 Ibid.

37 See, for example, a resolution passed by the Waffle-controlled Beaches-Woodbine Riding Association on 2 June 1972, QA (CCF/NDP).

38 Statement of the Ontario Waffle in reply to the Ontario NDP executive report, 8 May 1972, QA (CCF/NDP).

39 Pitman and Harney to fellow New Democrats, 21 June 1972, QA (CCF/NDP).

40 Administrative Committee minutes, 14 June 1972, now in QA (CCF/NDP). The author, as a vice-president of the Ontario NDP, was present at that meeting.

41 Those actually attending the meeting and their titles were David Lewis, federal leader; Bill Mahoney, national director of the United Steelworkers; Fred Dowling, Canadian director of the Canadian Food and Allied Workers; Larry Sefton, director of District 6 of the United Steelworkers; Lynn Williams, a vice-president of the Ontario NDP and Sefton's assistant; Don Taylor, Mahoney's assistant; Don Montgomery, Toronto area supervisor of the United Steelworkers and president of the Toronto and District Labour Council; "Bud" Clark, assistant to the Canadian director of the Textile Workers Union of America; Sam Fox, Canadian vice-president of the International Ladies Garment Workers Union; David Archer, president of the Ontario Federation of Labour; Dennis McDermott, Canadian director of the United Auto Workers; Gordon Vichert, president of the Ontario NDP; and Stephen Lewis, leader of the Ontario NDP.

42 Lewis interview.

43 Council minutes, 23 June 1972, QA (CCF/NDP).

44 See Morton, *Social Democracy in Canada*, 134–5.

45 For a discussion of the psychological effects of colonialism on a colonial people, see Franz Fanon, *Black Skin, White Masks* (New York: Grove Press 1967), esp. chap. 4.

Chapter 9
The Significance of Party Personality

1 See Max Black, *The Social Theories of Talcott Parsons* (Englewood Cliffs, NJ: Prentice-Hall 1961). For an analysis of Parsons's work, see Alvin Gouldner, *The Coming Crisis of Western Sociology* (New York: Basic Books 1970).

2 See David Easton, *The Political System* (New York: Knopf 1953), *A Framework for Political Analysis* (Englewood Cliffs, NJ: Prentice-Hall 1965), and *A System Analysis of Political Life* (New York: Wiley 1965).

3 See David Easton and Jack Dennis, *Children in the Political System* (New York: McGraw-Hill 1969).

4 John Maynard Keynes, *The General Theory of Employment, Interest and Money*, rpt. ed. (London: Macmillan 1957).

5 John Kenneth Galbraith, *The Affluent Society* (Boston: Houghton Mifflin 1958).

6 Milton Friedman, *Capitalism and Freedom* (Chicago: University of Chicago Press 1962).

7 David Riesman et al., *The Lonely Crowd: A Study of the Changing American Character* (New Haven: Yale University Press 1956).

8 Samuel Beer, *Modern Political Development*, chap. 8.

9 M. Ostrogorski, *Democracy and the Organization of Political Parties*, edited and abridged by S.M. Lipset (New York: Doubleday 1964).

10 This phrase is inspired by J.E. Hodgetts's "structural heretics," an apt image used to describe nondepartmental bureaucratic forms in Canada. See J.E. Hodgetts, *The Canadian Public Service: A Physiology of Government, 1867–1970* (Toronto: University of Toronto Press 1973). Hodgetts's physiological analogy implies an interaction between the institutions of government and the external environment and provokes a similar analytic framework as my personality analogy.

11 See Young, *The Anatomy of a Party*, chap. 6.

Index